"One generation of leadership looks at another—from experience to emergence. Eddie Gibbs brings experience and scholarship to understanding changing church culture and younger church leaders."

LEITH ANDERSON, *pastor, Wooddale Church, and author of* Leadership That Works

"Eddie Gibbs has done it again! First he helped see the church of the future with *ChurchNext* and now he shows us the kind of leadership necessary to bring that church into being. *LeadershipNext* is nothing short of a primer on leadership. I fully intend to absorb its content because now I have a blueprint to live into."

GREG OGDEN, *executive pastor of discipleship, Christ Church of Oak Brook, and author of* Discipleship Essentials *and* Transforming Discipleship

"Eddie Gibbs has God's heart for our hurting world, and a tactician's head for winning the war for souls on the frontline in the materialistic West. He is absolutely right: it is a new day demanding fresh ways to talent-spot, mentor and release the missional leaders needed for the apostolic work Jesus has left to his church. Young apostles arise! Older leaders, treasure and release your Timothys to their harvest duties! The Lord of the harvest has given them the help and strength of the Holy Spirit!"

BRIAN DODD, *author of* Empowered Church Leadership

"*LeadershipNext* tells it like it is. It's a great resource for leaders who want to be both biblical and adaptable to the culture. I especially recommend it to any pastor who is starting out or burning out in ministry."

SARAH SUMNER, *associate professor of ministry and theology, Haggard School of Theology, Azusa Pacific University, and author of* Men and Women in the Church

"No matter what time period or culture we are in, there is always a need for leadership. However, how we lead does change depending on the people, the place, and the culture and values. In our emerging culture ⋯ ⋯ ⋯ ⋯ ⋯ many aspects of leadership in our churches ⋯ ⋯ ⋯ ⋯ w to do that."

DAN KIMBALL, *author of* The Emergin⋯ ⋯rch

"*LeadershipNext: Changing Leaders in a Changing Culture* by Eddie Gibbs is a book to be placed in the hands of every young leader with the words 'Walk in the light of Eddie's words and you will work effectively and not go off the path.' I've known and profited from a friendship with Eddie for twenty years; he is a competent guide to effective ministry in contemporary society."

TODD HUNTER, *president, Alpha USA*

"Eddie Gibbs is a wise and seasoned observer of the church throughout the world. He has worked with and trained several generations of leaders across all denominational boundaries and many cultural contexts. This book identifies the challenges confronting leaders in a rapidly shifting world. With a passion for the kingdom and a love for the church, Eddie outlines a way forward for leaders in a complex and swiftly shifting world. This is an important and helpful book."

ALAN ROXBURGH, *president, Missional Leadership Institute*

LeadershipNext

CHANGING LEADERS IN A CHANGING CULTURE

EDDIE GIBBS

InterVarsity Press
Downers Grove, Illinois

InterVarsity Press
P.O. Box 1400, Downers Grove, IL 60515-1426
World Wide Web: www.ivpress.com
E-mail: mail@ivpress.com

InterVarsity Press® is the book-publishing division of InterVarsity Christian Fellowship/USA®, a student movement active on campus at hundreds of universities, colleges and schools of nursing in the United States of America, and a member movement of the International Fellowship of Evangelical Students. For information about local and regional activities, write Public Relations Dept., InterVarsity Christian Fellowship/USA, 6400 Schroeder Rd., P.O. Box 7895, Madison, WI 53707-7895, or visit the IVCF website at <www.intervarsity.org>.

Design: Cindy Kiple

Images: Gary S. & Vivian Chapman/Getty Images

ISBN 0-8308-3283-1

Printed in the United States of America ∞

Library of Congress Cataloging-in-Publication Data

Gibbs, Eddie.
  LeadershipNext: changing leaders in a changing culture / Eddie
Gibbs.
      p. cm.
  Includes bibliographical references (p.   ) and indexes.
  ISBN 0-8308-3283-1 (pbk.: alk paper)
  1. Christian leadership. 2. Leadership—Religious
aspects—Christianity. I. Title: Leadership next. II. Title.
BV652.1.G53 2005
253—dc22

                                                                    2005008304

P 19 18 17 16 15 14 13 12 11 10 9 8 7 6 5 4 3 2 1

Y 19 18 17 16 15 14 13 12 11 10 09 08 07 06 05

Contents

Acknowledgments

First, I want to express my thanks to Andy Le Peau, editorial director of InterVarsity Press, for prodding me into action in response to a radio interview on the topic of the emerging church he saw reported on *Christianity Today's* website. In response to a question on the reasons for the loss of so many of the under-thirty-fives from the church, I replied that one factor is that they are reacting against a culture of control. Andy thought that one observation contained the seed for a book. So here is the expanded version!

As a sixty-six-year-old I undertook the task with some misgivings, feeling that someone who represented those in their thirties or twenties would be much better qualified to explore the issues. On further consideration I realized that there might be some value in an older person being both an interpreter and an advocate. But I would not have dared to undertake the task without the encouragement, counsel and comments of both younger and older leaders who are respected by those under thirty-five, and who have demonstrated their leadership ability as acknowledged leaders of networks. In particular I would like to express my thanks to Todd Hunter, Mike Breen, Rick Marshall and Peter Brierley for reading and commenting on an earlier draft of this text. I am sure if any of these individuals had been the author, it would have been a much different and possibly better book. But I thank them for their patience with me and for their valuable comments. I have also benefited from the responses of the anonymous readers. It goes without saying that I take responsibility for the final version of the text.

My son-in-law Brian Auten did valiant service in checking the text and contributing his editorial skills to make sure that the text made sense and that the grammar passed muster. Renee, my wife of forty-two years, demonstrated her usual forgiving spirit as I pounded the keys when we should have been spending time together.

I also wish to thank Fuller Seminary for their generosity in granting me a ten-week sabbatical that was largely devoted to producing the first draft and to giving my thoughts some public airing during ministry to younger leaders in Denmark and Norway.

Most of the initial writing was undertaken in Wales and England. So I wish to thank my sisters-in-law Betty Jenkins in South Wales and Marie Henson and Jean Treadgold in the East Midlands for providing hospitality to my wife and me so that I could work undisturbed, while sisters caught up on news of family and friends.

Also I express my appreciation to my daughter Helen, son-in-law Joe and grandson Andrew for our time together during the birth of our fourth grandchild, Emily—an event that provided added inspiration and an irresistible distraction.

Eddie Gibbs

Introduction

Where Have All the Leaders Gone?

Leadership is a nerve-racking and exhausting business. Each new day, leaders face fresh challenges and yet more decisions, making it difficult to maintain momentum. Once leaders begin to tire or stall, they are in danger of becoming obstacles or diversionaries. If this is true under the most routine conditions, it is even more the case when the surrounding culture is in turbulent transition. Today, there is abundant evidence that such cultural change is rapidly occurring on a global scale, particularly throughout the developed nations and in cities that are worldwide centers of technological innovation.

For many institutions this sea change in culture has precipitated a crisis in leadership. Most of the leaders who have made it to the top of hierarchical institutions arrived there after decades of faithful service. During those decades, they developed insights and skills based on their accumulated experience. But now these leaders have emerged only to discover that the conditions under which they must operate are significantly different from those they have previously worked under. They are not only unnervingly unfamiliar but at times incomprehensible, having changed beyond all recognition. The ministry training I received over forty years ago was for a world that now no longer exists, and even at the time it was undergoing radical change. Consequently, the major challenge for leaders is not only the acquisition of new insights and skills but also unlearning what they already know. Today's leaders need the courage and ability to risk their false sense of confidence and to surrender their predetermined, "wired" responses, and outdated and inaccurate mental maps.

For the vast majority of leaders this is extremely hard. Hence, training has become a major industry—one that seeks to address two key questions. First, how can leaders now in place best be retrained so that they understand the global trends that affect them? Second, how can a new generation of leaders best be identified, resourced and eventually empowered to use their insights and entrepreneurial skills? Warren Bennis asks, "Where will the next generation of leaders come from?"[1] This is the question that must be on the mind of leaders in every institution, whether business, education, health care, military, government or—the concern addressed in the following pages—the church.

While this book is concerned with leadership in the church, the overall issue of leadership must be placed in a much wider context so church leaders understand that the turmoil they face is not confined to organized (or increasingly disorganized) religion. Rather, the cultural tumult is a pervasive one. It is not merely the consequence of the church's marginalization in the West. Neither is it due primarily to dwindling numbers or overstretched resources. It arises from the fact that the church faces cultural shifts of seismic proportions. Many of the changes occurring all around us are no longer predictable and incremental, but unforeseeable and chaos-producing.

Churches that fail to read and accurately interpret the signs of the times risk a bleak future. Throughout Europe and Australasia, this has been evident for some time. There, we have witnessed the steady weakening and near collapse of denominational structures—structures designed for a very different kind of world. Now, however, this cultural change is having as profound an affect on traditional North American denominations. Granted, this trend is more advanced in Canada than in the United States, the latter being still an anomaly in the Western world in terms of the numerical strength of its churchgoing population. But the United States is not immune.

Few people would dispute the fact that the churchgoing population has been in decline during the past three or four decades. The only debate is regarding the actual percentage of the population that attends a worship service on an average week. The pollsters put this figure at between 39 and 43 percent, whereas those who base their estimates on attendance data reported by the churches put the figure at around 18 percent, with a figure of more than once-a-month attendance at around 25 percent. When these figures are broken down by region, the Midwest and South represent the highest figure, with the seaboard states of the Northeast and the Southwest registering the lowest church attendance.

Since the mid 1960s, North America has experienced four trends that when taken together point in the direction of the European and Australasian experience. The first trend has been the numerical decline of the major denominations. Those traditional denominations that used to be called the "mainline" are now "sideline."[2] Second, in keeping with their European counterparts, North American churches are losing their under-thirty-fives at an alarming rate. Third, as a result of dwindling congregations and higher operating costs, an increasing number of churches are struggling to keep their doors open. Finally, there are fewer and fewer seminary-trained leaders for those traditional denominations that struggle to replace aging clergy who are approaching or are past retirement age.

In the United States the serious nature of the situation is masked by a religious entrepreneurship that has brought into being a significant number of megachurches and spawned a church-planting movement that has recorralled a percentage of those who had left congregations to find their own way in life. The success of these initiatives, however, does not represent new growth for the most part. Instead, it is built on the redistribution of the existing churchgoing population. Furthermore, they have not made an impact to the extent that they have been able to reverse the downward trend.

Unlike the conditions of decline in the churchgoing population that prevail in other Western countries, the churchgoing population in the United States is in flux. With the rapid expansion of the suburbs after World War II, evangelical attention and church-planting efforts followed "white flight" from the cities to the suburbs. This in turn left behind elderly and poor whites to struggle to maintain their urban churches. These older inner-city neighborhoods were also home to vibrant African American congregations that were eventually joined by storefront churches established by the fresh waves of immigrants from Central and South America, Asia (especially South Korea), and sub-Saharan Africa. Many of these new congregations rented and later purchased the church buildings of those congregations that had either left the cities or whose numbers had dwindled almost to the point of extinction.

The negative church trends in the United States have also been masked by the phenomenon of returning baby boomers. In a movement that gathered momentum in the 1980s and the early 1990s, boomers who had abandoned the church in large numbers during the era of Vietnam and Watergate began their return. For many of these boomers, church took on fresh meaning after they married and started their own families. Moreover, it is estimated that 80 percent of these returning boomers selected a church of a different tradition from that in which they were raised. In fact, many were no longer influenced by the denominational label of a church, being attracted instead by its seeker-friendly ethos and the quality and range of its programs that addressed their felt needs.

This consumer-focused approach to ministry successfully attracted crowds, but it has failed for the most part to transform lives or construct significant personal relationships that provide encouragement, spiritual growth, accountability and avenues for Christian ministry. The old adage "easy come, easy go" has proven very true in terms of many churchgoers, especially the boomer returnees. Many wander from church to church, seeking fresh religious stimuli, entertainment and diversion. The United States may have a vibrant religious marketplace compared to the rest of the Western world, but more and more people spend their time just shopping around, looking for diversion while avoiding commitment.[3]

On both sides of the Atlantic as well as across the southern Pacific, churches are losing their under-thirty-fives.[4] Many explanations are offered for this loss; the most common of them focus on either archaic styles of worship or preaching that ignores the everyday life of younger people and leaves the pressing issues of the day unaddressed, issues such as ecology, sexuality, quality of life, the Internet and virtual communities.

This book focuses on a frequently overlooked factor, the relationship between leadership and the loss of the under-thirty-fives. Younger adults are walking away from those institutions characterized by a culture of control and a style of delegation that is considered disempowering—the prevailing leadership style of those who are over forty (whether they are boomers or the two previous generations, often called the "silents" and "builders"). Their concept of leadership and management most commonly follows the acronym PLOC (Plan, Lead, Organize and Control). That older style of leadership might have worked—more or less—in a cultural context where information was restricted and privileged, circumstances to a large degree were predictable and change was orderly. Those conditions no longer exist. As Gary Hemel asks in relation to the business world, "Are we learning as fast as the world is changing?"[5] In the midst of a cultural maelstrom, the church must not lull itself into a sense of false security on the misguided assumption that its leadership structures are firmly entrenched and biblically authenticated.

In addition to focusing on younger leaders, this book's particular concern is with those leaders who are in start-up congregations and new movements, or are working on an experimental basis within established churches with the liberty to develop new structures that are appropriate to the missional challenge. It would require a whole book to explore leadership issues within various traditions, be they Presbyterian, Episcopal, Congregational, or staff- and board-governed churches.

Our received understanding of the ministry of apostle, prophet, evangelist and pastor-teacher might be far more culturally conditioned by the mindset of modernity than we realize. It is my contention that we need to reexamine these roles in light of first- *and* twenty-first-century contexts. How is it possible that the early church developed and deployed so many leaders within such a short span of time, thus multiplying local congregations throughout the Mediterranean world? How did the Christian movement of the first century expand so rapidly at a time when it was culturally marginalized, faced the challenges of pluralism and owned no real estate or training institutions?

In contrast to the first two centuries of the church, why has the twenty-first-century church been unable to produce leaders in sufficient numbers and caliber to revitalize existing congregations and birth new communities throughout the Western world? Furthermore, what can the churches of the Northern Hemisphere learn from those in the South that, despite their many problems, are sustaining incredible rates of growth? In the face of unprecedented missional opportunities and challenges, what should be the defining characteristics of the next generation of church leaders? And how can the churches in both the South and the North develop authentic followers of Jesus who will be faithful to the gospel in a rapidly changing world?

In attempting to address these issues, I wish to acknowledge my indebtedness to many younger leaders who are pointing to new ways of seeing and doing as well as to older mentors who have poured their wisdom into the lives of those who are so eager to learn on an ongoing basis. My oral sources are almost exclusively drawn from the church, while much of my reading outside of the Bible has been from thinkers in the business world. Indeed, similar questions are being addressed in the business world, both by Christian writers as well as by those searching for spiritual values in reaction to the moral confusion and spiritual wasteland that has been created by the secularization of Western societies.

I am all too aware that this is a work in progress. Considering the changes and chaos of this fleeting world, it cannot claim to be anything more. Furthermore, the "emerging church"—the phenomenon that has surfaced within some traditional denominations and has also taken the form of new networking movements—is recent and evolving. Some observers have concluded that it does not have sufficient cohesion to be designated a "movement" and is by definition decentered. Some prefer to speak of it more in terms of a "conversation." It represents a spectrum of initiatives that share some common values and priorities, while displaying considerable differences.

I have refrained from identifying individuals in deference to the fact that so many of the younger leaders experience a high failure rate as they embark on steep learning curves while feeling their way around. To all those who are no doubt relieved to find that I did not name them, I want to express thanks both for their enthusiasm and their vulnerability. Both of these are refreshing and energizing traits.

I have written with two primary readers in mind. The first is those leaders whose worldview has been shaped by the presuppositions and challenges of modernity and who continue to understand ministry to the flock and evangelization from a Christendom mindset. Such leaders consist mainly, but by no means exclusively, of the over-forty generations. There are also many younger church leaders who share this worldview because of the influence of traditional understandings of "church" and the presuppositions on which their training for ministry were based. For these readers, with whom I most closely identify, I have attempted to provide some insights as to why emergent church leaders see things in a very different light and demonstrate contrasting leadership styles.

Second, this book is written as a word of encouragement from an older guy to younger leaders, especially to those who are plowing a lonely furrow and wonder whether their risk-taking and the misunderstanding they encounter are worth the effort. I also want to offer some cautions and point out some blind spots that I believe need to be identified for the future direction of the emerging church. In reality moderns and postmoderns need to be in conversation and in a listening mode because each has valuable insights to contribute. This is especially important at the present time when worldviews exist side by side to the extent that all ministry has become crosscultural. The critique we offer regarding our various understandings of the church must be deeply theological, yet from the standpoint of a missional and kingdom-embracing theology, rather than a Constantinian and Christendom ecclesiology. The particular focus of this book is on leadership issues as they relate to the breaking of the traditional maintenance mold in order to engage contemporary culture. In so doing I will offer a theological critique that applies to the approach of younger leaders within the emerging churches in their responses to the challenges posed by traditional understandings of church.

Finally, I write this book after forty years of ordained ministry in the Anglican church. Despite the many tensions and uncertainties at the present time, I would not exchange today's challenges and opportunities for any other period. The church in the West is emerging from the misplaced certainties of the Christendom era to become the church that the Lord intended—shaped by our call to trust Christ unswervingly, our willingness to follow him into an unknown immediate future and our desire to invite others to join us in the adventure of the spiritual journey in the steps of the One who calls us to follow him as "the way, the truth and the life."

OVERVIEW

In the opening chapter I redefine leadership in response to the current cultural context of rapid change, much of which is unpredictable. This requires leaders who are able to discern the signs of the times and to respond in prompt and appropriate ways. It presents a challenge to older leaders who must question their assumptions about leadership and adopt new attitudes and learn new skills. It also highlights the different assumptions and styles of leadership between those who look to established institutional models and those who are shaped by the broader cultural context. This divide is partly, but not exclusively, generational.

Chapter two argues that change in leadership roles and styles is not an option but an urgent necessity. The information age is characterized by ambiguity. On the one hand globalization highlights the megatrends affecting our world through economic and religious power blocks, resulting in a clash of civilizations. Another factor is the emergence of communication networks, some of which are controlled by centralized media channels such as CNN or Al Jazeera, while others are decentralized and unregulated, such as the Internet. On the one hand large institutions, such as multinational companies and the militaries of Western nations, wield enormous power. On the other hand, networks of terrorist cells grab global attention and inflict significant damage, and small companies each with a handful of employees create 80 percent of the new jobs in North America and Europe.

In relation to the growth of the church around the world, we see the emergence of megachurches in the global South as well as in the North, but also the proliferation of small fellowships of Christians meeting in homes, cafés, schools, community centers, pubs and bars, business offices, hotels, and in the open air. Whereas the "elephants" get most of the attention, the most significant growth may come from the multiplication of the "fleas." For the most part emerging church leaders represent the fleas rather than the elephants. This is not because of a remnant theology that justifies smallness as the inevitable result of faithfulness to the gospel; rather it reflects the conviction that the church must be structured in small, reproducible units consisting of people committed to engaging the broader culture.

Chapter three reexamines the Great Commission as recorded in Matthew's Gospel from the standpoint of the missional understanding of the church outlined in chapter two. It emphasizes the challenge that Commission presents to the contemporary church in terms of reordering its priorities to transform church members into disciples who are learning to walk with God on a daily basis. In so doing these churches are also equipping them to translate their witness into the life situations and languages where God has already strategically placed them. It represents a shift in perspective from *going* to church to *being* the church.

In chapter four I address the need for churches to move from a hierarchical and often highly controlling style of leadership to one that is far more decentralized and that encourages ground-level initiatives. It is a style represented by strong relationships and high accountability. Chapter five takes up a major implication of this change in style, emphasizing the need for team building, not only among the paid staff but among the volunteer leaders and throughout the membership. A congregation must not be considered a crowd of people but a federation of teams. While the concept of team building is simple, its development and sustenance is complex.

Chapters six through eight focus on those leadership traits, activities and attitudes modeled by many younger leaders. The lists and profiles outlined in these chapters are not randomly generated but represent cohesive clusters shaped by the response of younger leaders to the missional challenge of a postmodern cultural context.

In many ways the younger leaders have a distinct advantage over older leaders because they are a product of the information age. It is the only cultural context they have ever known, whereas most older leaders—this author among them—have had to shed many of the assumptions of the past, learning from the example of younger leaders and listening to their explanations and interpretations of postmodernity.

At the same time the learning is not all one way. Older leaders have much to contribute and need to raise their valid concerns regarding the weak points and blind spots of younger leaders. Furthermore, many younger leaders have not had the benefit of missions training and may be so immersed in their cultural context that they are not able to provide a critique from within. Our contextualization of the gospel and of the church must be critical rather than naive, recognizing that every culture, whether modern or postmodern, includes good, neutral and destructive elements.

Chapter nine addresses the issue of the price tag on leadership. There is always a cost associated with the very nature of the gospel and the world's antipathy to the message of the cross. In the present cultural climate there are particular costs arising out of misunderstandings within the church, and new initiatives and alternative structures entail risk taking.

The final chapter then turns to the issue of how new leaders will be identified and equipped for ministry in the twenty-first century. It identifies a number of innovative approaches being developed in the United Kingdom, North America and Australia. It speaks to established leaders and seminaries about the responses they might want to consider and also encourages younger leaders to avail themselves of new opportunities for learning. Many are committed to lifelong learning and have developed interdisciplinary learning skills, but this needs to be expanded beyond a pick-and-choose learning style to include communal learning (virtual and face-to-face) and areas of study that they would not have selected on their own but that will expand their conceptual horizons and provide valuable insights.

It is always difficult to write from within a context of cultural transformation. Twenty-twenty vision is much easier with hindsight. But the changes taking place are so significant that we must not live in denial or downplay the signs of the times. If we succumb to these temptations, we will wake up one day to discover that we did far too little, much too late. And that won't be the first time in the long history of the church.

1

Redefining Leadership

We might think that leadership is so self-evident that it doesn't need to be defined. We might assume a leader is simply the person at the head of the pack who determines the direction and persuades those in tow to follow faithfully. But that assumption is seriously inadequate and could be thoroughly misleading. It provides an apt description of a tour guide holding aloft a brightly colored umbrella for a group of people who need clear direction and the security of one another in an alien land. But it does not apply in the much broader context of leadership within movements that are looking to engage, infiltrate and transform culture—the task of the church engaged in mission within Western contexts.

As we consider the complexity of leadership in contemporary cultural settings, we will draw on biblical insights and secular wisdom. In regard to the latter it is recognized at the outset that the church should not simply follow the leadership insights and models of the business world. Yet we may discover we have much to learn from recent thought in secular business literature concerning such issues as values-based leadership, which recognizes the gifting of others and the fact that leadership is not simply confined to the pinnacle of the hierarchy but rather emerges at every level of an organization. Christian thinkers also have a valuable contribution to make by both affirming these insights and subjecting them to a discerning theological critique.

The relationship between the secular and spiritual is a symbiotic one rather than a clash of opposites. In the secular realm many significant changes in thinking have occurred. For example, the management-by-objective philosophy that proved so demanding, manipulative and destructive for so many in the business world has now been largely superseded. In the course of reading a large number of recently published books on leadership in the for-profit and nonprofit worlds, I have been struck by their emphasis on humility, a servant attitude, spirituality and consistently upheld values as essential ingredients for leadership visions to be actualized. This welcome development is in line with leadership values made explicit in the New Testament.

LEADERSHIP IN TRANSITION

Leadership is a complex issue; it cannot be defined in one short sentence. It takes on different forms in diverse situations in which individuals demonstrate contrasting leadership traits. We can more readily identify the characteristics of leadership by their absence since, unfortunately, we have more experience of both leadership vacuums and leadership muddles than we do of leadership that has a clear sense of direction and empowers the community it leads.

Kenneth Cloke and Joan Goldsmith provide two broad categories that describe the absence of leadership in any organization or community—zombification and atrophication. These terms describe the protective response encountered in organizations where leadership has become either laissez faire or controlling. They observe that "numbing oneself to experience is a natural response to unfulfilled expectations, unprocessed pain, unfinished grieving, unresolved conflict, and repetitive disappointment."[1] In other words people have stopped thinking for themselves and have become lethargic. These two conditions are all too prevalent in many churches. The authors provide a range of telltale symptoms, which I have listed (with slight modification):

- People are punished for being aware and being authentic. In other words, telling it as it is.

- [Leaders] stop telling the truth and lie or keep silent about things that matter.
- Feedback is no longer oriented to how [people] can succeed but to how they have failed—not just in their work but as human beings.
- Performance assessment becomes judgmental and hierarchical rather than supportive and participatory.
- Honesty is separated from kindness, integrity from advancement, and respect from communication.[2]

If these indicators are accurate in relation to the business world, they are even more applicable and widespread with respect to the church. The casualty rate among church leaders has reached disturbingly high levels as leaders leave local church ministry because of burnout, stress-related illness and disillusionment. When churches become dysfunctional and toxic, they are prone to project their problems onto the leaders, whom they hire and fire with increasing rapidity. Or else trapped leaders, with nowhere else to go, simply curl up and sit it out until retirement, like hedgehogs without the benefit of protective spines.

Yet the scenario is not all doom and gloom. Some older leaders have successfully made the transition and are today leading vibrant congregations. A few leaders of seeker-sensitive megachurches that came to the forefront in the 1980s and 1990s are in the throes of taking a second—and equally radical—step into the twenty-first century to retain and reach out to those under thirty. However, some of the most adventurous leaders to engage the counterculture movements of the 1960s have since become the most conservative in reaction to the present cultural challenges. They still bear the scars of their previous phase of entrepreneurship, and they don't have the energy reserves to face a fresh challenge.

I am aware of two or three megachurch pastors who are reconsidering their ministry priorities, recognizing that there is a growing desire for church structures that are more relational, with less emphasis on a stage-managed professional performance and a greater focus on the need for active participation in the worship experience, ministry to one another and mission in the world. This shift is evident not only among boomer pastors but also among some younger leaders who have been successful in attracting a younger congregation but are aware of a high turnover rate.

One perceptive member of a thriving Gen-X congregation meeting as part of a megachurch writes of a prevailing success-driven gospel and self-help Christianity, with a lack of authenticity in relationships and members of their small groups seldom holding one another accountable. She states in a paper submitted as a class assignment in my course on the emerging church that although their music is upbeat, "without an authentic, life transforming relationship with Christ and the Church, worship becomes little more than singing songs to a rock band and conjuring up an emotional high rather than being in the awesome presence of God." These are not the views of a judgmental person; at the outset she includes herself among those whom she describes.

At the present time God is also raising up a new generation of leaders who are acutely aware of the inadequacies of a consumer-driven church model. With the exception of those who have been safely corralled in the Christian subculture or were enculturated into the world of yesterday in their seminary training, it is a generation that is aware of the growing chasm between the church and popular culture. (I hasten to add that not all seminaries are exerting a retrograde influence!)

The church of the twenty-first century needs missional thinkers and apostolic leadership. By missional leadership, I mean leaders who can read the Scriptures with fresh eyes, relating the story of redemption to the human condition in its present cultural contexts—contexts that are increasingly multicultural and influenced by global trends. Whereas theology of mission was once taught as a specialist course, we now need to teach our entire repertoire of Bible, theology and church history courses from a missional perspective. One of the greatest tragedies in theological education has been the separation (to their mutual impoverishment) of ecclesiology from missiology. This separation has resulted, on the one hand, in a missionless church and, on the other, in a churchless mission. Here we can learn valuable lessons from the churches of the Southern Hemisphere—if we are prepared to set aside our intellectual elitism or, more bluntly, snobbery.

DEFINING LEADERS AND LEADERSHIP

It is possible to define *leadership* in such a way that it applies across time in relation to the church regardless of its particular tradition or context. J. Robert Clinton provides the following definition: "A Christian leader is a person with a God-given capacity and the God-given responsibility to influence a specific group of God's people toward God's purpose for the group."[3] This definition draws attention to the initiative of God in calling forth leadership, a point that is strongly emphasized throughout Scripture.

We have only to think of the call of Abram, Joseph, Moses, Gideon, David, Isaiah, the Twelve and the apostle Paul as well as the leadership roles played by Miriam, Deborah, Dorcas and Priscilla and the prophetic ministry of the evangelist Philip's four daughters. Many of these individuals were not obvious choices in terms of their innate abilities and experience, but in each case, having been called, they were equipped by God in order to fulfill their calling. Their role was to "influence," not dominate, the group among whom they were given leadership responsibilities. Clinton's use of the term *group* leaves open the extent of their leadership. Some individuals exercise leadership behind the scenes by advising and mentoring other leaders who have a more public and extensive sphere of influence.

This is very different from much of the leadership literature of the 1980s that focused on high-powered, entrepreneurial leadership exercised by larger-than-life "charismatic" personalities. In its secular usage *charismatic* does not apply to spiritual gifting but to fast-talking persons with magnetic personalities, inflated egos and the big ideas necessary to provide them with a sense of personal fulfillment. Thankfully, this understanding of leadership has been strongly challenged in recent years. There is increasing evidence demonstrating that such high-profile, charismatic leadership is not sustainable in the long term and ultimately has a debilitating effect on the entire organization over which it has been imposed.

James Kouzes and Barry Posner emphasize that "leadership is not the private reserve of a few charismatic men and women. It is a process ordinary people use when they are bringing forth the best from themselves and others. Leadership is your capacity to guide others to places they (and you) have never been before."[4] Steven Bernstein and Anthony Smith express the same point of view:

> Leadership is now understood by many to imply *collective* action, orchestrated in such a way as to bring about significant change while raising the competencies and motivation of all those involved—that is, action, where more than one individual influences the process.[5]

In attempting to define leadership, especially within the contemporary church context, it must be understood as applying to every level of the church's structure. On the assumption that every disciple of Jesus Christ will exercise some kind of influence on the people around them, they are *de facto* leaders. All it requires to constitute an individual as a leader is for one person to be following! Furthermore, the choice of who functions as a leader within a particular situation depends to some extent on the nature of the task at hand and the availability of a person with the appropriate gifts. Robert Banks and Bernice M. Ledbetter, in offering their definition of leadership, embrace this broader concept. For them "leadership involves a person, group, or organization who shows the way in an area of life—whether in the short- or the long-term—and in doing so both influences and empowers enough people to bring about change in that area."[6]

At the outset it will be helpful to draw a distinction between the narrower and broader definition of leadership. Walter Wright expresses the distinction well:

> If by leader we mean one who holds a position of authority and responsibility, then every Christian is not a leader. Some are—some are not. But if by leader we mean a person who enters into a relationship

with another person to influence their behavior, values or attitudes, then I would suggest that all Christians should be leaders. Or perhaps more accurately, all Christians should exercise leadership, attempting to make a difference in the lives of those around them.[7]

Here my concern is primarily with the narrower definition of leadership, although many of the observations will equally apply to every Christian who influences others. Wright's definition of leadership encompasses both the narrow and broader understanding. "Leadership is a relationship—a relationship in which one person seeks to influence the thoughts, behaviors, beliefs or values of another person."[8]

Leaders don't function in isolation but with the backing of a team whose roles may change from time to time. Sometimes a leader will deliberately step aside to take a breather, much like an athlete during a cycle race who for a time cedes leadership to a teammate in order to relieve the pressure. Migrating geese demonstrate the same strategy out of instinct, when the lead goose in a typical V formation drops back and another takes the lead.

Among athletes functioning as a team, this is not a self-serving, competitive move but rather one that is made out of consideration for the person who has been setting the pace and needs a respite before assuming the leadership role once again. In contrast, when athletes compete as individuals, their constant jockeying for position represents a trial of strength, a clash of temperament or a ruthless pursuit of advantage by exploiting a moment of weakness. The leadership scenarios within the emerging church require sharing leadership responsibilities among a team. We will consider in some detail the significance of team leadership within the local church in response to the solo-pastor model of leadership that has prevailed in the past.

REEXAMINING THE CONCEPT OF SERVANT LEADERSHIP

In reaction to the prestige-seeking and domineering style of leadership that has prevailed in some ecclesial traditions, the servant-leadership model of Jesus provides a welcome correction. Sometimes the use of this servant concept has resulted in an abdication of leadership, particularly when it was mistakenly understood to imply that the servant's primary role was to meet the demands of those he or she was called to serve. This is a serious misunderstanding of the servant role of Jesus, who was first and foremost the servant of his heavenly Father.

Jesus unswervingly sought his Father's guidance for the direction of his ministry. Rather than simply responding to popular demand, he took the initiative in terms of his overriding purpose. The morning after Jesus had ministered to the sick in Capernaum, Simon appealed to him to meet the pressing needs of the crowds who had again gathered. Jesus responded by declaring, "Let us go somewhere else—to the nearby villages—so I can preach there also. That is why I have come" (Mk 1:38). The demand for Jesus was so relentless in Galilee that had he allowed pressure from the crowds to determine the future course of his ministry, he would never have completed the work his Father had entrusted to him. As a servant leader his primary allegiance was to his heavenly Father. Jesus knew that his path of obedience would lead to Jerusalem, where he would be betrayed, rejected and crucified.

Serving as a Christian scholar in a business school, Shirley Roels critiques the common understanding of servant leadership:

> Is it really an accurate representation of Jesus as portrayed in the Bible? Frequently, we use servant leadership to mean leaders should simply absorb and carry out the ideas of others. That model is attributed to Jesus. It seems to me that Jesus wasn't *just* a servant of people. His example of servanthood was defined very differently because of his unique connection to the will of God.[9]

First and foremost Jesus was committed to doing his heavenly Father's bidding, not to meeting the demands of his followers and the crowds. He came to fulfill the role of the "servant of the Lord." The idea of the servant of the Lord as understood in the Old Testament was by no means a demeaning one. To the contrary, it was a title of honor, applied to Israel's national leaders and, even more significantly, to the servant king referred to by Isaiah. It referred to the special messenger sent by God with whom Jesus identified—an identification that was also assumed by the early church.

We need to exercise care when applying the notion of servant leadership to leaders within today's church. We are not Jesus. Consequently, we are prone to be selective in our obedience, we display sinful tendencies, and we are limited in our understanding of God's will for our lives; thus we struggle to interpret and follow his day-to-day guidance. Servant leadership can neither be made a justification for whatever we are doing nor become a pious cover for human weakness, false humility or abdication of responsibility.

Roger Greenleaf, the Quaker author of the groundbreaking book *Servant Leadership* and a thinker ahead of his time, expounds the concept with discernment and contemporary application. Writing in 1977, Greenleaf explained the insights he gained during his time as a manager at AT&T, but it took a decade for his ideas to begin to make an impact on secular leadership. He drew inspiration for his model from the life and ministry of Jesus. For Greenleaf true servant leaders are those who are prepared to take the initiative. But before embarking on a course of action, they listen to God and to the voices around them in order to determine what God requires of them. They are committed for the long haul, maintaining faith and hope, patience and fortitude. They also make time, no matter how busy their schedules, to withdraw from the relentless demands of daily life in order to refocus and renew their strength.

Such discipline enables servant leaders, who are all too aware of their limitations, to demonstrate foresight and anticipate their next steps. As they exercise discernment, servant leaders are constantly making connections between isolated pieces of information, looking for a coherent pattern to emerge. Gifted with intuition that Greenleaf perceptively defines as "a feel for patterns," they conceptualize rather than simply critique. Greenleaf chides:

> Too many settle for being critics and experts. There is too much intellectual wheel spinning, too much retreating into "research," too little preparation for and willingness to undertake the hard and high-risk

tasks of building better institutions in an imperfect world, too little disposition to see "the problem" as residing *in here* and not *out there*. In short, the enemy is strong natural servants who have the potential to lead but do not lead, or who choose to follow a non-servant.[10]

LEADERSHIP SHAPED BY CONTEXT

Though it can be defined in general terms, leadership is profoundly influenced by the context and the personality of the individual. We cannot simply transpose one style of leadership from one particular time, location and cultural setting and apply it to another. Herein lies one of the problems in trying to impose biblical models of leadership without distinguishing universally valid elements from those that are context specific. The models of leadership seen in Scripture are not always reproducible, but there are valuable lessons to be learned that can be adapted to situations in our own lives where similar circumstances prevail.

Abraham, for instance, demonstrated a style of leadership that was appropriate for a patriarchal, extended family. Joseph, before he was liberated by Pharaoh to function as a grand vizier over all of Egypt, emerged as a leader first as a household slave and then as a long-term prisoner. During his long years facing adversity, he demonstrated fortitude, patience, trustworthiness, God-given knowledge and extraordinary gifts of strategic planning. Moses, after an even longer period of preparation, was called by God to become the liberator of his people from enslavement in Egypt. Joshua, Moses' loyal lieutenant, succeeded him as a military commander and led Israel to victory over the Canaanites through a succession of skillfully led campaigns. David became Israel's greatest king within a theocratic context. For years after, the prophets of Israel exercised leadership as bold, antiestablishment figures that told the nation and its leaders what they needed to learn from God but were so often unwilling to hear or heed.

Moving to the New Testament, we encounter Jesus' model of leadership. Jesus proclaimed the good news of the kingdom. Jesus chose twelve unlikely individuals as pillars of his church and prepared them for leadership by having them observe all that he did, listen to his teaching and eventually go out as his representatives.

In the contemporary situation, traditional pastoral leadership is often shaped by inherited patterns of hierarchy, status and indispensability, resulting in a dependent, disempowered and disgruntled following. When churches are dysfunctional, traditional leaders buckle under the weight of the unreasonable demands laid on them. Among the consequences are a high percentage of pastors leaving from burnout or moral failure, taking early retirement, or seeking alternative employment outside of the local church. By contrast the emerging leaders are concerned not with institutional maintenance but with missional effectiveness. They focus on ministry *by* the church in the world rather than ministry *in* the church that is largely confined to the existing members.

TYPOLOGY OF LEADERSHIP

Different situations require distinctive leadership gifts. One complex array of challenges might require a range of leadership expertise, necessitating a team approach. In order to tackle an unfamiliar or new set of circumstances, highly *creative* individuals are needed. These are people who can think "outside the box," who are prepared to experiment and take risks.

Then there are the *executive* types who are the principal decision makers. Their skill is in their ability to see the big picture—the capability to distinguish the crucial elements and evaluate options. Besides the macro, they also see the micro, which keeps them anchored in an unswerving and passionate commitment to "keep the main thing the main thing." But executive types need people alongside them who have *managerial* skills, who can determine the steps that need to be taken in order to achieve what Jim Collins and Jerry Porras describe as the BHAG—the "Big Hairy Audacious Goal." They write, "A true BHAG is clear and compelling and serves as a unifying focal point of effort—often creating immense team spirit. It has a clear finish line."[11] The leadership team needs to identify and pursue unswervingly the primary goals that undergird the movement's vision.

The creative and executive types of leader rely on individuals with managerial skills who are *task oriented*. Task-oriented leaders need to be served by leaders with *interpersonal skills,* who will function as the team-builders, consolidating, resolving conflict and restoring the group's morale. Such individuals encourage and reassure so that each person feels valued.[12]

CHARACTER, CHARISMA AND COMPETENCE

It is unreasonable to expect that all of these gifts and skills will reside in one individual, which is one of the fundamental reasons why leadership must be team-based rather than attempted solo. Whatever the local church context, irrespective of size, leadership represents a daunting challenge. Unlike leadership within the business environment or in the military, church leadership must embrace all comers, from the cradle to the grave. Also the BHAG in question is nothing less than the communication of the good news of Jesus Christ, accomplished through credible communicators who demonstrate in their own personal and corporate life the accessibility, sufficiency and attractive reality of that message.

Leaders who attempt such a daunting task in their own strength set themselves up for failure. With every step they need the strength and guidance of the Holy Spirit as well as the support of a team of people who share their values and commitment. Leaders are constantly challenged to sacrifice values in the interests of expediency. Within the context of the church, as well as in business and political spheres, leadership failure arises more out of character failure than unwise decision making. Yet *character* must not be divorced from *competence*. We must not lose sight of the need for visionary, entrepreneurial, risk-taking and Holy Spirit-inspired leadership. These leadership qualities are especially needed as the present church suffers from a loss of sense of direction, as an increasing percentage of local churches struggle for survival, and as the church finds itself increasingly marginalized and its influence evaporating. Who will step in to turn the tide?

Throughout history we have seen God raise, call and equip the next generation of leaders to attempt great things in his name and power. Writing primarily in reference to the business world, Jean Lipman-Blumen observes that charismatic leaders who espouse a decidedly radical vision often appear in times of great distress. Their contribution is needed precisely when society's ordinary coping mechanisms are out of kilter. She describes their response as a devotion born of distress.[13] An increasing number of senior church leaders recognize that the potential leaders emerging from traditional channels do not have the vision, passion and risk-taking qualities necessary to shape and direct the church in an uncertain future.

Using Lipman-Blumen's language, we need to move from a *transactional* to a *transformational* leadership model.[14] The former represents those who work within a given structure, meet the needs of their followers and are skilled in striking compromises in order to keep everyone on board. On the other hand the transformational leader, prepared to think "outside the box," works to transform structures. Transformational leaders shape the lives of individuals around them, providing them with intellectual stimulation and presenting them with significant challenges.[15] This style of connective leadership is more evident among the under-thirty-fives, and women tend to be more adept at it than men. The controlling style of leadership that is so prevalent among the builder and boomer generations, and that typically determines the church's corporate culture, must give way to this empowering, connective style if the church is to reinvent itself to meet the missional challenges and opportunities of a new day.

LEADERSHIP MATRIX

For too long the church has operated with a long list of requirements that an individual must meet in order to be considered for leadership. This flies in the face of the evidence of how significant leaders have emerged among the people of God over the course of history. Jesus did not start out with such a list; otherwise he would not have chosen any of his original team of disciples. Instead, he selected unlikely individuals who were teachable and whose lives he could shape through his presence among them. But until he had ascended into heaven and imparted his Spirit to them, his ministry could not become their ministry, which is why he insisted that they wait in Jerusalem until they had received this promise of the Father (Lk 24:49; Acts 1:4).

Leith Anderson argues that there is no definitive list of qualities and qualifications precisely because leadership is not just about leaders. Rather, "it is about a matrix of followers, organizations, circumstances, power and history."[16] Such a radical rethinking about the nature of leadership in today's fast-paced and unpredictable world is not confined to those addressing the needs of the church. Peter Senge, who is famous for his contribution to systems theory, comments:

> We are coming to believe that leaders are those people who "walk ahead," people who are genuinely committed to deep change in themselves and in their organizations. They lead through developing new skills, capabilities, and understandings. And they come from many places within the organization.[17]

Warren Bennis, contributing to the same volume, urges: "We need to move to an era in which leadership is an organizational capability and not an individual characteristic that a few individuals at the top of the organization have."[18] Such thinking is in line with our understanding of the church as the body of Christ. It is a living organism, in which all members (1) find personal significance in the context of relationships, which enables them to (2) develop their full potential as they (3) make their distinctive contribution in conjunction with others.

This understanding provides the urgently needed antidote to the individualized and privatized religion that has crippled the life of so many churches. Personal identity and significance can never be achieved by "navel gazing." The individual is made whole and healthy within a community that has both a shared history and a shared hope—a timeline and a channel through which corporate identity and purposeful activity can be expressed.

NEW LEADERS FOR CHANGING TIMES

Yesterday's styles of leadership will not be adequate for the opening decades of the twenty-first century. The future is too unpredictable for the predetermined parameters once provided by long-range planning. The church, along with the business world and other institutions, has to learn the skills of just-in-time planning as well as the creation and consideration of alternative scenarios. The original meaning of the word *manage* needs to be recovered. Before the controllers purloined the word to signify "control," it meant "coping," responding promptly and appropriately to unforeseen circumstances over which we have no control. In the area of pastoral care, we still use the term in this sense. We ask someone who is faced with a domestic crisis or tragedy how they are managing—that is, how they are coping.

It is evident in rapidly changing times that knowledge does not necessarily flow from experience. Yesterday's solutions and procedures may not provide an adequate or appropriate response to present challenges. Hence, the biggest hurdles facing long-time leaders may not be in learning new insights and skills, but in unlearning what they consider to be tried and true and what thus provides them with a false sense of security.

Some church leaders begin their ministry with the best of intentions in terms of changing their style of leadership from controlling to empowering. But the entrenched dependency system they inherit causes them to take matters into their own hands on account of shortage of volunteers, incompetence of those who have assumed responsibility or long-entrenched expectations of members. Leaders who allow themselves to become trapped in this system work on the assumption that if *they* don't do it, it doesn't get done. Empowering leaders must be prepared to challenge any separation of responsibilities, which leaves the pastor to attend to the "spiritual" and "sacramental" areas, while laypersons shoulder some of the responsibility for practical matters such as finance and property maintenance. Pastors and layleaders stand together in addressing the spiritual and practical aspects of ministry, maintenance and mission.

Warren Bennis, considering the challenges that organizations face in the wake of the knowledge revolution and globalization, insists that we need new leaders—not just younger leaders, but leaders with new competencies.

In fact, he urges all of us to listen to the under thirties and over seventies.[19] The younger generation brings a fresh perspective, whereas the old folk bring insights without the temptation to grasp power, being content for younger people to take their lead.

GAINING WISDOM AND BUILDING TRUST

While we understand Bennis's call to heed younger voices, we might be surprised by his highlighting of the "over seventies." Seniors bring two distinctive contributions: their broader perspective and the wisdom of their years. They can often think more objectively because they no longer have to defend their positions. Some octogenarians are spectacular visionaries because they are ready for their final fling in life. They are no longer nervous about change because they won't have to live with it for very long! As I have dialogued with younger leaders, many have expressed their longing for mentoring by older leaders. (This is especially true among those who have had a tense relationship with their boomer parents but who love their grandparents.) Keeping this in mind, it is a mistake to regard the emerging church as a passing youth phenomenon. A single generational cohort makes for a very self-serving church. Those churches that have the most significant influence among the under-thirty-five-year-old generation are those with 15 to 20 percent of the members in the over-sixty-year-old category. These seniors provide much-needed mentoring, accountability, encouragement and wise counsel.[20]

Younger leaders typically provide a very different style of leadership from that of their elders. One matter of great concern is the lamentable disconnect between the leadership generations at present. Bill Easum comments that "many of today's most significant leaders are under 30 and we have never heard of them."[21]

Many younger leaders realize that authority does not come with a position and a title but that it has to be earned. It is established on the basis of trustworthiness and competence. They understand that leadership emerges as power is shared rather than as authority is exerted. That power may arise from the application of one's area of expertise, but it is based on trust and is reinforced as personal relationships are deepened and extended. Charles Handy uses the example of the rowing crew of eight going backward steered by a cox who cannot row. When he used this illustration an oarsman in the audience responded: "How do you think that we could go backward so fast, without communicating, if we were not completely confident in each other's competence, committed to the same goal, and determined to do our best to reach it? It's the perfect description for a team."[22]

The leaders of the future must grow and flex with a changing context. They recognize the need to respond rapidly to the unexpected. They are risk takers who maintain a low profile because they take so much flak. They are also individuals committed to change precisely because they recognize the need for change within themselves. Motivated by their insatiable curiosity— a curiosity that drives them to see connections between apparently unconnected pieces of information—leaders of growing organizations are committed to lifelong learning. This in turn results in a refreshing humility; rather than simply make statements, they admit the limitations of their knowledge and continually ask questions. Leaders are constantly growing and making course corrections as they incorporate their new insights. If they stop learning, they eventually stop leading.

LEADERSHIP CHALLENGES

The chapter began with generic definitions of leadership and then explored the various dimensions of leadership, emphasizing how profoundly influenced it is by context. Now we will highlight the leadership challenges that arise when we compare and contrast the traditional church with our postmodern and increasingly neopagan culture.

Church leaders in the twenty-first century must be prepared to reexamine all of their established assumptions, policies and procedures. They must initiate change by asking those they serve whether the church and its leadership are obstacles or channels to becoming a more effective missional presence in their specific cultural context. In many cases the task of the leader

may involve bringing churches to face a painful reality or to overcome determined resistance that stems from ignorance or reluctance.

*Beyond preserving the inherited institution: Leading a mission-focused commu-
nity of disciples.* The primary task of the leader is to reconnect ecclesiology
and missiology in order that the church be defined first and foremost by its
God-given mission. Under the centuries-long influence of Christendom, a
disconnect developed between church and mission. Mission is God-given in
that it represents the heart, initiative and patience of God's relationship to
humankind throughout the ages. It is a mission in which all three persons
of the Trinity work inseparably and distinctively.

Consequently, if the church is to carry out its commission faithfully, it
must draw its models, inspiration, motivation and wisdom from the earthly
ministry of Jesus in relation to his Father and the Holy Spirit. The apostle
John emphasizes this point by recording Jesus' declaration to his heavenly
Father concerning his disciples: "As you sent me into the world, I have sent
them into the world" (Jn 17:18). John then records Jesus' assurance and his
challenge to the disciples gathered in the upper room on the day of his resurrection: "Peace be with you! As the Father has sent me, I am sending you"
(Jn 20:21).

At the heart of Jesus' mission was the training of a group of close followers who learned by (1) listening to his teaching, (2) observing his interactions with people from all walks of life (which included responding to their
needs as well as challenging their assumptions) and (3) working under his
personal supervision. They were first disciplined learners (disciples) before
they were sent out as his personal representatives (apostles).

It is precisely those who had been disciples themselves that Jesus commissioned to make disciples among all peoples. In other words, in order to
invite others to join our ranks, we have to have been through the discipling
process ourselves. Furthermore, Jesus envisages that the communities of believers will continue to take their message and ministries into the world in
order to become a transformative presence. In proclaiming the good news of
the reign of God made present in Christ, those communities function as ser-

vants and anticipatory signs of a God-ordered future in which Christ will reign supreme on earth.

If response to this call of Jesus is the message and mission, how should potential leaders be identified and prepared? Clearly, they need to have been transformed and redirected by that message; otherwise, they will have no credibility. Their training must also relate closely and comprehensively to the mission for which they are being prepared. It must provide both a thorough theological understanding as well as the missiological insights necessary for crosscultural communication from the margins of society. By contrast, so much ministerial training has focused on caring for the flock of God and on maintaining the "shop." So much of our traditional theological agenda has been shaped by a Christendom-context mentality and has been largely confined to an internal debate between various theological factions. A missional theology, on the other hand, focuses on dialogue with unbelievers and those of other religions.

Beyond ideology-driven evangelism: Leading a values-based community of disciples. I confess to a growing disquiet about the time-honored term *evangelism.* When we refer to the good news of Jesus Christ as an *ism,* we are in danger of reducing it to an ideology. The heart of the gospel comprises news to be proclaimed and received rather than abstract propositions to be affirmed. This news is bound up with a story and a person, of which we are invited to become a part. Instead of evangel*ism,* we should retain the verbal form, which is the way the term is used in the New Testament. Evangel*ization* signifies the proclamation of the good news that is actualized in the life, death and resurrection of Jesus Christ.

In contrast, so much of contemporary evangel*ism* has consisted in bringing individuals to a point of decision—turning to Jesus as the Savior, who secures forgiveness of our sins and assures us of a place in heaven. While the gospel includes those important truths, it embraces so much more. It is as much concerned with how we live our lives *before* death as with *after* death. In its true New Testament meaning, eternal life embraces the here and now as a prelude to eternity.

The task of the leader is to spell out the dimensions of personal and community identification with the death and resurrection of Jesus Christ that is our baptismal covenant. Baptism bears witness to what God has done on our behalf and also signifies our identification with Christ. But that identification cannot be confined to an internalized and individualized commitment. We are baptized not only into the person of Christ but also into his body, constituted as the church here on earth, with all its diversity and imperfections (1 Cor 12:13). Baptism is a profoundly corporate act that signifies for all believers their new identity as members of a community of faith. Furthermore, as members of Christ's body, they are baptized into his mission, equipped by the Spirit to make their distinctive contribution to the totality of the ministry of the church.

If the church is to be credible as it communicates the message of the good news of the reign of God, it must demonstrate the values of the kingdom, including humility, honesty, integrity, purity of life, justice and compassion. Not only must leaders explain these values and qualities in light of the baptismal covenant, they themselves must model such qualities and live in relationships of mutual accountability with the churches they serve. Such an understanding of leadership has profound implications for the identification of potential leaders and for the way they are trained. The traditional route—the academic environment based on competitive performance and individual effort—will need to be carefully reevaluated in light of the pressing need for character formation, relational skills and ministry competencies.

Beyond dispensing information: Seeking spiritual formation rooted in Scripture. In most Protestant churches the overwhelming emphasis in ministry is imparting information. The pastor serves as the teacher, communicating knowledge and wisdom through sermons, Bible studies and other classes. In the missional church the concern to relate biblical and theological content is broader than information output. Missional leaders focus as much attention on "intake" as on "output." What is being received, reflected and acted on? They are constantly asking the "So what?" question. Knowledge, missional leaders understand all too readily, can be made an end in itself. Once again, this attitude—dispensing information—is often reinforced by the course content and grading criteria in seminary education.

I well remember a conversation with a highly successful pastor of a megachurch in a traditional denomination. He was a founding pastor who had led his church from a handful of people to a congregation of over twelve thousand members. Many leaders would envy his success in growing a church, yet he had become increasingly restless. He was haunted by the question "Where is the life transformation?" Were his church members living a qualitatively different life from the general population? What profile was the "watching world" likely to construct after observing and interacting with those who professed to follow Christ? Were professed followers more trustworthy or sincere? Did they live a simpler lifestyle, demonstrate a healthier family life by giving high priority to being a spouse and parent, and live out gospel values in the workplace? Or were they indistinguishable from those who made no profession of faith in Christ?

We need to select building materials carefully to ensure that we build a durable construction on the foundation laid by the apostles.

> If any man builds on this foundation using gold, silver, costly stones, wood, hay or straw, his work will be shown for what it is, because the Day will bring it to light. It will be revealed with fire, and the fire will test the quality of each man's work. If what he has built survives, he will receive his reward. If it is burned up, he will suffer loss; he himself will be saved, but only as one escaping through the flames. (1 Cor 3:12-15)

Church planters therefore should not be driven by show and speed but by concern that the faith communities they have helped establish survive in the midst of adverse circumstances—and even more importantly, that they pass when the Lord gives the ultimate test on his return to earth.

The lack of adequately discipled church members is a widespread problem, not only in the Western world but also within the rapidly growing churches of Africa, Latin America and Asia. If life transformation is to take place among believers, the all-encompassing nature of the life of discipleship needs to be taught from the Gospels and the rest of the New Testament. The Gospel of Matthew is particularly helpful in this regard. It fills out the concept of discipleship, instructing communities of first-century believers in the establishment of their new identities as Christ followers. Only after the Twelve have experienced the life-changing impact of the discipling process are they in a position to embark on their mission of making disciples among all peoples.

However, the conditions of first-century discipleship do not establish a comprehensive list of rules. Issues change with time and situation. For this reason the individual believer needs the wisdom and discernment of a community of faith and relationships of mutual accountability. It is through such interactions that profound transformation begins to take place. This is borne out by research conducted in 1987 that indicated that there was no statistically significant difference in values between a churchgoer and nonchurchgoer. Gallup reported at that time, "Church attendance, it appears, makes little difference in people's ethical views and behavior with respect to lying, cheating, pilferage, and not reporting theft."[23] It was only among those who were committed to their church in activities beyond the worship service that a statistically significant difference was found in terms of truth telling, the absence of racial prejudice and the ability to see beyond materialism.

The reduction of discipleship to an itemized list of "dos and don'ts" can readily lead to legalism and judgmental attitudes. The latter occurs when followers of Christ within one cultural context judge other believers living in very different contexts by their own criteria. With patience in listening and in a spirit of mutual understanding, each must hold the other accountable according to the values of the reign of God spelled out in the New Testament. Last, there can be no life transformation resulting in a person becoming more Christlike without the indwelling of the Holy Spirit in the person's life as well as within the community of disciples (Rom 8:5; 1 Cor 6:19; Gal 5:22-25; Eph 5:18). Believers must cultivate the attitude of abiding in Christ in relation both to the values they uphold and the mission they are committed to.

Beyond the controlling hierarchy: Leading empowered networks of Christ followers. Younger leaders are presently demonstrating much more egalitarian models of leadership. In today's diverse and rapidly changing world, people on the frontlines must be informed and empowered to make the right decisions promptly. This is a challenge facing many organizations. The church is not alone in its need to develop new models and provide better leadership selection and training.

In order to lead in today's fast-changing world, leaders must not project an aloof, know-it-all image. We are all in a learning mode, especially when facing situations not previously encountered. To empower others effectively, leaders must have demonstrated competence in their own area of specialization. But they not only must be aware of what they know, leaders must readily acknowledge what they don't know. Both elements are essential for the empowerment of others.

Indeed, leadership largely consists in making connections, connecting the dots between isolated pieces of information and bringing together people who have the combined resources to address the challenge. The task of the leader is (1) to seek the wisdom of the leadership team when assessing the overall situation, and (2) to bring together those with the necessary task, organization and people skills. Because of this, leaders need to be trained to think in a lateral rather than a linear mode. They must learn to work across disciplines for the simple reason that real-life challenges may cover a broad range of issues.

Beyond the weekly gathering: Building teams engaged in ongoing mission. The New Testament emphasizes that a local congregation is not merely a group or crowd of people who meet together for an hour or two each week. Rather, a congregation should be viewed as a federation of teams—people who support and encourage one another as they live out their faith commitment and minister to the people they are in contact with. Within the body of Christ, ministry and mission flow out of relationships. Frances Hesselbein notes that in addition to being mission focused, values based and demographics driven, the organization of the future will be relationship centered, led by individuals who always find time for people.[24]

Team building requires considerable skill. It is so essential to ministry that it needs that to be a foundational part of leadership training. In a healthy team, each individual feels valued and believes that he or she is engaged in a worthwhile endeavor. Each knows his or her distinctive contribution and also the skills, wisdom and insights that other members can provide. Team members affirm one another in mutually enriching relationships. A synergy develops as they combine their efforts to find solutions and to develop strategies to tackle specific issues. Team building, a challenging prospect when working with paid employees, is even more so when working with volunteers. Consequently, the next generation of leaders must be trained in such an environment in order to develop the ministry skills appropriate for leading the contemporary church.

Beyond a gospel of personal self-realization: A service-oriented faith community. Younger leaders see the manifold ministries of Christ in a far more holistic way than have many of their predecessors. They do not think in hard and fast categories, which separate the Great Commandment (to love our neighbors as ourselves) from the Great Commission (to go into all the world to make disciples). The authentic disciple does not consider them distinct. God so loved the world that he gave his only Son, and in turn the Son pours his love into our hearts that we might continue his mission.

For younger leaders, the greatest concern isn't how to get people to come to church but how best to take the church into the world. Their emphasis is not on extraction from the world but on engagement with society. This emphasis on engagement needs to be reflected in the church's criteria for selecting leaders and training them for ministry. For example, those who seek ministry in the church as an escape from the pressures of secular employment need to be weeded out. At the same time, those offering themselves for ministry without any significant life experience outside of the church need to immerse themselves in the secular world—just as a missionary candidate would be encouraged to have prefield, crosscultural experience.

The greatest commandment, to love our neighbors as ourselves, is not a means to evangelization in the sense that conditions are attached in order for material benefits to be received. But disciples of Jesus, engaged in such service of compassion and social justice, do so in the spirit of Christ so that their acts of service become the good news of the reign of God that point unmistakably to Jesus as the source, to whom disciples openly bear witness. If there is a hidden agenda, then their actions flow more from manipulation than from love. True love takes the initiative without conditions, demanding nothing in return. When people turn to Christ as Savior and Lord, their response to the gospel comes as a byproduct. Usually this occurs because of the distinctive manner in which the service is offered in the name of Christ. The people engaged in the ministry of feeding the hungry, providing shelter for the homeless or refuge for the outcast and the abused reveal the very character of the Lord they serve.

The personal qualities and selfless commitment of the followers of Jesus raise questions and are powerfully attractive. Those engaged in these ministries are more than willing to speak appropriately about the Christ they serve. But the service is offered unstintingly and unconditionally whether or not that spiritual response is forthcoming. There is no hint of discrimination in responding to the needs of those they are called to serve. They seek to glorify the Name, whether or not they have opportunity to name the Name.

Beyond the inwardly focused church: Leading a society-transforming community of disciples. Every local congregation should ask this question: If the Lord were to remove us overnight from our neighborhood, in what ways would the surrounding community become aware that we were no longer in their midst? A missional church does not simply meet the needs of its own members but equips groups of disciples in order to affect the worlds they inhabit.

Most of the time the church is dispersed and deployed on its many mission tasks. It is as much the church when it is in dispersion as it is when it gathers week by week for its corporate worship. The task of leaders is to help church members identify their mission and function as agents of the reign of God in their place of employment. By establishing appropriate structures that enable these ministries to function, they facilitate the building of Christ-following teams who work out the implications of their discipleship in their vocation.[25]

This is the broader agenda within which leadership needs to be defined. It will not suffice for leaders to serve as institutional guardians and functionaries. Instead, they are called to exercise an apostolic role, which requires them to send and accompany the church into the world, operating on the frontiers where the people of faith engage the communities in which they work and live.

SUMMARY

I have identified a range of challenges that must be addressed if established, traditional churches are to transition into "mission-shaped faith communities." The advent of the information age underlines the necessity to see leadership as a team function, recognizing the distinct contribution of each team member in terms of their personality, gifting and experience. We have seen that leadership combines character, charisma and confidence. In the context of the emerging church most leadership will emerge from within the congregation. At one level or another every person is exercising some measure of leadership. Consequently, the church must understand leadership to be a value that permeates the whole community.

2

Why Leadership Styles Must Change

In this chapter we will examine in greater detail the extent and radical nature of the global changes of the twenty-first century. The church must resist the temptation to retreat into its own cultural cocoon in the mistaken belief that it can escape the impact of this transformation. Leadership styles must change in light of the fresh challenges the church faces. This is as true for leaders of established churches as for entrepreneurial emerging churches. We don't need new leaders but *different* kinds of leaders. This has implications not only for the next generation of leaders but also for current leaders, who need to gain new insights and skills to more effectively lead their churches into increasingly complex ministry contexts.

The church is no longer one of the central institutions that shapes values and meets the social, emotional and spiritual needs of the Western world. It has ceased to provide the primary reference point of identity for people. In this post-Constantinian era, the church's role has become much more modest and marginal, at least as it is perceived by the society at large and increasingly by church members themselves.

As the church assesses its present position and looks to the future, it must ask itself whether it will degenerate and eventually fossilize or whether it will undergo the radical renewal necessary for it to recapture the dynamism that characterized its life in New Testament times, enabling it to make a significant impact on the Roman world during the first three centuries of its existence. What course the church follows will largely depend on the quality and vision of its emerging leadership.

Given that the current cultural context is far less cohesive and is characterized by fragmentation into many jostling subgroups, transformation is more likely to come about through grass-roots initiatives by local churches and informal cohorts. Bottom-up, innovative initiatives have the potential to gain momentum and successfully reproduce, whereas directives that filter down through the decision-making process of ponderous church bureaucracies mostly run out of steam. A one-size-fits-all approach does not work in a highly diversified environment. Consequently, senior church leaders must learn to operate as permission-givers as well as initiative-takers while at the same time requiring a high level of accountability.

FLEAS AND ELEPHANTS

Charles Handy notes that most innovations in the commercial world originate from fleas rather than elephants: "The world of organizations is fast dividing itself into fleas and elephants!" Handy argues that while elephants get all of the attention, "the new ideas come mostly from the fleas." Fleas tend to live on the outside of elephants, not in their bodies. Just as fleas need elephants, so every society needs both inventive fleas and efficient elephants.[1]

Although Handy made this observation in relation to the world of commerce, it translates effectively into the current context of the church, where most of the exciting innovations are the result of ground-level initiatives. Leaders of hierarchical church structures need to keep in touch with these innovations and provide them with support—and with the needed criticism and accountability. At the same time traditional church leaders need to go further, recognizing that the demands of the church in transition require new ways of identifying and encouraging innovative "flea" leadership.

This may be a day of small things in the sense that most changes begin on a small and localized scale, but smallness does not necessarily indicate insignificance. While small things do not always become big, fleas reproduce at a much faster rate than elephants and as a consequence have the potential to make a more far-reaching impact!

THE WESTERN CHURCH'S ENCOUNTER WITH RELIGIOUS PLURALISM

Although the process is less advanced in the United States than in Europe, Canada and Australia, secularization has marginalized the church and eroded its traditional influence over Western society.[2] Nonetheless, even though secularization has successfully dismantled Christendom, it has not destroyed the desire for the transcendent. In recent decades spirituality has reemerged as a potent societal force.[3] *Spirituality* is defined as an inner quest for meaning and the exploration of options. Typically, this leads either to a commitment to a religion of the individual's choosing or else to the creation of an eclectic mix of religions—an option sometimes described as "mix-and-match" or "smorgasbord" spirituality.

Unlike the cultural context that prevailed under Christendom, increasingly marginalized churches now find themselves competing in a pluralistic religious environment. To see indications of marginalization and competition, glance at the considerable amount of shelf space and the range of literature devoted to the "religion and spirituality" section of major chain bookstores. Religious pluralism is fueled by global immigration trends, with many new arrivals in Western countries being Muslim, Hindu, Sikh, Buddhist, Confucian and so forth. Consequently, many Christians find themselves in daily contact with sincere adherents of other faiths.

Such a smorgasbord spirituality does not readily respond to traditional styles of Christian outreach. A come-to-us strategy of invitational evangelization is less and less effective. We need a new apostolic style of leadership which recognizes that ministry in the surrounding community is increasingly crosscultural and Christians need appropriate insights and training for it. In short, we need to move beyond marketing to missional strategies. Take, for instance, the challenge of engaging in apologetics in a religiously pluralistic society. It is no longer a case of theism versus atheism, but of relating one's Christian understanding within a context of many different understandings of deity and the human condition. Canadian theologian John G. Stackhouse Jr. poses the challenge of engaging in apologetics in a context of religious pluralism:

> No one can possibly list, let alone understand, much less master, the range of ideological options on offer to North Americans today. Thus the claim that "my ideology is superior to all others" proves immediately difficult, if not flatly impossible to demonstrate. So one's enthusiasm for one's own ideology ought to be expressed in a way appropriate to this situation.[4]

Therein lies the skill of the well-trained missionary.

Both in the United States and in the United Kingdom, overseas mission agencies and returned mission personnel are sharing their insights with the church and deploying personnel to engage in urban church-planting initiatives. Examples include the Southern Baptist Mission Board, the Church Mission Society of the Church of England and such groups as Operation Mobilization and Youth With A Mission. Of equal significance is the commitment of young people who have grown up in a multicultural urban environment and, having grown up alongside of people of other ethnicities, bring crosscultural sensitivity to the church. This is perhaps the best training school of all. The church in the West has much to learn from churches in other areas of the world where Christians have always lived as a minority community in cultures dominated by other religious traditions.

This kind of pluralistic interaction pushes Western Christians in a variety of ways. Groups in the minority may close ranks in order to survive in a cultural context that they believe is at odds with their convictions. Their place of worship and religious observances reinforce their social identity—a place of group support where their faith is renewed and their beliefs are reasserted. Others may react with suspicion, feel threatened and even respond with intolerance and hostility. And other individuals or families are tempted to compromise their beliefs and practices in order to make social or economic headway in the host culture; thus they slide into nominality.[5] Nominal Christians may be fascinated and challenged by those of other faiths who are far more committed than they. Young people are particularly vulnerable to nominalization as they navigate the issues of self-identity and question whether they will allow themselves to be shaped by the dominant globalized youth culture or reassert their cultural identity.

TOLERATION, OR INDIFFERENCE

In the West, monotheistic, revelation-based faiths are challenged in the name of tolerance. It is widely held that religious exclusivism must be resisted, whether that exclusivism is expressed within Christian traditions (Catholic, Orthodox or Protestant) or between other religions (Muslim, Hindu or Sikh). However, for many Westerners, such tolerance is simply another term for religious indifference or an expression of a general philosophical relativism. Such religious indifference is as likely to affect the atheist as the theist.

Jonathan Rauch, writing in the *Atlantic Monthly,* describes his own position when someone asked him about his religion.

> "Atheist," I was about to say, but I stopped myself. "I used to call myself an atheist," I said, "and I still don't believe in God, but the larger truth is that it has been years since I really cared one way or another. I'm—that was when it hit me—an . . . apatheist!"

He then accuses his Christian friends of the same condition of apathy.

> I have Christian friends who organize their lives around an intense and personal relationship with God, but who betray no sign of caring that I am an unrepentantly atheistic Jewish homosexual. They are exponents, at least, of the second, more important part of apatheism: the part that doesn't mind what *other* people think about God.[6]

A MISSIONAL RESPONSE

The church in the West has not seen itself as a marginalized group in a pluralistic society since the time of Constantine. Consequently, many conservative Christians are prone to respond with aggression or conspiracy theories, both of which are born out of insecurity. Conspiracy theories are generated out of the conviction that there are groups in existence, such as secular humanists or Muslim extremists, for example, who are secretly plotting and strategizing to tip the balance of power. While some conservative Christians may wistfully hope for the restoration of the prestige, privileges and power of a former age, it is unlikely that this will take place. Church leaders must set aside such fears and aspirations and learn to look to the future with faith-generated hope, firmly convinced that the church will not only survive in its emerging context, but will also be able to thrive.

This conviction arises from two sources. First, the church was birthed in an environment that was just as pluralistic as the present one. Second, the early church—in that very environment—experienced phenomenal expansion as it worked from the margins of society. Given this radical change of perspective, the church needs to identify, empower and provide resources to a different kind of leader—one who has a missional conviction and the crosscultural training required to operate in today's pluralistic environment. Missional leaders do not look for social affirmation but are prepared to take risks with the realization that mission often entails a launch into uncharted waters against the prevailing tide of public opinion.

The task of leadership is further complicated by the fact that many congregations comprise as many as four generations, each of which has its own distinctive cultural characteristics. In many congregations we find the silent generation (1924-1945), the boomer generation (1946-1964), Generation X (1965-1981) and finally Generation Y—the oldest of whom are now in their mid twenties.[7] Each of these generations has been shaped, to a greater or lesser extent, by attitude-forging social and political movements and global affairs (such as wars, scientific developments and economic ups and downs). In an environment of rapid social change one of the tasks of a leader is to serve as an interpreter among these generations, helping each to understand the positions and the presuppositions of the others. Charles Handy highlights this challenge, commenting that "the paradox of aging is that every generation perceives itself as justifiably different from its predecessor, but plans as if its successor generation will be the same."[8]

SIGNS OF THE TIMES

As I began to write this chapter I asked Rick Marshall, who served for more than a decade as the crusade director for Billy Graham and who has his ear to the ground in regard to cultural trends, to provide me with a list of what he considered to be some of the most significant cultural developments. He confirmed many of my impressions, which are included in the following paragraphs.

Economic developments. In the area of economics we have seen a dramatic rise in the standard of living of those in the middle-income range. Higher expectations have led to consumerism and increasing financial pressures, with most families needing two incomes to maintain or enhance their standard of living. This in turn has put pressure on marriages and given rise to a generation of latchkey kids, an increased divorce rate, single parenting, and insecure and resentful children who have suffered through the trauma of the conflicts and separation of their parents. In addition, we have seen a rise in cohabiting couples, same-sex partnerships and children born out of wedlock. This leads to the growing difficulty in recruiting volunteers because people have less discretionary time. Churches that continue to hold up the ideal of the stable nuclear family find that, in so doing, they are alienating a significant percentage of their congregation.

Demographic changes. In terms of demographics, the populations of Europe and North America are aging, not only due to lower birthrates but because people are living longer. Congregations are simply growing older. This has two implications for ministry: (1) pastors must meet the needs of a large group of aging members, and (2) seniors want their church to remain unchanged. The demands of seniors means that the church is experiencing a severe disconnect in relating to those under forty.

The ethnic makeup of our society is also changing. Global economic pressures have triggered significant migrations from parts of Asia, Africa, Latin America and Eastern Europe. The waves of migrants create new permanent residents and citizens, and also seasonal workers. Many church members find themselves working and living alongside people of other faiths, and some of their children date children of other faiths. Consequently, pastors, even those of predominantly Caucasian congregations, face more and more crosscultural-ministry challenges. Thus pastors need to be sensitive to the potential cultural misunderstandings and tensions within their surrounding communities.

Information age. We have moved from an industrial to an information age. There is an avalanche of new information and exponential growth in new technologies. The gap between what we feel we need to know and what we actually know grows wider daily. For controlling leaders who feel that they need to know everything, this is a huge anxiety-producing challenge.

Another feature of the information age is that knowledge on every conceivable subject is now widely available through the Internet. With this "democratization of knowledge," the privileged few aren't the only ones "in the know." The implications for today's leaders are obvious. We can no longer know everything, but we can identify people with knowledge and experience that we do not have. In the New Testament, church leadership was not invested in one individual but in a range of persons with particular gifts and experience. If such a leadership style was appropriate in the first century, it is essential in the twenty-first century.

The rapid transfer of information (and economic resources) on a global scale has had a profound effect on how institutions operate. Hierarchies are too ponderous and job descriptions too restrictive for the information age. This is an era of rapid response, alternative scenarios and just-in-time planning. Even in the context of the church, which represents an island of relative calm and stability, leaders must detect significant change and respond in an appropriate and timely manner.

The knowledge revolution and the fluctuations in the global economy are also causing increasing numbers of people to seek alternative employment and learn new skills in order to remain employable. The search for work and the relocation demanded by employers mean that growing numbers of people have to move more frequently. This causes economic problems for churches. Those that embark on capital campaigns experience the cost firsthand.

The communication revolution—the Internet, satellite television, cell phones and DVDs—coupled with the youth-dominated demographics in Asia, Africa and Latin America, has given rise to the global dominance of pop culture. Our high-tech culture is also having a profound effect on human relations and community life. Young people establish virtual relationships on the Internet rather than connect face-to-face with family and friends. And the stimulus overload from television and video games has contributed to neurological disorders as well as to a loss of childhood through participation in violent video games and pornographic websites.

CROSSCULTURAL DISCERNMENT

Today's leaders must be students of cultural movements. While some aspects of postmodernity cause concern and need to be challenged, not everything should be dismissed in a defensive reaction. In fact, some aspects of postmodernity affirm biblical insights and challenge contemporary Christians to examine their basic beliefs with more care. All of us have biases related to our own cultural conditioning; hence we should heed any source that will help us sort the treasures of the gospel from our own cultural baggage. The church must constantly engage culture, seeking to contextualize its message without losing its unique message and distinctive lifestyle.

Missionaries draw an important distinction between *naive* contextualization and *critical* contextualization. In the former, Christian beliefs simply merge with the broader culture in question, becoming little more than a veneer that leaves deep issues unchallenged and unchanged. The latter, though, recognizes the complexity of the relationship between gospel and culture. Leaders need spiritual discernment to distinguish between (1) those elements of a culture that the gospel affirms, (2) aspirations that only the gospel can fulfill and (3) those elements that represent the demonic, which must be challenged. Many younger leaders within the emerging church movement are vulnerable to naive contextualization due to their lack of crosscultural training. For example, a number of emerging church leaders have been profoundly impressed by the gentleness and simplicity of devout followers of Eastern religions. But they are prone to see those religions in romanticized forms rather than in their more popular and radical forms. Of course, the same can be said of Christianity. We must be prepared to come to terms with the dark episodes, repent of past actions and renounce current behavior that contradicts the gospel we profess.

Today's church leaders must be trained to observe and interpret the cultural changes taking place throughout society. The combined impact of these changes is so powerful that Andrew Grove, former CEO of Intel Corporation, has described them as a "strategic inflection point."[9] This is the point at which a curve moves in another direction due to a shift in the balance of forces. Times of transition are also referred to as the "sigmoid curve," in which the future represents either decline or the beginning of a new trajectory. If church leaders fail to respond appropriately to such changes, they are likely to lead the church into decline as they cling to outmoded ways of thinking and working.

Evidence of this changing trajectory began with the decline of traditional denominations in the mid 1960s. This decline has not abated during the subsequent decades. Today many of those denominations have lost a quarter to a third of their membership. Attendance figures are even more sobering; typically less than a third of the members are in church on an average Sunday. At the same time that the majority of churches have been in decline, the number of megachurches has increased dramatically, and new church networks and independent church-planting initiatives have appeared. Despite the combined impact of these growing churches, the overall numbers continue to decline.

The younger generation is far more adept than the old at handling two further challenges: multimedia and the Internet. The preboomer, "silent" generation was given that label because their voice is seldom heard. They were passed over because they failed to make the transition from the industrial to the information age. Both the silent and boomer generations represent word-dominated cultures; they find it difficult to handle communication that is multichanneled. That said, in the case of the Internet, boomers represent a transitional generation who are far more comfortable than church leaders in their late fifties to mid seventies. (But remember, we are looking for a distinct *type* of leader with different and varied skills, not simply a *younger* leader.)

REACTION OR ENGAGEMENT

Many conservative theologians and church leaders react negatively to postmodernity. Often their response is visceral and condemning. They dismiss it out of hand rather than asking where God is at work in this movement. What can be learned? What valid questions and challenges does it bring to the contemporary church? We can begin to identify and engage with the darker side of postmodernity only after we have addressed the issues raised by such questions.

Most mainline denominations are led by leaders in their fifties to seventies who were schooled in the tenets of modernism and who thereby address contemporary issues with outmoded presuppositions based on rationalism and relativism. Many other senior leaders in traditional and long-established churches have also succumbed to the culture of modernity, embracing its presuppositions. In some cases they have fought against its conclusions, but with modernity's own weapons. First, they have responded programmatically to troubling issues, but without a relational component, which would bring about deeper change. Second, their approach is abstract and highly propositional rather than grounded in the life issues and questions people face daily. In contrast, the postmoderns engage in dialogue and seek to build relational support among group members addressing the issues. They are also more ready to live with ambiguity and mystery rather than insist on clear-cut, definitive answers. Their worldview is far less black and white.

MODERNITY AND POSTMODERNITY

Modernity. Modernists regard the transcendent and the supernatural as superfluous. It is assumed that the scientific method provides certain knowledge, and when wisely applied, that knowledge renders human progress inevitable. Our self-contained world can be explained and, even more importantly, controlled by rational processes. Nature's incredible energy has been increasingly harnessed in the service of technological, economic and social progress. Modernists' focus on human potential encourages individuals to draw strength from their own resources and release their latent powers. It encourages each individual to regard him- or herself as autonomous, self-determining and free. The loss of a sense of dependency on a God also encourages denials of human sinfulness as well as its long-range and comprehensive consequences.

In the face of overwhelming evidence to the contrary, modernists assume that humankind is inherently good and that any unfortunate mistakes that have tragic personal and social consequences can be eradicated through education and societal reintegration. Those generations making up much of today's present church leadership—the builders, silents and boomers—collectively represent modernity's "can-do" mentality, with all of the advantages and drawbacks that such energy and self-confidence engenders.

Wade Clark Roof, in his long-term study of the boomer culture, assesses the impact of modernity. He claims that its rationalistic approach has stifled the experiential dimension of faith; its extreme individualism has severed connection to place and community, and alienated people from their natural environments. Its creation of autonomous spheres has separated life from work; diluted ethical values; caused the synthesis of moral, religious and civic values to fall apart; and redefined religious identity by severing the roots of historic Christian traditions.[10]

Postmodernity. Today, the self-confident assumptions of modernism are crumbling in the face of current events. Postmodernists question the misguided self-confidence of modernity with both insight and humor. Much that was once assumed to be true is now being reexamined. Truth claims are questioned, and the motives of those who make such claims are scrutinized. Postmodernists believe that the assertions of the modernists are little more than attempts to exert power. Within the cultural context of radical pluralism, "truth" is merely a subjective or community-based assertion, but it is not universally binding: "That is fine for you, but it is not true for me." In fact, the bolder and more expansive the claims made, the greater the suspicion. "Big" stories, that is, overarching metanarratives, are rejected as attempts to invalidate the "little" stories that shape and claim the allegiance of another individual or group. Big stories that provide an explanation of life and that demand the total allegiance of "true believers" are assumed to be controlling devices or power grabs.

One consequence of this suspicion is that many pre-Christian postmoderns reject the gospel when it is framed in propositional statements. A more promising approach is (1) for an individual to begin with his or her own story of God's grace at work, and (2) for that story to be reinforced by the witness of other people who have different backgrounds, temperaments and life experiences. We should introduce the gospel not as a sequence of propositions but as a series of significant "little" stories, which make up most of the Bible, leading to the story of Jesus himself, including the kind of life he lived and the statements he made about his mission and his identity.

Thus the gospel is shared, not imposed, as a story worthy of serious consideration. By telling the stories of our own experience in relation to the biblical stories of the people and events spanning two millennia, and by recounting the impact of the gospel on the lives of countless individuals from a variety of ethnic, intellectual and socioeconomic levels, we can begin to address the postmodern suspicion about the gospel.

The challenge comes in finding ways to communicate that story. In order to do this effectively, church leaders need to engage and wrestle with the prevailing mindset, whether modern or postmodern, rather than addressing it from a safe distance. An understanding of the postmodern cultural context helps us tell God's story with the rich texture of the biblical account. It must deal honestly with complex issues, using a diversity of evocative images unencumbered by the straightjacket of modernistic presuppositions and overtones.

COMMUNICATING THE BIG PICTURE

Within this climate of suspicion, postmoderns above everything else want to experience authenticity. They are interested not so much in our truth claims as in the extent to which our lives correspond to the truth we proclaim. Postmoderns still possess a deep hunger for a metanarrative that can provide them with a sense of significance, purpose and freedom, but they are highly sensitive to inconsistencies (which they often rightly label hypocrisy). Credible communication therefore requires honesty, humility, deep respect for the individual as a person of intrinsic worth, and the assumption that God is already at work in that person's life. At the same time people who share the good news of Christ also need insight into the overarching spiritual battleground, discerning the reality of malevolent spiritual deception and domination.

In the current cultural climate, credible gospel communication does not *impose* an absolute but *proposes* an alternative. Any attempt to share the good news that gives the impression that the witness has wholly packaged the message and has a ready response to all previously unanswered questions will be regarded with suspicion and treated with ridicule. Authentic witnesses do not have the "whole story" but bear testimony to what they have grasped and have been obedient to in their own lives. This is why individual witness is limited and needs to be filled out by the corporate testimony of the church. That testimony must be continuously enriched, celebrated, reenacted and corrected from the Big Story that unfolds in the two Testaments that make up Scripture.[11] One further important element needs to be added, namely, the need to listen to the witness of those who follow Jesus in cultures other than our own, particularly those who have lived under dehumanizing poverty and persecution.

Postmodernity speaks the language of "perspectivalism," which asserts that what you see depends on where you stand. It is true that this presents a challenge to the absolute truths of the gospel, but that challenge can be addressed by presenting the good news from a variety of perspectives. The collective witness of the church is reinforced by the testimony of people from across the centuries and around the globe.

Those who witness to the authority, relevance and power of the gospel represent an impressive diversity of cultures as well as every intellectual and economic bracket. Within the Bible, we find individuals and groups responding to various elements of the message with different levels of understanding. The broader our embrace of that revelation, as well as of the witness of the church in every age, the richer our understanding will be of the gospel.

Given all of this, tomorrow's leaders must be prepared to live with not only humility but also ambiguity and contradiction. I remember a number of local churches in the 1950s and 1960s that held evangelistic outreach weeks under the slogan "Christ is the answer." Such a statement exuded the confidence of modernity. At one level it enshrined an important truth: Christ is the answer to the human predicament. God has made himself known, has made full provision for our salvation and presents the pathway that we must walk in order to know him. But as an open-ended statement, it promises more than it can deliver. Christ is not the instant answer to everything. Those who follow Christ continue to struggle with unanswered questions, and we will take some of those questions to heaven.

In every area of human inquiry, we find that we have to live with the inexplicable and the irreconcilable. The closer we come to questions of a fundamental nature, the more this is the case. There are profound mysteries at the heart of the universe as well as within the nucleus of a single atom, not to mention the complexities of interaction within living organisms and inanimate objects. It is all too easy to resort to reductionistic explanations; however, I am no scientist, so I have probably already said too much along this line.

The challenges that tomorrow's leaders face are as complex as they are compelling. People are increasingly vulnerable and disoriented in these confusing and uncertain times. Their personal liberation has produced more compulsive anxiety than boundless freedom. Consequently, with a future too uncertain and terrifying to contemplate, the overwhelming tendency is to focus on "now." Change and flux are normative and endless. Unassailable truths have been reduced to mere collective hunches. There is no solid ground, but simply a restless sea. Such is the postmoderns' sense of inadequacy; they have to constantly reinvent themselves in order to survive from day to day. Dominic Crossan captures the postmodern predicament with the following lines:

> There is no lighthouse keeper.
> There is no lighthouse.
> There is no dry land.
> There is only people living on rafts
>   made from their own imaginations.
> And there is the sea.[12]

While so many people in centuries past found a rock-firm faith in the midst of similar storm-tossed seas, this anxiety-producing predicament provides a challenge and an opportunity for the communication of the biblical message.

FROM HIERARCHIES TO NETWORKS

Western cultures are exceedingly complex and chaotic, and they present an unnerving picture for the well-ordered mind. However, hierarchical organizations are too cumbersome and monolithic to operate effectively in a context of diversity and rapid, often unpredictable, changes. Networks, on the other hand, are flexible, responsive and empowering precisely because they have no control center and are able to grow exponentially. In order to facilitate the expansion of networks, current organizational structures need to be highly flexible, smaller and flatter.

Networks may branch out from a common center (which provides inspiration and resources but avoids control) or have no center at all. In the latter case their identity represents the sum of the parts. Rather than developing and replicating an organizational machine by way of an expanded bureaucratic hierarchy, network expansion is more akin to the growth of an organism. In this regard leaders have been likened to gardeners who plant, prune, fertilize, cultivate and harvest. The leader does not *control* but *cultivates*. Leadership in such an environment of complexity and chaos "is a matter of how to be, not how to do it," observes Frances Hesselbein.[13] Hesselbein's leaders

> long ago banned the hierarchy and, involving many heads and hands, built a new kind of structure. The new design took people out of the boxes of the old hierarchy and moved them into a more circular, flexible and fluid management system that released the energy and spirit of our people.[14]

These leaders build dispersed and diverse leadership, distributing leadership to the outermost edges of the circle to unleash the power of shared responsibility.

FROM COMPARTMENTALIZATION TO CONNECTIVITY

Harlan Cleveland also provides some helpful insights on leadership and management within a culture of chaos. "Chaos," he writes, "describes that inferno of unfathomable complexity laying just beyond the flat world of empirical evidence."[15] Because leaders cannot order, explain or control that inferno, they need to relax. Cleveland further observes: "The compartmentalization of the vertical disciplines gets in the way of understanding reality."[16] Such compartmentalization is produced and reinforced by modernity. Life, however, does not come in such manageable units. In reality we are faced with a complex intertwining of issues. Consequently, we need interdisciplinary responses. That is one of the reasons why churches may be more effective if they move beyond the concept of a single leader to one in which leadership is exercised by a team with one individual serving as *primus inter pares*—first among equals.

The temptation faced by any individual who exercises leadership is, in Cleveland's words, to "neglect the 'externalities'—those naggingly relevant facts that don't fit into our logical modes of thinking."[17] On the other hand, the effort to embrace more data than we are intellectually and emotionally able to handle can cause "analysis paralysis." "The biggest danger to systematic thinking," Cleveland insists, "is information entropy."[18] "Analysis paralysis" and "information entropy" are particular occupational hazards for controllers, who are overwhelmed by their need to know everything. New generation leaders, by contrast, are content to know to whom they can go in order to find what they need to know.

Some theorists discuss two-level leadership. At the second, lower level, leaders use their individual expertise in order to address a particular challenge. With some, this expertise is technical in nature. Others are systems people, who are skilled at connecting and sequencing. Still others are effective at establishing and furthering good working relationships. The first, or primary, level of leadership involves the ability to "keep the main thing the main thing." First-level leadership is concerned with challenges or insights that influence and at times threaten to subvert the overall operation.

Cleveland describes this primary level of leadership as "the art of getting-it-all-together." Consequently, the leader functions as a generalist. But, as Cleveland explains, there is a catch in that "there is actually no generalist ladder to leadership."[19] How then do first-level leaders emerge? Typically, they begin by demonstrating their competence in a specific area, but that competence also spills over to embrace a broader perspective. Often they demonstrate not only technical skill but also strategic thinking. In the context of industrial management, enterprises usually suffer when technical managers who lack this broader perspective and are woefully inadequate in "getting-it-all-together" are promoted to senior management. Within the context of the church, a senior pastor cannot afford to become immersed in his or her particular area of interest, be that preaching, pastoral counseling or evangelism, for example, but must serve as a generalist concerned for the overall development of the Christian community in a balanced way.

LEADERSHIP WITHIN A MOVEMENT

As we look to a future in which the church is no longer a central institution of society but rather a movement operating from the margins, we see that this shift has enormous implications for the role of leadership in churches or mission agencies. A prestigious institution provides status, security and established operational procedures, but a fledgling movement is a dynamic, changing, explorative organism that requires a radically different temperament, new motivational drives and a wider range of skills. By definition, movements "move" and therefore require leaders who are not stuck and insecure when it comes to change and adaptation.

Cleveland provides a list of eight attitudes that he believes are indispensable to the management of complexity. They apply equally well to leadership among the people of God.

- A lively intellectual curiosity; an interest in everything—because everything really is related to everything else and therefore to what we are trying to do, whatever it is.

- A genuine interest in what other people think and why they think that way—which means you have to be at peace with yourself for a start.

- A feeling of special responsibility for envisioning a future that's different from a straight-line projection of the present. Trends are not destiny.

- A hunch that most risks are there not to be avoided but to be taken.

- A mindset that crises are normal, tensions can be promising and complexity is fun.

- A realization that paranoia and self-pity are reserved for people who don't want to be leaders.

- A sense of personal responsibility for the general outcome of your efforts.

- A quality I call "unwarranted optimism"—the conviction that there must be some more upbeat outcome than would result from adding up all the available expert advice.[20]

These points are worth pondering as a personal checklist and also as criteria to assess emerging leaders. From my own interaction with younger leaders, the correlation seems extremely close. This checklist can be used to help recognize and then develop future church leaders who have the vibrancy and creativity necessary to engage in mission in these chaotic times. The church needs navigators tuned to the voice of God, not map readers. Navigational skills have to be learned on the high seas and in the midst of varying conditions produced by the wind, waves, currents, fogbanks, darkness, storm clouds and perilous rocks.

WHAT LEADERS MUST PROVIDE IN CHAOTIC TIMES

Warren Bennis says people want direction, trust and hope from leaders. Even in postmodernity, there can be no leadership without an appropriate exercise of authority. Such authority does not arise from a leader's position or title but originates in the trust built up on the basis of character, competence, respect and consistency. Authority is based on the twin pillars of responsibility and influence, and leaders are not simply those who impose their own wills but are individuals from whom opinion is sought. Furthermore, if authority is not devalued but jealously guarded, it thwarts the leadership potential of others. In such a case others often find themselves disempowered, and any display of initiative is regarded with suspicion.

The worst course of action that leaders can take in times of radical change is to deny that change is happening and to believe that everything will eventually return to "normal." Spencer Johnson's amusing parable *Who Moved My Cheese?* emphasizes this point. It is the story of two mice named Sniff and Scurry, and two little people named Hem and Haw, who are habitually sent to a certain place to obtain their daily supply of cheese. They fail to notice that changes are taking place and that the supply of cheese is diminishing. Instead, they insist on going to the same place. Hem and Haw wait long after the supply has been exhausted and constantly complain, "Who moved my cheese?"

Eventually, because they are too afraid to explore the maze in search of other cheese stations, Hem and Haw starve to death. Sniff and Scurry meanwhile go in search of other sources. The moral of Johnson's story is that change happens and that we must be observant enough to see it coming and adapt accordingly. "If you do not change," Johnson warns, "you can become extinct."[21] Hem and Haw resented change and felt threatened by it, but Sniff and Scurry enjoyed it and treated it as an adventure.

In the midst of chaos, leaders provide vision that rises beyond the present circumstances that threaten to overwhelm and capsize the movement. Such vision provides a sense of purpose, resilience and exuberance. In order for the church to remain on even keel, keep its bows to the waves and stay on course, it will have to "keep the main thing the main thing."

SUMMARY

In this chapter I have identified the far-reaching changes that are taking place within Western cultures and have sought to indicate how such changes affect the nature of leadership within the church. At the present time there are at least two paradigms in operation: one is shaped by the assumed certainties of modernity; the other recognizes that many of those certainties are beginning to crumble, and our only certainty arises from the grace of God and the faith in God that the Holy Spirit generates within us.

Throughout the Bible those who have responded to God's grace in obedience have been described as those who "walk with God." Enoch walked with God. Noah walked with God. Abraham walked with God, not knowing what his destination would be (Heb 11:8). When Jesus called his first disciples, he invited them to "follow me," with no indication as to where he was going. While moderns most likely will ask "Where to?" postmoderns will query "Who with?" In regard to the second question, Jesus leaves his followers in no doubt, whether we be first- or twenty-first-century pilgrims. He says, "Follow *me*." After Jesus' ascension, the disciples, with much initial hesitation, ventured forth around the Mediterranean world, and in so doing discovered that the Lord Jesus was true to his word: "And surely I am with you always, to the very end of the age" (Mt 28:20).

3

Leaders Passionate About the Great Commission

Younger leaders within the emerging churches are seeking to bring their own generation into the community of faith. Within traditional church settings their task is especially challenging, largely on account of the church having its own culture shaped by modernity. However, that cultural perspective does not relate to the worldview of younger generations, whose worldview has been shaped both by the information age and by the popular culture of postmodernity. Out of a sense of frustration, some have left traditional churches to become church planters of independent churches, while others have been released to establish satellite congregations of a mother church.

Some of these younger leaders aim to help former church attenders renew their commitment to Christ; others are working hard to assist those making that commitment for the very first time. One strategic approach has been to develop young-adult and youth-oriented churches, whose primary goal is to retain teens and twenty-somethings. This is a valid and important ministry, considering the extent to which the under-thirty-fives are leaving institutional religion.

Churchgoing parents of these young people are anxious about these trends and are looking to their congregational leaders to develop worship options and relevant ministries that will bridge the cultural and generational gap. In established churches many associate pastors who work among young people find themselves under heavy pressure to integrate these young people into the larger church fellowship. Most of the emerging churches that operate under the organizational umbrella of a megachurch fall into this category. They often have impressive resources that enable them to craft services appealing to youth, but under the surface they are much like the parent organization. Bill Hogg, a Youth for Christ director in Seattle, described such churches as "pigs with lipstick." In other words, they are the same old thing "dolled up" to make them apparently culturally relevant and attractive.

The church's evangelistic strategy of seeking to retain its youth by the creation of a culturally appropriate worship experience (I describe this as the "minder church") is basically an invitation to come to us on our terms. Control is firmly in the hands of those who maintain the church culture, and communication is still punctuated with "churchspeak" or "Christianese." While the "minder church" remains a valid and significant ministry for stemming the leak of young people, my primary concern in this chapter is the challenge facing the church to reach out to those who have already abandoned it—or have been abandoned by it. An even greater challenge relates to those who have never been involved in the life of a local congregation. In the United States most of the never-churched are only one generation removed from church, whereas their European, Canadian and Australasian counterparts may be two or three generations removed.

THE CHURCH'S MANDATE

Some missiologists divide the church's mission into two mandates: the *cultural mandate* to love our neighbors as ourselves, described as the greatest commandment, and the *evangelistic mandate,* identified with the Great Commission. I challenge this view on two counts. First, the Great Commission cannot adequately be described as the evangelistic mandate. Its goal isn't the mere presentation of the good news of Jesus Christ for the purpose of bringing people to the point of decision but making disciples of Jesus Christ. Second, a distinction between the two mandates creates a separation that weakens the integrity of the disciple-making process.

The Great Commission must not be textually separated from the preceding chapters of Matthew's Gospel. David Bosch underlines this point, declaring:

> It is inadmissible to lift these words out of Matthew's Gospel, as it were, allow them a life of their own, and understand them without any reference to the context in which they first appeared. Where this happens, the "Great Commission" is easily degraded to a mere slogan, or used as a pretext for what we have in advance decided, perhaps unconsciously, it should mean.[1]

The entire Gospel shows what it means to be a disciple. At heart it means to "love the Lord your God with all your heart and with all your soul and with all your mind." Jesus said, "This is the first and greatest commandment. And the second is like it: 'Love your neighbor as yourself.' All the Law and the Prophets hang on these two commandments" (Mt 22:37-40). And when Jesus talks about "neighbor," his concept extends beyond family and tribe, including Samaritans as well as the entire non-Jewish world. For Jesus and his disciples the issue is not "Who is my neighbor?" but "To whom can I become a neighbor?"

MATTHEW'S TARGET READERSHIP

It is clear that Jewish readers were the primary audience of Matthew's Gospel. The majority of New Testament scholars now believe that Matthew's original readers were Jews of the Diaspora rather than Palestinian Jews.[2] The earliest copies to survive originate from Syria. This is not surprising, because after the fall of Jerusalem and the destruction of the temple by the Roman armies in A.D. 70, the Jewish followers of Christ fled to that neighboring region.

Once they were dispossessed from the land and the temple was destroyed, the Jews experienced a growing identity crisis. The sense of dislocation and disaffiliation grew even more acute for the disciples of Christ as they found themselves under increasing attack from the Pharisaic party. Jewish Christians at that time "understood themselves primarily as a renewal movement within Judaism rather than as a separate religion."[3] The Pharisees, who had now assumed power, had become increasingly strident in their attempt to buttress Jewish identity around their interpretation of the Law. Around A.D. 85 the Pharisees issued a bitter polemic, known as the Twelfth Benediction, against Jewish Christians. It declared, "Let the Nazarenes and the heretics be destroyed in a moment. . . . Let their names be expurgated from the Book of Life."

INTROVERSION AND EXCLUSIVISM REBUKED

In this climate of uncertainty and vulnerability, Jewish Christians were under incredible strain. The more Jewish the congregational makeup of a church, the greater the pressure to "circle the wagons." As Bosch explains, "It is for this community that Matthew writes, a community cut off from its roots, its attachment to Judaism exposed to the harshest test possible, divided in itself as to what its priorities should be, groping for direction in the face of previously unknown problems."[4]

Matthew challenges his readers' tendency toward introversion at a number of points. At the outset, it is in this most Jewish of Gospels that we read of the visit of the magi from the East (Mt 2:1-12). From the beginning of the story the significance of Jesus' birth for non-Jews is clearly indicated. It is made even clearer as Jesus' ministry unfolds. When the centurion takes the initiative and sends his servant to ask for Jesus' help, Jesus announces to his followers:

> I tell you the truth, I have not found anyone in Israel with such great faith. I say to you that many will come from the east and the west, and will take their places at the feast with Abraham, Isaac and Jacob in the kingdom of heaven. But the subjects of the kingdom will be thrown outside, into the darkness, where there will be weeping and gnashing of teeth. (Mt 8:10-12)

Jesus also denounces the Jewish cities that serve as the hub of his ministry, comparing them unfavorably to the despised cities of Tyre, Sidon and, even more strongly, Sodom, the Old Testament city that had been totally destroyed by God on account of its wickedness.

> Woe to you, Korazin! Woe to you, Bethsaida! If the miracles that were performed in you had been performed in Tyre and Sidon, they would have repented long ago in sackcloth and ashes. But I tell you, it will be more bearable for Tyre and Sidon on the day of judgment than for you. And you, Capernaum, will you be lifted up to the skies? No, you will go down to the depths. If the miracles that were performed in you had been performed in Sodom, it would have remained to this day. But I tell you that it will be more bearable for Sodom on the day of judgment than for you. (Mt 11:21-24)

As the Jewish believers in Syria and elsewhere pondered these words, they undoubtedly found a powerful incentive to transcend their narrow Jewish nationalism and recognize their God-given mission as bearers of the good news of Christ to their own people *and beyond.*

On another occasion Jesus tells the Pharisees and teachers of the law that they represent a wicked and adulterous (i.e., spiritually faithless) generation. He draws an unflattering comparison between them and the people of Nineveh, the capital city of Israel's enemy Assyria and the city Jonah had been so reluctant to confront. "The men of Nineveh," Jesus states, "will stand up at the judgment with this generation and condemn it; for they repented at the preaching of Jonah, and now one greater than Jonah is here." He then contrasts the unresponsiveness of the Pharisees, the teachers and the generation as a whole, with the eager initiative of the Queen of the South (also referred to as the queen of Sheba in 1 Kings 10:1). She "will rise at the judgment with this generation and condemn it; for she came from the ends of the earth to listen to Solomon's wisdom, and now one greater than Solomon is here" (Mt 12:41-42).

On another occasion a Canaanite woman approaches Jesus on behalf of her demon-possessed daughter. As with the centurion, Jesus also commends the Canaanite for her great faith (Mt 15:21-28). In his parable of the workers of the vineyard, Jesus rebukes those in Israel who are envious of those who seem least deserving. In this we see the contrast between the Jews who have anticipated the Messiah's coming and the Gentiles who find him at this late hour (Mt 20:1-16).

The parable of the wedding banquet presents a further challenge to Israel's exclusivism. As God's people, the children of Israel thought they had reserved seats in God's kingdom banquet, yet when the invitation is given with the coming of Jesus, they respond negatively. Consequently, the servants are commanded to go out into the streets to gather all the people they could find (Mt 22:1-14). In the final days of his earthly ministry, the Lord reminds his Jewish disciples that "this gospel of the kingdom will be preached in the whole world as a testimony to all nations, and then the end will come" (Mt 24:14).

In the town of Bethany a woman anoints Jesus' feet with her hair, an act of sacrifice, humility and humiliation. When the disciples criticize her for what they judge as extravagance and exhibitionism, Jesus responds with these memorable words: "I tell you the truth, wherever this gospel is preached throughout the world, what she has done will also be told, in memory of her" (Mt 26:13). This nameless woman of ill-repute becomes an example of devotion to Christ and a challenge to Jewish religious exclusivism. Finally, in response to the midday darkness and the earthquake that follows Jesus' death on the cross, a pagan centurion, a member of the execution party, exclaims, "Surely he was the Son of God!" (Mt 27:54).

THE CHURCH'S MISSION AMONG THE PEOPLES OF THE WORLD

These words of Jesus scattered throughout Matthew's Gospel present an equally poignant challenge to the church today. Whenever it is prone to judgmental detachment and self-preoccupation, whenever it forgets or abandons its mission, the church stands under the judgment of God. Western church leaders must not only emphasize ministry among the people of God, but they also need to mobilize the people of God for mission in the world.

In sending out his twelve disciples, Jesus anticipates the mission that will be entrusted to the whole people of God. Matthew's Jewish readers would not have missed the significance of the number twelve. Just as the people of God had been divided into twelve tribes, so the church of Jesus Christ is built on twelve foundational pillars, twelve disciples who become apostles to the nations. Their mission, initially restricted to "the lost sheep of Israel" (Mt 10:6), is a precursor to the much wider and inclusive mission to "all peoples everywhere" (Mt 28:19 GNB). Bosch observes that, for Matthew, *disciples* referred to more than the Twelve. "The first disciples," in Bosch's mind, "are the prototype of the church."[5] The Good News Bible translation more clearly shows that "going to all nations" (as the phrase is more commonly translated) does not refer to modern nation states but to "all peoples" with a shared sense of identity. In this mission, which was undertaken in the first place by Jewish Christians, fellow Jews are included but they are now no longer a specially privileged people.

Matthew mentions the proclamation of the gospel to "all nations" as a prelude to the end of the age (Mt 24:9, 14). Embarking on that task only becomes a possibility after the death and resurrection of the Messiah of the Jews.[6] This Gospel does not conclude in Jerusalem, where we might expect, but in Galilee, or as only Matthew refers to it, Galilee *of the Gentiles* (Mt 4:15; see Is 9:1-2). Galilee had a cosmopolitan population and a strategic location. It bordered Syria, and its location on a trade route linked it with Damascus to the east and Syrian Antioch farther north.

Jesus intentionally concludes his ministry where he had started out, meeting with his disciples in "Galilee of the Gentiles" by appointment. We can hardly imagine that the disciples who meet with him in their homeland keep the incredible news of Jesus' resurrection from their families and neighbors on their return home from Jerusalem. Indeed, as reported by the apostle Paul when he listed some of Jesus' postresurrection appearances, it is possible that this is the occasion when more than five hundred of Jesus' followers meet with him (1 Cor 15:6). Most of these disciples were still alive at the time of Paul's writing, some twenty-five years later. Considering the life expectancy of their period, this suggests that mainly young people were at this meeting. Matthew also emphasizes the significance of the meeting when he mentions that Jesus meets with his disciples on a *mountain,* which according to Craig Keener "recalls the other sites of revelation in the Gospel" (Mt 5:1; 17:1).[7]

All of the Gospel authors focus on the mission Jesus entrusted to his followers, but they each bring their own distinctive emphasis. Matthew highlights the process of formation, as he shows the Lord drawing alongside his disciples in order to continue to teach them. Mark focuses on the announcement of the good news (Mk 16:15-19).[8] Luke's emphasis is on empowerment through the promise of the Holy Spirit (Lk 24:45-49), while John stresses the continuity between the heavenly Father's sending of Jesus into the world and the church's own worldwide mission (Jn 20:21). However, it is only in Matthew's Gospel that the mission is presented as a command to be obeyed, because obedience is at the heart of discipleship.[9] In the Gospels the disciples are those who follow in the footsteps of Jesus, whose first commands are "Come, follow," and whose last is "Go" (Mt 4:19; 28:19).

Bosch insists that Matthew's Gospel is essentially a missionary text. He argues that "it is primarily because of his missionary vision that Matthew sets out to write his gospel, not to compose a 'life of Jesus' but to provide guidance to a community in crisis on how it should understand its calling and mission."[10] Matthew understood that mission primarily in terms of disciple making.

LEADING GREAT COMMISSION CHURCHES

An encouraging percentage of younger leaders are passionately committed to the fulfillment of the Great Commission to make Christ followers among all peoples. They understand this call to mission in local, regional and global terms. However, we are not simply talking about the addition of more programs to an already-existing structure. Furthermore, the emphasis on disciple formation cannot be confined to an emerging church. Rather, it presents a discomforting challenge to the entire church.

We in the majority of churches in the West face a communication crisis. We are failing to make known the good news with credibility and conviction. Most traditional denominations are in decline. Those churches that are experiencing growth—whether independent congregations, newer movements or revitalized traditional churches—are growing by virtue of their ability to contact and attract those in transition. If we categorize those outside the church in terms of the *loose,* the *lapsed* and the *lost,* the church is mainly preoccupied with the *loose,* those who still attend church occasionally. The *lapsed* present a greater challenge in that many of them have had negative church experiences. However, when they are invited to (or stumble on) a church that is significantly different from those they have previously known, many find their way back. The *lost,* by definition, do not know the way back, and so need to be found.

Why does the church face this crisis in communication? Why has the Great Commission become the Great Omission in so many Western churches? Considering the many good things that churches do, why have they lost sight of what is central? Some might challenge the assertion that obedience to the Great Commission is *the* central function of the church, arguing instead that worship is primary. I have some sympathy with this position, yet authentic worship is inseparable from mission. When we come near to the heart of God in worship, we cannot but feel God's heartbeat for the world. The mission of the Son of Man was "to *seek* and to save what was lost" (Lk 19:10, emphasis added). The church is the very outcome of that mission.

From Decision to Discipleship

The contemporary church has to face its failure to turn *decisions for Christ* into *disciples of Christ.* We have to recognize that the term *disciple* is not restricted to super-Christians but is the way to describe ordinary believers.[11] The way that church growth was popularly perceived—and widely misunderstood—contributed to the current problem. Thousands of pastors became skilled in growing a church numerically, which resulted in larger crowds but untransformed lives. It appears that most of the growth achieved by "successful" churches reflected their ability to capture a greater share of the local religious market, at the expense of other churches that found themselves unable to compete.

Many pastors of growing churches have failed to ask the basic question, "Where is our growth coming from?" They should have read Donald McGavran, founder of the church growth movement, who emphasized that healthy church growth consists of (1) making disciples of Jesus Christ and (2) incorporating them into biblically faithful churches where they can grow into spiritual maturity and become part of its ministry to the world. McGavran reminded us that discipleship entailed not only stepping out but also being prepared to cross the bridges that God himself provides for mission.[12]

Many today argue that we have moved in our thinking beyond "church growth" to "church health." If this means moving beyond the popular 1970s to early 1990s version of church growth, I could not agree more. Unhealthy churches led by ego-driven and manipulative pastors may grow numerically, but this does not represent significant or sustainable growth. On the other hand, I disagree just as strongly if "church health" implies that we are no longer giving high priority to making new disciples.

In a therapeutic culture such as the United States, churches are prone to preoccupation with self-analysis that often arises from ecclesiastical hypochondria. Healthy churches do grow, but not by stealing adherents from other churches. They grow by going into the world, loving people as their neighbors and responding to their needs. This includes people's greatest need, which is to yield their lives to Jesus Christ as Savior and Lord. The current preoccupation with church health appears to have diverted attention from the priority of obedience to the Great Commission.[13] McGavran's original challenge to the churches in the 1950s and 1960s needs to be heeded afresh.

FAILURE TO MAKE DISCIPLES

In contemporary Western Christianity, we have little understanding of the concept of discipleship. Those who are "evangelized" are brought to the point of decision, go through membership procedures and then continue as part of the worshiping congregation, but the vast majority remain in a passive role. Only 10 to 30 percent of a typical congregation is regularly involved in ongoing Christian education classes, small groups or ministry teams. For those who settle just for the worship experience, there is little evidence of life transformation. Those "socialized" into the church through family or community involvement are likely to have stronger relational bonds, but this does not always translate into faith development. Western churches suffer from a chronic problem of undiscipled church members, an environment that serves as the perfect breeding ground for "nominal Christianity."[14]

Many younger leaders are acutely aware of the church's failure to disciple its members and have seen the serious consequences. They react against the privatization of faith, the focus on material benefits, the substitution of pop psychology for biblical content in preaching and teaching, and the apparent absence of significantly changed lives. They realize that our understanding of church must be more radical and dynamic. In the first three centuries of the church the emphasis was not on *going to* church but on *being* the church. The church is not a building or an institution but a body to which one belongs. From the standpoint of the emerging church movement, church cannot be reduced to a weekly sixty- to ninety-minute gathering; instead, it is a seven-day-a-week identification. As the *ekklēsia,* the "called-out ones," we are commissioned to be God's people when we are dispersed as much as when we are gathered.

For many Christians today, discipline is too close to the term *discipleship* for comfort. Discipline entails setting priorities and making commitments. It requires vigilance and consistency. Yet it must not be allowed to degenerate into legalistic, judgmental and grim determination. In contrast to the burdensome legalism and unreasonable demands of the Pharisees, Jesus invited the weary to take his yoke upon their shoulders, and promised that they would find it surprisingly light (Mt 11:29-30). To the extent that we submit ourselves to the yoke of Christ, we will find an exhilarating freedom. Such is the paradox of discipleship.

Younger leaders are seeking to address the lack of discipleship as part of the emerging church movement. Many of them are determined to ensure that their primary calling is "to prepare God's people for works of service, so that the body of Christ may be built up" (Eph 4:12). They recognize that such preparation is not primarily achieved through knowledge-based programs. In that type of classroom situation there is little or no personal accountability. As Greg Ogden has observed out of the frustration of his own early disciple-making efforts, "Unless disciples receive personal attention so that their particular growth needs are addressed in a way that calls them to die to self and live fully to Christ, a disciple will not be made."[15]

Eugene Peterson's *A Long Obedience in the Same Direction* presents an incisive challenge to the shallow evangelism and self-focused misrepresentation of the Christian life. The title of his book provides his working definition of discipleship. Peterson sees the Christian life in terms of discipleship and pilgrimage, which he defines as follows:

> For recognizing and resisting the stream of the world's ways there are two biblical designations for people of faith that are extremely useful: *disciple* and *pilgrim*. Disciple (*mathētēs*) says we are people who spend our lives apprenticed to our master, Jesus Christ. We are in a growing-learning relationship, always. A disciple is a learner, but not in the academic setting of the schoolroom, rather at the work site of a craftsman. We do not acquire information about God but skills in faith.
>
> *Pilgrim* (*parepidēmos*) tells us we are people who spend our lives going someplace, going to God, and whose path for getting there is the way, Jesus Christ. We realize that "this world is not my home" and set out for the Father's house.[16]

For the original disciples of Jesus, there was no mystery or misunderstanding regarding the Great Commission. They knew what he was referring to because they themselves were the products of a three-year journey of discipleship. On the day they were called, Jesus invited them to follow him, and in so doing they learned how to fish for people (Mt 4:18-22). This call to follow reminds us that discipleship is both relational and transformational. The initiation into discipleship is the call to "follow" in his steps, but his last word is to "go" into all the world. Learning and pilgrimage belong together. The disciples were privileged to be Jesus' closest and constant followers. Consequently, they could not face the prospect of continuing on their own when Jesus returned to heaven. But discipleship is never about going it alone. As he was about to ascend into heaven, Jesus assured them, "And surely I am with you always, to the very end of the age" (Mt 28:20).

THE ELEMENTS OF DISCIPLESHIP

The basic concept of discipleship was not hard to understand for those who had followed Jesus during the years of his earthly ministry. In contrast, Christians today have little appreciation of the challenges of discipleship. Church leaders need to analyze what must be done to bring discipleship to the forefront in the life of every Christ follower. In the first place, leaders themselves must personally and publicly demonstrate what it means to follow Jesus in today's world. Naturally, the specifics will vary, but there are basic elements that are valid for each place and all time.

1. *Discipleship entails a personal response to Jesus' call to follow him.* Evangelicals have emphasized new birth and conversion. But new birth is intended to lead to growth in Christ, and conversion is meant to lead to a journey in a new direction in Christ's company. Discipleship is not confined to a select group of supersaints; it is the calling of every believer. It is not simply about meeting Jesus at our journey's end but our response to Jesus' invitation to be with him throughout life's entire journey.

2. *Discipleship is lifelong learning.* We do not graduate this side of heaven. As we journey with Jesus, there are always new things to learn and fresh challenges to face. We never "arrive," which is an important consideration not just for our own sense of adventure but also because it injects a necessary note of

humility as we readily acknowledge that our own lives are still in process and our understanding is partial. This humility is vital when we share what we have learned with seekers or those who are at an earlier life stage of their walk with Christ. Matthew does not conceal the fact that disciples have weaknesses. He records moments when the disciples have "little faith," when they are "afraid" and when their behavior is inconsistent with their discipleship. Even after the resurrection, Matthew reveals that while they worshiped Christ, "some doubted" (Mt 28:17). Donald Hagner interprets this doubt to mean hesitation and indecision. He writes, "It seems clear that Matthew wanted members of his community to apply the truth to themselves."[17]

3. *Discipleship involves learning in community.* This is a necessary corrective to the one-on-one emphasis that has been so prevalent in contemporary models of discipleship. Among the Twelve there is great variety in temperament and viewpoint. The disciples learn from each other as they respond to the questions Jesus poses and as they share together with him. They learn through mutual interaction. They are a community gathered around Jesus himself. This fellowship enjoyed by Christ's disciples forges a community that has no parallel or equal outside of the church of Jesus Christ.

The disciples' learning environment does not take place in a classroom but during the course of their travels with Jesus. He does not want them to learn by rote but rather to reflect on his teaching and apply it to their lives. Jesus' teaching is not meant simply to inform the mind but to redirect the will toward changed lives. Neither does Jesus allow us to be selective in our application of his teaching; he instructs his disciples "to obey everything I have commanded" (Mt 28:20). Such obedience is not to a new Torah but to the teaching and person of Jesus. Learning discipleship from Jesus entails listening obediently to him, following wherever he leads and forsaking all that would hinder our response. It represents the formation of a lifelong habit of action and reflection, or in other words, learning through life's experiences.

4. *Discipleship means a life of service and self-giving.* The disciples learn the lessons of discipleship by being in close contact with Jesus, who demonstrates self-giving love and service throughout his ministry but supremely in

the cross. The disciples understand that Jesus not only calls them to follow but also to "fish"; by following they will learn how to draw people into the "net" of the kingdom of God. When the church today makes disciples who are not themselves making disciples in turn, we are not making disciples as Jesus taught.

5. *Discipleship means teaching as Jesus taught.* Jesus demonstrates a variety of communication approaches: storytelling, proclamation, demonstration, riddles, aphorisms and penetrating questions. Moreover, he does not just set us an example, but he promises to continue with us as we venture into the world in his name. Craig Keener comments, "If many Christians today have lost a sense of Jesus' presence and purpose among us, it may be because we have lost sight of the mission our Lord gave to us."[18] Those leaders who are called of God to take the church into the future need to sense the priority of the Great Commission: "teaching them everything I have commanded you."

More Than Obeying a Command

Matthew's Gospel alone expresses Christ's commissioning of his disciples as a command. Furthermore, no other New Testament passage specifically refers to the Great Commission. Neither the book of Acts nor any of the Epistles directly exhorts the churches to go into all the world to make disciples. An echo of the Great Commission appears at the conclusion of Romans, but it is in the form of a doxology, not a command:

> Now to him who is able to establish you by my gospel and the proclamation of Jesus Christ, according to the revelation of the mystery hidden for long ages past, but now revealed and made known through the prophetic writings by the command of the eternal God, so that all nations might believe and obey him—to the only wise God be glory forever through Jesus Christ! Amen. (Rom 16:25-27)

What are we to make of this silence? Clearly, it should not be interpreted as a lack of concern for the spread of the gospel. There are clear and repeated references to the ongoing communication of the gospel and the establishment of new churches throughout the Mediterranean world. Exploring the significance of the New Testament's silence regarding the Great Commission, Harry Boer writes that the early church was not motivated by a sense of obligation but rather out of a spontaneous desire to share the good news—a desire implanted by the Holy Spirit, the true driving force for mission.[19]

The explicit and direct command to Matthew's Jewish readers may represent a challenge to their tendency toward introversion. If so, then the command was not necessary for the churches described in Acts and of the subsequent postapostolic period. Nevertheless, the introversion that was an exception in the first century has now become commonplace in contemporary Western churches. Today's younger church leaders must challenge it, and indeed many are determined to do exactly that. They may prove to be an indication of God's investment in the future, provided they remain true to their vision and calling.

Yet the response of Christ's disciples is more than mere obedience to a command. The Twelve do not simply follow Jesus as other disciples follow a teacher or as people look for a model. They do not so much emulate as worship him. Christ's disciples are worshipers before they become witnesses. Matthew emphasizes the disciples' relation to Jesus not only as "teacher" but also as "Lord." Bosch observes that "where Matthew's sources have 'teacher' or 'rabbi' in the mouth of the disciples, he has changed this to 'Lord.' There is only one exception; Judas Iscariot twice calls him "Rabbi," and both times are in the context of his betrayal of Jesus" (Mt 26:25, 49).[20] Jesus' disciples venture forth in the name of the One to whom all authority has been given on heaven and on earth. It is this monumental fact that moves them forward. To the extent that they take bold steps in venturing to all peoples everywhere, they discover that the Lord is with them constantly and permanently.

RESHAPING AND REDIRECTING THE CHURCH

What are the characteristics of churches that are taking seriously this broader understanding of the Great Commission and the recognition that the church is both the product of and agent for mission? What are the leaders of the communities and movements that comprise the emerging "mission-shaped church" inculcating?[21] In the past twenty years, working groups on both sides of the Atlantic have launched initiatives endeavoring to respond to the missionary challenges presented to Western churches by the changing cultural context.

The late Bishop Lesslie Newbigin was a pioneer thinker who applied his missionary insights to the situation in Western societies.[22] Newbigin's work stimulated the formation of the Gospel and Our Culture network in the United States and Canada, a group that has produced a number of books addressing the relationship of church and mission. At the University of Aberdeen, Andrew Walls has drawn attention to the challenge of reevangelizing the West, which he considers to be one of the world's most difficult missionary fields.[23] Darrell Guder, Craig Van Gelder, George Hunsberger, Alan Roxburgh, Wilbert Shenk, George Hunter and Charles Van Engen have each made major contributions to the literature. These authors also represent a wide range of ecclesial traditions: Lutheran, Baptist, Mennonite, Methodist and Reformed. In reviewing their contributions, we can summarize their insights under the following headings:

- The church is shaped by the mission of God rather than by a self-serving agenda of numerical growth or defensive isolation. In other words growth is a byproduct and should not be the primary focus. At the same time nongrowth raises legitimate questions regarding the church's faithfulness to its calling.

- The church defines its mission in relation to the Trinity. It recognizes the interrelationship of the Persons in the outworking of salvation, and in its own life it embraces the community and diversity expressed in the Godhead. Mission cannot be privatized or individualized.

- The church establishes the inseparable connection between worship and witness. The praise that the church addresses to God leads to proclamation and communication of the gospel to the world. In the Psalms there are a number of examples of praise flowing into witness. For instance:

Sing to the LORD a new song;
> sing to the LORD, all the earth.

Sing to the LORD, praise his name;
> proclaim his salvation day after day.

Declare his glory among the nations,
> his marvelous deeds among all peoples. . . .

Say among the nations, "The LORD reigns." (Ps 96:1-3, 10)

What is anticipated by worship in the temple and the synagogues is not actualized until the day of Pentecost. On that occasion it becomes evident that overheard praise is a powerful form of witness. The close connection between praise and witness represents more than a theological integration of ecclesiology and missiology; it establishes a spiritual dynamic. In the emerging church, a prioritization of worship does not result in the *marginalizing* of mission but in the *energizing* of it.

- The church recognizes the rich and colorful diversity in God's creation. As it engages with the cultural mosaic and the kaleidoscopic interplay of cultures, it realizes that it must itself demonstrate both diversity and reconciliation.

- The church is challenged to take up an incarnational approach. Using the example of Jesus' ministry and the struggles of the New Testament church to relate the gospel to both non-Jews and Jews, the church today must not extract inquirers and seekers from their cultural context only to invite them into a secure cocoon. Instead, it must permeate the cultural context in order to learn its values and aspirations in order to relate the gospel effectively. In so doing, those who are engaged in mission will come to a fresh understanding of the gospel and will face the gospel's challenges afresh in their own lives.[24]

- The church must reach out in an attitude of unconditional love. It must not only reach people *where* they are but also accept them *as* they are.

This stance, however, must not be interpreted as an attitude of tolerance toward any lifestyle that may be obsessive or self-destructive. Inclusion always has a view toward transformation, because the message of the gospel brings liberation and empowerment.

- The church's commitment to transformation is not limited to individuals but extends to the geographic communities in which the church is located and the nongeographical networks in which it is engaged. Missional churches recognize that they are signs and servants of the reign of God, but because they themselves are in the process of becoming, they are ambiguous signs and unworthy servants. When drawing people to it, the missional church must always point beyond itself.

- The church must give high priority to the Great Commission. We do so as Jesus followers sent into the world, guided and empowered by his Spirit. This entails a firm commitment to relationship building and the recognition that disciples do not exist in isolation but in communities of mutual support, accountability and commitment. The emerging church is more concerned with ministry *by* the church than ministry *in* the church.[25]

NOT A FAD BUT A FRONTIER

Before reading further, it is important to grasp that when I speak of the emerging church I am not talking about trendy forms of worship or of holy huddles of like-minded people seeking spiritual experiences and developing creative events. Rather, I am speaking of communities committed to being authentic expressions of the mission of God in the world. Neither am I focused exclusively on churches designed to stop people under thirty-five from leaving, to reengage the formerly churched or to attract the never-churched.

Mission engagement is aimed at every generation that has been alienated from the life of the church or at those to whom the church seems irrelevant and discredited. The particular focus of this book is on those under thirty-

five years old because they represent the most pressing challenge that
churches on both sides of the Atlantic and in Australasia face. In a few years,
with an aging population in the Western world, mission and ministry among
seniors will become an equal priority. Authentic expressions of the emerging
church are shaped by and committed to mission, a point that represents
such a challenge to the established order that it is the ecclesial equivalent of
a Copernican revolution.[26]

In addition to the rejuvenation and redirecting of existing churches, we
will also need to establish new churches. These will not simply be the off-
spring or clones of existing congregations, but they will represent faith
communities that are custom-built for mission. The *Mission-Shaped Church*
report of the Church of England suggests the following definition of church
planting:

> Church planting is the process by which a seed of the life and message
> of Jesus embodied by a community of Christians is immersed for mis-
> sion reasons in a particular cultural or geographic context.
>
> The intended consequence is that it roots there, coming to life as a
> new indigenous body of Christian disciples well suited to continue its
> mission.[27]

Bob Hopkins, in his critique of this report, suggests that the definitions
could be further strengthened by highlighting the notion that such churches
need to reproduce within their contexts. That way, church growth happens
through multiplication rather than by addition. As Hopkins explains, "only
to focus on making the first cross-cultural bridgehead as the report tends to,
perpetuates operating only in the dynamic of *addition* and misses the practical implication of the crucial recognition that one mark of the church is to
multiply."[28] A *come-based institution* is reshaped into a *go-shaped movement.*
The church needs to repent for its failure to be the church, and not just for
its moral failures but also for its missional ineptitude. It has to wake up to
the fact that with the dawn of the postmodern era and the passing of the
Constantinian and Christendom eras, the world has changed dramatically.

SUMMARY

The church must reestablish the priority of the Great Commission. It is the Lord's mandate that *defines* the church as people who follow Christ in every area of life with a local and global vision for Christ's reign on earth. It also *drives* the church to turn from an inward focus that invites the world to come to enjoy its benefits to a church that disperses and infiltrates every power center and every segment of the culture.

4

What's Different?

Leadership is always challenging, but it has become even more so in the current climate of discontinuous and unpredictable change. Under these drastically changed conditions, decisions can no longer be made on the basis of well-established precedents. Now, leaders must be capable of creative and independent thinking. Peter Drucker describes the profound and all-encompassing nature of present-day societal change in the following way:

> Every few hundred years throughout Western history a sharp transformation has occurred. In a matter of decades, society altogether re-arranges itself—its worldview, its basic values, its social and political structures, its arts, its key institutions. Fifty years later a new world exists. And the people born into that world cannot even imagine the world in which their grandparents lived and into which their own parents were born.[1]

Our age is such a period of transformation.

Many leaders who vainly endeavor to be all things to all people will soon discover that they have raised unrealistic expectations and have set themselves up for failure. In their struggle to survive, increasing numbers of these leaders burn out, and many of them withdraw from full-time ministry. Some observers estimate that nearly 50 percent of those who train for local church ministry are no longer serving local churches ten years later. Thus for a person to survive, let alone thrive on, the demanding call of church leadership, discernment and discipline are critical.

DECISION MAKING UNDER TIME PRESSURE

The church is not the only entity struggling with the precarious and hazardous nature of leadership. In recent years leadership-training courses have proliferated and become a multimillion-dollar business enterprise. Jean Lipman-Blumen, professor in the prestigious Drucker School of Management in Claremont, California, highlights the pervasive challenges to leadership. She writes, "Like early morning fog, the changing demands upon leaders seep through every cranny of society: families, schools, churches, grassroots political movements, corporations, and governments."[2]

In the high-paced business world, Lipman-Blumen explains, leaders have to operate with shorter and shorter time frames. This rapid pace shrinks the amount of time that leaders have for making decisions. The pressure of having to make quick decisions, some of which may have far-reaching consequences, often means fewer second chances. If leaders blow it, it is often with the destructive force of an explosion rather than a puff of wind. Therefore, leaders live with the dilemma of having to think for the long term despite being under relentless pressure to succeed in the short term.[3]

While church leaders typically are not exposed to a similar level of pressure, they are often faced with having to make decisions in an environment where (1) it is increasingly difficult to raise budgets, (2) it is hard to enlist and maintain the support of volunteers, and (3) there are conflicting agendas among church members. Furthermore, the pool from which to draw volunteers continues to shrink. The overwhelming majority of congregations number less than 120. In North America the average is just under 100, while the United Kingdom's average is even smaller. Given this, the future of many congregations is increasingly precarious. As in the commercial world, many churches are currently poised at what is called the "strategic inflection point," referring to the point at which trends have shifted from an upward to a downward direction.[4]

At such times, decisions have far-reaching consequences. A decline can accelerate if leaders fail to discern the shifting trends, or if they lack the courage to recognize the urgency of the situation. This is very evident in the United Kingdom, where so many churches and chapels have closed their doors and sold their buildings. The question remains whether, before long, churches in the United States will find themselves in a similar situation.

NAVIGATION IN MISTS AND STORMS

Under modernity, humankind believed that it was in control and that it was able to bring order out of chaos. Our transition into a culture of postmodernity has arisen partly out of the sobering realization that chaos is beyond our control. The chaotic nature of postmodernity requires movement away from compartmentalization to the acceptance of a world of complexity and interaction.[5]

The problem with so much of our ministry training is that it is still based on the assumptions of modernity. In seminaries and other ministry-training schools, knowledge is compartmentalized into a range of specializations. Methods are taught with the expectation that they can (and will) deliver predictable outcomes. From this perspective leadership is about "following the road map," that is, defining the problem and developing a series of steps by which it might be solved. Unfortunately, real life is far messier. Harlan Cleveland observes: "The world of human relationships is always untidy." Those of us who insist on tidiness and control are prone to ignore relevant facts that do not fit our theories. Indeed, the clues needed to address a challenge effectively may lie precisely in those "bits of messiness that interfere with our neat picture."[6]

Bill Easum's insights have helped church leaders understand and operate within this chaos and confusion. He insists on addressing it in positive terms, as a challenge to faith and as a springboard for creativity. Easum turns the attention of church leaders to chaos theory, stating that "instead of the enemy of order and beauty, chaos is an essential early element in the birthing of everything new. The chaotic, unpredictable, and sometimes destructive dynamics of flow are not 'tamed' or 'controlled' by rules, resolutions, or policies."[7] There is no place to run to in order to avoid the impact of chaotic change. While its major effect is experienced in the urban context, suburbia, small towns and rural communities are no longer safe havens.

Mike Regele insists that this culture of chaos is global; there is nowhere to run. Furthermore, Regele adds that (1) the pace of change is so rapid that there is no time to reflect, (2) the complexity of change presents us with too much information to absorb, (3) chaotic change is comprehensive and affects every area of life, and (4) change in a culture of postmodernity is both unpredictable and discontinuous, which means that it cannot be anticipated ahead of time.[8]

LESSONS FROM HISTORY

Younger leaders in the emerging church movement are rediscovering the relevance of the early Christians for our times. They are learning the fundamental elements that enabled the church to be such a dynamic movement, and are seeking to translate those into contemporary settings. As we examine the social conditions of the Roman world of the first and second centuries, it is clear that the *Pax Romana* masked a seething cauldron of turbulent humanity. This was especially evident along the empire's frontier, in places like Israel. Under the Roman imperial system, the majority of Israel's population eked out a precarious, hand-to-mouth existence. The general populace was crushed by an intolerable burden of taxation, intimidated by an occupying army and exploited by local officials who benefited personally through graft and corruption. For most people a poor harvest or a downturn in trade meant that they were no longer able to pay their taxes, a situation that only added to personal and familial debt.[9]

We must remember when we read the Sermon on the Mount that when Jesus encourages the common people not to be anxious about food, clothing and aging (Mt 6:25-34), these are very real concerns for his hearers. Many have painful, haunting memories of their own experience as well as the privation of family members and their entire community. Jesus calls his disciples from among these common people, people from the margins of society. With one possible exception, all of them are from the northern region of Galilee. They are not chosen from the societal center of Jerusalem. They are not raised in the religious establishment and are not part of the influential lay movement of the Pharisees. Instead, they are common trades people who, when later examined by the court of religious leaders, are despised as uneducated folk (Acts 4:13).

The apostle Paul describes the members of the early church as weak and poor. However, this did not mean destitute. Most in the early church belonged to a "household." This meant that they had roots as well as the support of an extended family system, representing a more secure and privileged class.[10]

The first century was indeed tumultuous, but it is important to note that chaotic times prevailed for long periods in the history of God's people. Abraham, Isaac and Jacob were constantly on the move. Israel's slavery in Egypt brought a sense of security, but at the price of servitude. Israel wandered in the wilderness of Sinai for forty years after the liberating experience of the exodus. During the period of the judges, everyone "did that which was right in his own eyes" (Judg 17:6; 21:25 KJV). The kingship of Saul ended disastrously, and his successor—David—could trust neither his counselors nor members of his own family. Soon after, chaotic conditions increased as regional powers like Assyria and Babylon grew in strength. First, Assyria threatened and subsequently conquered the northern kingdom of Israel. Though spared this initial onslaught, the people of Judah suffered the same fate when Babylon, after vanquishing the Assyrian Empire, sacked Jerusalem.

The prophets of the Old Testament addressed Israel and Judah during this chaotic period. Calling on God's people and their leaders to face the consequences of their injustice, oppression and broken covenant, prophets such as Jeremiah, Ezekiel, Isaiah and Amos warned the nation of the inevitable judgment of a holy God on his people. They also called the people and their leaders to look beyond the Lord's judgment to a time when God would rebuild their fortunes through a faithful remnant.

Turning to the New Testament's prophetic vision of the future, we see a similar picture, but on a global scale. Chaotic times will prevail. Jesus talked about future wars, famines, earthquakes and increasing conflict between good and evil (Mk 13:3-27). But once more the outcome is assured. Jesus Christ will return as Lord to establish his universal reign.

In the history of God's people, those chaotic conditions were sometimes the direct consequence of human sin and of God's judgment on his people and other nations. At other times, the chaos arose out of times of social upheaval occasioned by technological advances, the demise of old industries and the emergence of new knowledge-based business enterprises. A changing job market often brings great opportunities to some but excludes others from the economic benefits because they lack the necessary education and training. In our present circumstances, we find both elements at work, and yet we can see God's redemptive purposes being worked out in the midst of the confusion and uncertainty. It is imperative that church leaders be able to read the signs of the times. Many younger leaders with new styles of leadership appear to be at the forefront because they are not weighed down by traditional structures and expectations. The fact that many of them are bivocational enables them not only to keep in touch but to personally feel the pressures.

Younger leaders handle chaos, vulnerability and uncertainty better because they are the products of the current cultural milieu, embodying both its strengths and weaknesses. Much like the early church, they are comfortable functioning from the margins; for them the church has become an increasingly marginalized institution. They do not operate with the top-down mentality so typical of their predecessors. Moreover, they are prepared to make do with limited resources. While older generations struggle to adapt to the new social reality, younger leaders wonder what all the fuss is about.

THE TWILIGHT OF THE HIERARCHY

The fragmentation of society into a multiplicity of subcultures and interest groups, and the widespread availability of information, has contributed to the current questioning of traditional authority. In *Nobody in Charge,* in a section titled "The Twilight of the Hierarchy," Harlan Cleveland highlights the effect of the culture of chaos on authority and organization. Cleveland explains, "The shift is now more than obvious: from top-down vertical relationships towards horizontal, consensual, collaborative modes of getting people together to make something different happen."[11]

Every institution has had to adjust to this new reality, including those that have operated in the past in a hierarchical and authoritarian manner. And these adjustments are not merely cosmetic; many are unmistakably radical in nature and often represent complete shifts in modus operandi. Existing leaders have discovered that they can no longer operate by means of command and control but instead have had to learn to communicate, debate and negotiate. Regimentation has become less effective as people expect to be treated with dignity and respect in recognition of their individual uniqueness and intrinsic worth. This sensitivity is especially important given our increasingly ruthless and economically competitive world. Such ruthlessness undermines morale and strips people of energy.

As society fragments and people exercise their freedom of choice, hierarchical structures crumble. The turfism of hierarchical organizations can especially frustrate younger people. According to Gifford Pinchot, they are sensitive to the fact that "the system of measurement and control . . . impede[s] cooperation and the free flow in information that is necessary to achieve productivity in the information age."[12] They recognize that lateral and flexible structures are required to maintain unfettered access to the knowledge, wisdom and resources necessary in today's fast-paced environment.

Though Pinchot is writing for the business context, we find parallel developments among younger leaders in the church who instinctively operate beyond their congregation and denominational structures. Internet blogging provides an example: younger Christians are conversing with others outside their local church and denominational contexts. I know of one young leader engaged in urban ministry in Miami who has denominational and congregational ties in terms of finances and local volunteers, but his primary peer mentors are young leaders in Northern California and Wellington, New Zealand. Neither of these individuals is in his denomination, but both attend emerging church conferences, have set up working groups on urban development and a range of other topics of mutual interest, and record their thoughts in blogs. The young leader in Miami can contact his two urban ministry "knowledge people" on a daily or weekly basis by e-mail and chatrooms, or by visiting their websites.

THE IMPACT OF COMPREHENSIVE AND CHAOS-PRODUCING CHANGE

Today, we live in a culture of chaotic change that is comprehensive and deep-rooted. It affects every human institution. Self-protective and identity-preserving exclusiveness is being replaced by inclusiveness. Organizations can no longer afford to look within to determine their future. They need to invite a diverse group to participate in their conversations. Traditional, strongly cohesive institutions are being replaced by short-term coalitions and temporary groupings. Furthermore, Lipman-Blumen comments that the major discontinuities produced by the current upheaval can cause people to sever links with their own traditions.[13] Yet that same cultural storm also causes some to turn to organizations that offer security and safety. Herein lies a danger for evangelical Christians and other conservative traditions.[14] A time of cultural upheaval challenges us afresh to see what we have misunderstood (or missed completely) due to our cultural blinders.

HOW NETWORKS FUNCTION

Organizations that are best able to operate within the new cultural reality are flexible, fast-moving and sensitive to the changes taking place in their environment. They are interconnected and inclusive. As I reread the book of Acts and the letters of the New Testament, I was impressed by the abundance of evidence that the churches of the Mediterranean world operated as clusters and networks rather than as a centralized hierarchy. Given the slow and precarious communication channels of the time, they could not have been organized differently. Paul did not exercise authority in a heavy-handed or controlling way. Rather he left churches to work things out for themselves, intervening only when situations were getting out of hand.[15]

In the providence of God it may be that the networked-cluster structure was God's way of protecting the early church under persecution. There was no "head" for the Romans to use counterinsurgency techniques against— that is, "kill the head, destroy the body." There was no central hierarchy that could be rooted out. Destroying small nodes wouldn't do the trick; there were far too many, they could be quickly replaced, and they were able to re-group organizationally. Also the New Testament house churches, consisting of extended households, were small but close-knit, which means that they were extremely difficult to infiltrate for the purpose of subversion and de-nunciation. (This is one reason why the church in China will most likely continue to grow at a phenomenal rate.)

Network structures are invariably untidy and sometimes downright messy. Leaders who have been forged by a hierarchical culture find them es-pecially difficult. Thomas Stewart makes a helpful distinction between net-works and hierarchies: "Networks, by definition, connect everyone to every-one. Hierarchical organizations, by definition, don't do that—they create formal channels of communication, and you're expected to follow them."[16] Stewart observes that within hierarchies, positions substitute for persuasion and the rule of law trumps grace, whereas in networks, relationships depend much more on cooperation than control.[17]

One problem with the network approach, however, is this lower level of control. Unless there is a high level of trust in place, the cooperative charac-ter of networks can lead to loss of cohesion and momentum. Trust therefore is critical, but it can be built only through strong communities. The essential building blocks of successful communities include commitment, compe-tence, dependability, communication and affirmation (see chap. 5).

THE "BODY" IMAGE

There is a point of tension between the loose networking structures that are increasingly evident in Western societies and communities with strong bonds of commitment built on trust. When addressing community development, the New Testament relies heavily on the metaphor of the body, which emphasizes unity, diversity and interdependence. Paul describes the church as being one body consisting of an amazing variety of members who each have a specific location and function (Rom 12:4-5; 1 Cor 12:12-27). Such an image defies analysis and yet fires the imagination. The church is not only bound together by vision and mission statements but also by the Spirit of Christ, who gives each member a common identity within the family of God (1 Cor 12:12-13; Eph 2:18; 4:4).

Authentic community begins with the frank recognition that loose connections are not robust enough to provide cohesion. There must be strong bonds of mutual commitment that will endure times of strain and upheaval. Unconditional commitments are not made within alliances of convenience. (We see the consequences of loose connections in Western marriage, which has shifted from a solemn covenant to a mere social contract.) Only within a secure environment can we safely drop our defenses and take off our masks. Until we find a home and establish a family identity, authentic community is unlikely to develop. The covenant community provides a context within which individuals can find affirmation and learn to truly forgive. It is an environment of giving as well as receiving. In community we also hold each other accountable, because affirmation that lacks discernment and integrity is destructive to the other person.

Authentic community has porous boundaries. Margaret Wheatley and Myron Kellner-Rogers provide helpful insights into the way boundaries function in living systems. Rather than being self-protective walls, boundaries become the place of meeting and exchange. We usually think of these "edges" as the means of defining separateness: what's inside and what's outside. But in living systems, boundaries are something quite different. They are where new relationships take form, an important place of exchange and growth.[18]

A community that uses its boundaries as a self-protective wall and ceases to include others becomes a clique. In authentic community, as people receive the benefits of the care of other members, they are obliged to share those benefits and include others on the other side of the boundary. The boundary between the community and the outside world is not a defensive shield but a frontier for engagement. By such involvement, the community becomes both a sign and a servant of the reign of God.

Life forms are dependent on relationships. The individualism and privatization of Western society is dehumanizing and has tragic consequences. Wheatley and Kellner-Rogers argue that life is systems-seeking and that independence does not belong to the living world; it is an invented political concept. They caution that species that ignore relationships, act in greedy and rapacious ways, and exhaust themselves while striving for conformity simply die off.[19]

Thus the church must demonstrate its fundamental relational character as both the *body* and the *bride* of Christ. Doing so is profoundly countercultural, not by being isolated and insular but as a missional presence in the world. In order to do this, the church must constantly reaffirm its own distinctive nature, recognizing the extent to which it has been subverted by the cultural values of individualism and narcissism.

FROM CONTROL TO EMPOWERMENT

Churches must be prepared to dismantle many of their hierarchical structures. These hierarchies, whether local, regional or national, have become too inflexible and unresponsive. William Bridges asks, "What does it take to lead an organization where people forget their job and do what needs doing?"[20] Church leaders need to reexamine established patterns of working and their insistence on inflexible job descriptions. As church leaders begin to make this shift, they will become acutely aware of their need for the skills and insights of other people. "Networked technology," adds Bridges, "takes power from the *head* of an organization and distributes it among those who comprise the *hands*."[21] Empowering others inevitably means yielding one's own power.

Moses realized this truth after delegating authority to other leaders (elders) in Israel (Ex 18:13-27; Num 11:16-17, 25-30). Delegation in itself was not enough; it had to be linked with the empowerment of others, which in turn entailed a loss of control. ("The LORD said to Moses: '. . . I will take of the Spirit that is on you and put the Spirit on them' "—i.e., the seventy elders of Israel [Num 11:16-17].) When two leaders, Eldad and Medad, began to prophesy among the people, Joshua urged Moses to stop them. "But Moses replied, 'Are you jealous for my sake? I wish that all the LORD's people were prophets'" (Num 11:26-30). A leader cannot delegate what God has already empowered people to do.

The act of empowering others can be tainted with an attitude of control. James Kouzes and Barry Posner highlight this tendency:

> The problem with empowerment is that it suggests that this is something leaders magically give or do for others. But people already have tremendous power. It is not a matter of giving it to them, but of freeing them to use the power and skills they already have. It is a matter of expanding their opportunities to use themselves in service of a common and meaningful purpose.[22]

Empowerment includes valuing others, removing constraints and granting opportunities.

ADVENT OF THE INFORMATION AGE

Today, the flow of information is increasingly difficult to restrict. Authoritarian governments are painfully aware of their growing inability to keep truth from their population. Harlan Cleveland notes some of the reasons this is so: The Internet and its powerful search engines significantly reduce the control of hierarchies and their leaders. The volume of available knowledge and its speed of transmission make it impossible for leaders to assimilate everything they feel they need to know. Furthermore, knowledge is not a commodity that is lost once it is exchanged; it grows exponentially through the process of sharing.[23] The Internet operates as a counter to mass media and the corporate world of advertising, entertainment and filtered news precisely because it is decentralized and cannot be controlled.

Virtual communities play a significant role in the information age. For many, virtual communities are simply off the radar screen. Those who are not computer literate generally underestimate the strength and significance of chatrooms and blogs. Older pastors need to wake up to the fact that over 50 percent of the population in Europe, North America and many areas of Asia are regularly surfing the Web. This percentage rises to 70 percent among teens. The net-savvy generation has already surpassed the baby boomers and is becoming the dominant influence in pop culture.

I recently stood in front of a series of very gifted street preachers in a Canadian city. Hardly a person stopped. The street is no longer the public forum; the Web has provided the new marketplace for the exchange of ideas. Spirituality is a hot topic on the Web, and Christians need to play a significant role in the ongoing discussion. Yet Tom Beaudoin alerts us to the fact that discussions on "alternative spiritualities" vastly outnumber those on orthodox Christianity.[24]

While many churches have websites, the great majority are nothing more than electronic bulletin boards, with no place for interaction. In contrast, I remember a conversation with a pastor from Southern California who had a special service to mark the first anniversary of the 9/11 attacks on the World Trade Center and the Pentagon. There were several thousand at the service, but an even larger congregation—people around the world who were viewing the service via the Internet—was unseen. And these virtual congregants could communicate in real time with the pastor, who was able to respond to their comments in the course of his sermon.

In my assessment, virtual communities have both advantages and disadvantages over face-to-face communities. They provide access for people who wish to engage in exploratory-type conversations. Howard Rheingold notes that since we cannot see one another in virtual communities, we are unable to form prejudices. Such a forum allows us to establish initial links with people in order to learn something about them before we decide to meet physically. They allow us to learn and engage at a speed and level with which we feel comfortable.[25]

At the same time, there are obvious limitations. Whereas the strength of virtual community is in providing anonymity, its weakness lies in its inability to build trust and accountability. Anonymity allows the participants to feel secure to the point that deception can be a real problem. In a virtual community, we can never be sure about our knowledge of another person.[26]

Near the end of the twentieth century, Howard Rheingold wondered about the future public role of virtual communities:

> The advent of the mass media and of the manipulation of public opinion through publicity and advertising led to the commodification and deterioration of the public sphere. . . . Are virtual communities beautiful illusions that lull us into thinking that we are participating in discourse, or are they a step towards a rebirth of the public sphere? I can't think of a more important question to attempt to answer in the closing years of the twentieth century.[27]

The communities of the future will be far more complex than those that existed prior to the knowledge revolution. They will incorporate a variety of expressions and will reflect both the mobile nature of our society as well as the complexity of our communication networks. They will not be made up of friends and neighbors who live and work within the same community.

FLEXIBLE AND REPRODUCIBLE STRUCTURES

The new realities of postmodernity mean the future structure of the church must be fluid, flexible and capable of adjusting to diversity. It can expand as a movement only to the extent that it is made up of small reproducible units. However, the reproduction of these units must not happen through mass production and mere replication, but through a process of generation that, in accordance with particular mission challenges and cultural contexts, encourages great variety.

The language that is sometimes used to describe this process of reproduction is *fractal,* a term taken from biology. Bill Easum explains the fractal structure of leaves: "No matter how much you magnify the leaf, the pattern is repeated over and over as intricate geometric patterns."[28] It is immediately evident why the idea of fractal growth alarms controlling leaders in that the growth is not organized from the center but occurs from the inner dynamic of each cell. But church leaders who have come to understand the power of the dynamic and have developed church structures along the principle of fractal growth realize its potential.

One younger leader, Wayne Cordeiro, has provided us with an impressive model. On the Hawaiian island of Oahu, Cordeiro built his church using re-producible units of five individuals or couples. Each unit functions as a team, and each team has a leader who has demonstrated a vision for ministry and has recruited others on the basis of that vision. Each team is united by its shared purpose and mutual concern for its members.[29] Cordeiro is concerned that every member of the church finds their fit so that they can become integrated and functioning members of the church. He achieves this by means of a training and interviewing process based on the acronym *DESIGN*:

Desire—What we would like to do if given the chance

Experience—What we have done that has built our expertise and confidence

Spiritual gift—What the Spirit has given us in order to participate effectively in a ministry of the ascended Christ

Individual style—Our personality and temperament

Growth phase—Where we are in our spiritual journey

Natural abilities—Aptitudes we were born with and which develop early in life[30]

This type of church will grow only to the extent that it is successful in creating an ever-expanding base of leadership. Unlike a pyramid, this base follows the fractal model, comprising interrelated units that demonstrate creativity and initiative. This, as Suzanne Morse explains, is the gist of polycentric leadership:

Successful communities, even those with long traditions of organized community leadership, will continue to broaden the circles of leadership to create a system for the community that is neither centralized nor decentralized, but rather polycentric. The polycentric view of community leadership assumes that there are many centers of leadership that interrelate.[31]

In a period of confusion and complexity, leadership must not resort to simplistic solutions or rely on borrowed, success-guaranteed formulas. It requires constant course corrections in the midst of opposing currents and prevailing winds. Leaders must ensure that everyone is managing to keep up, pausing long enough to allow the stragglers to catch up. And as organizations become more complex and decentralized, it is also essential that leaders keep a broader picture in view. Above all, the current environment requires leaders who are skilled in team building.

SUMMARY

If the church is to regain lost ground it must find new ways to identify leaders and develop ministry forms that are reproducible and can morph in response to the cultural mosaic. A truly missional church requires a team-building philosophy of leadership in order to bring together the range of insights, skills and experiences that are needed to translate vision into reality. Churches must be sufficiently flexible and spontaneous to respond in a timely manner to the needs, challenges and opportunities of postmodernity.

The church needs to be led by those who can live with untidiness but can see organizational patterns in the midst of the apparent chaos. Leaders need to be familiar with the recurring and widespread themes in our culture, and connected with the wider conversations taking place in cyberspace.

5

Team Building

Leadership is about connecting, not controlling. It is about bringing people together for the purpose of creative synergy. Because the information age is fast-paced and knowledge and experience are highly diversified, leaders of the emerging church recognize their need to operate in a team context. Team-based ministry allows them to draw strength from each other and to contribute to the common good from their God-endowed gifts and life experience.

Discipling doesn't occur in isolation but in communities where there is encouragement and mutual accountability. The same is true in ministry; it flows from authentic community. Whereas a clique closes its ranks and faces inward, authentic community turns outward to welcome and serve others. In today's world, leaders must be skilled at bringing people together in order to pool knowledge and skills. They must struggle to create the right "chemistry" of human relations, so that those they lead spark ideas in one another, urging each other forward in ministry and outreach.

Team building is not just about improving productivity. It brings people together in a supportive and challenging environment so that they might realize their full potential. Teams create and are created out of a rhythm. The team members know when to work hard together, but also when to slow down and play. Over time, team members come to appreciate not only each other's skills but also the depths of their personalities and life experiences.

This process establishes, deepens and reinforces mutual appreciation and lifelong friendships. As the team continues to build trust and understanding, more sensitive issues are discussed openly. At times, even most unexpectedly, conflict between team members actually helps relationships to become symbiotic over time. Where there is trust and mutual appreciation, sharp disagreement germinates new insights.

However, in the process of moving from an independent leadership style to one of team building some people may need to leave—those not prepared for their personal fiefdoms to be challenged and dismantled. Some leaders simply are not ready to have their personal agendas challenged. Others refuse to become vulnerable or to recognize their dependence on the insights and skills of other people. There is also the possibility of personality clashes that cannot be resolved.

Building healthy, functioning teams is difficult because team membership demands a high price. Patrick Lencioni identifies five barriers teams face and describes their symptoms. (1) At the bottom, members of a dysfunctional team demonstrate inattention to results because of a self-centered concern for status and ego. (2) This in turn leads to avoidance of accountability and toleration of low standards, because questioning one member's performance exposes the others. (3) A refusal to be held accountable signifies a lack of commitment, which is evidenced by indecision and avoidance strategies. (4) Where relationships are fragile, team members fear conflict and therefore maintain a veneer of artificial harmony. (5) The prevailing atmosphere of mutual suspicion and lack of trust causes team members to be distant and defensive. They cannot risk making themselves vulnerable to the other team members, whom they suspect of seeking to gain advantage over them.[1]

THE DISTINCTIVE STYLE TYPICAL OF YOUNGER LEADERS

One prominent older leader among Gen Xers, in response to my question regarding the effectiveness of his leadership style, listed his three principles of leadership as "low profile, low budget and low maintenance." Earlier textbooks on leadership, many of which were based on hierarchical modes of thinking, talk a lot about loneliness at the top. Inevitably, if there is only room for one high-profile leader on the top rungs of the hierarchy-and-control ladder, two things occur. First, loneliness, but with it also comes an absence of accountability. This is why younger leaders emphasize *low-profile* relationship-building over high-profile control. They don't feel the need to occupy center stage but instead are content to work from the sidelines. This stance actually strengthens their leadership position because it broadens their network of contacts and expands their influence. It also keeps them tied in with more people—helping them fight loneliness and the temptation to engage in unethical behavior.

A number of younger leaders, as well as those who serve as their mentors, have observed reluctance on the part of younger leaders to accept leadership responsibility. Team-based leadership must be employed as a device to avoid personal initiatives and to sidestep accepting responsibility for decisions made. The members must work through their disagreements to decide together on a course of action when faced with tough choices. When operating in a culture of discontinuity and chaos there are few easy answers. But mistaken leadership is preferable to a complete absence of leadership.

It is unlikely that financial resources will be so readily available to support the ministries of the future. *Low budget* means that churches, parachurch and humanitarian organizations, and mission agencies in the West are going to have to learn to operate on a "shoestring," much like those in the non-Western world. They will have to be habitually creative with their finances. And, when a work of God experiences a windfall, it should be used wisely for maximum impact.

Low maintenance reflects vision, shared values and, most importantly, trust. Suspicious and insecure leaders are prone to empower others with one hand while taking it away with the other. They constantly interfere through micromanagement. But when team members keep each other committed to the organization's overarching vision and maintain each other's moral integrity through accountability, it allows a trusting leader to freely delegate authority and responsibility.

Edgar H. Schein says team leaders should be characterized by a "willingness and ability to involve others and elicit their participation, because tasks will be too complex and information too widely distributed for leaders to solve problems on their own."[2] This observation, made in relation to the business world, is just as true in the church. Paul reminded the Corinthians about this using the "body" imagery. "God," Paul explained, "has arranged the parts in the body, every one of them, just as he wanted them to be. If they were all one part, where would the body be? As it is, there are many parts, but one body" (1 Cor 12:18-20). Team building in the church involves, empowers and integrates each member of this body, but does so in a setting of mutual accountability.

When I speak of team leadership, I'm not restricting the discussion to clergy or paid staff, but embracing all who are exercising leadership—influencing others in their thinking and actions—in whatever capacity.

It takes a great deal of give and take as a leader to learn to operate as a team player. Leaders who are loner-types typically see themselves as the unquestioned head, no matter the task in hand. Team leaders, on the other hand, are often highly flexible. They are willing and able to switch from being a leader to being a follower, depending on the work that needs to be done. More often than not, by stepping aside they enable others to develop their own leadership in the area of their special competence. Effective team leaders recognize that diversity is essential for the accomplishment of complex tasks, and that emphasizing group conformity is a surefire route to ruin. We should note that diversity is about a group's range of skills as well as the different personalities and people-skills found among its members. For example, those who are more problem-focused or more vocal are valued equally with those who are quiet or more solution-oriented.

LEADING INTO AN UNCERTAIN FUTURE

People who lead must know where they are going, and they must inspire confidence in others to want to go with them. In periods of upheaval leaders must demonstrate extraordinary levels of perception and insight into the realities of the world. But mere perception isn't enough. By itself, perception can lead to a doom-and-gloom mentality and paralysis without a corresponding clarity of vision in formulating appropriate responses. Leaders' perception has to be combined with "extraordinary levels of motivation to enable them [i.e., the members of the community] to go through the inevitable pain of learning and change." This, Edgar Schein continues, is particularly important "in a world with looser boundaries, in which loyalties become more difficult to define."[3]

If leaders are to calm the anxieties of their followers and colleagues, they must have great inner strength and emotional stability. Jesus demonstrated such qualities in the days immediately preceding his crucifixion. When he met with his disciples in the upper room, his attention was focused on the disciples, their relationships with one another and their future ministry. He was not preoccupied with his own mental and spiritual anguish. In fact, he assured them of his own peace, which he bestowed on them: "Peace I leave with you; my peace I give you. I do not give to you as the world gives. Do not let your hearts be troubled and do not be afraid" (Jn 14:27).[4]

Jesus also explained to his disciples that his departure would not weaken their influence. He must have startled them with his assertion that because he was going to the Father, they would be able to "do even greater things" (Jn 14:12). This statement shouldn't be interpreted to mean that Jesus' followers would be able to perform even greater miracles than their Lord. Jesus was thinking beyond his present circumstances and his impending death to the glorious effects of his death, resurrection and ascension. These "greater things" were the result of Jesus' saving work and the ministry of his Holy Spirit. Jesus' Spirit-filled followers would see greater fruits on account of Christ operating through them. They would transform innumerable lives and affect the world with an ever-increasing number of communities of Christ followers.

Jesus also said that his disciples would experience fruitfulness only to the extent that they remained in an abiding relationship with him (Jn 15:4-7). We must be careful how we interpret *abiding*. In uncertain and anxious times, we often equate abiding with a place to hide. Instead, Jesus had in mind a relationship. He was referring not so much to a safe place or a refuge, but a secure position. *Abiding* carries with it the connotation of endurance, whatever the circumstances. Effective team leaders in the church, therefore, should not encourage people to lean on them but should instead teach them about what it means to abide in Christ individually and collectively.

When leaders face uphill battles and have to make tough choices, both of which may happen with some frequency, they must resist the temptation to hide the possibility of their followers having to face a difficult future. Jesus was very frank with his own disciples. He warned them clearly and repeatedly of the opposition and persecution that were in store for them. In his final upper room discourse, Jesus gave extensive teaching on the subject (Jn 15:18—16:4, 17-33), knowing full well that they would not want to hear what he had to say. Followers should not expect their leaders to keep them completely immune from bad news. Rather, leaders should be examples of endurance. They need to help their followers face the reality around them, not allowing them to live in denial by burying their heads in the sand.

Jesus' relationship with his heavenly Father determined both his priorities and his timing. This is why Jesus gave extended time to prayer. Prayer was especially prominent during his final week. He clearly intended his disciples to overhear his longest prayer, which is recorded in John 17. In that particular prayer, Jesus' petitions presaged the transition from his earthly ministry to the ongoing ministry of his disciples. It also emphasized the continuity between the two. "As you sent me into the world," Jesus called out to the Father, "I have sent them into the world" (Jn 17:18). Note that this sending is not expressed in the future tense. It was already anticipated when Jesus led the Twelve during his Galilean ministry (Mk 3:13-19; 6:7-11) as well as when he called for many more laborers to gather the spiritual harvest (Mt 9:35-38).

Prepared to Reexamine Assumptions

Edgar Schein writes that leaders need "new skills in analyzing cultural assumptions, identifying functional and dysfunctional assumptions, and evolving processes that enlarge the culture by building on its strengths and functional elements."[5] We must be prepared to reexamine our assumptions in light of continually changing circumstances. Given new or very different contexts, old solutions may not fix familiar problems. In the same way, past achievements might turn out to be our great liabilities. Faced with the unfamiliar, insecure leaders often react out of denial rather than with discerning and balanced judgment. Unwilling to become involved or be put in a position of vulnerability, they try to protect themselves by maintaining a stance of judgmental detachment.

Leaders who are unable to function in unfamiliar settings will find the future increasingly discomforting. This is why the emerging church must remain intentionally and intensively missional; otherwise it will retreat in search of safer and more familiar ground. Leaders of the future will require the same crosscultural gifts that we have traditionally identified with missionaries. In today's pluralistic world, cultural lines crisscross whole societies. Some of them are self-evident as we enter communities of different races and see signs and billboards in other languages. Other cultural lines are far subtler, yet just as significant. Only an insider or a person with a trained eye know they are there. For instance, someone from Australia or New Zealand has no difficulty in distinguishing between their peoples. All penguins look alike, unless you are a penguin.

COACHING THE TEAM

In the sporting world a team's coach invariably is a former player. The coach's athletic experience grants him or her credibility. Although no longer able to race up and down the field, the coach's role is nonetheless energetic. Coaches empathize with a player's every move as if they themselves were on the field of play. Coaches are not armchair critics. They stand alongside their charges, sharing their joys as well as their frustrations and sorrows. They face long hours, failures and mistakes, but do not abandon their teams during low points. Most of all, coaches are passionate about their team, urging them on to surpass their previous best. Coaches embody the very spirit of the team, conveying an energy that both empowers and provides cohesion.

Good coaches help players cope with chaos, and they facilitate an ordered, strategic approach to the game at hand. They also create a collective climate and restore morale when the going gets rough. The mood of the coach is not a reflection of that of the team. Should that occur he or she has ceased to serve as a coach and has become a liability. Some coaches overstep the line from offering encouragement to shouting abuse. Civility can never be sacrificed in the cause of achievement. Winning respect can be more important than winning the game.

A great team is not just a group of brilliant solo performers. Instead, a great team is built with individuals who understand their contribution in relation to the skills of other players around them. Peter Drucker distinguishes between three distinct types of teams, and he cautions those who consider the creation of hybrid types. His model uses various team sports to make his point.

In baseball, according to Drucker's understanding of the game, the players play *on the* team, but they do not play *as* a team. Each player has a fixed position; the pitcher as well as the batter plays a lonely role. This type of team requires high accountability and is inflexible.

In football, the players have assigned positions, but they play *as* a team. Football teams are more flexible than baseball teams, but the requirements demanded of each player are stringent. Star players must subordinate themselves to the team because it is the team that "performs" whereas the individual players "contribute."

In tennis doubles, each player has a primary role rather than a fixed position. Each covers and adjusts to their teammate.[6]

Respected coaches also work to achieve relational harmonies, a rhythm of movement and the ability to read the play. Each player, whether on the field or sidelines, gives full attention to the state of play. Each learns to play with the team in mind rather than to serve his or her personal ambitions. Coaches also work constantly to build and restore the level of trust between the players; they strengthen hope and build anticipation as they face upcoming games.

In their mind's eye, great coaches see what the team can become. They exude a confidence based on a realistic assessment of the situation and of the resources available for building the team. Coaches know the history of their team and recall high points to inspire the current players. But their exhortations must ring true in the ears of the players.

While demonstrating many qualities of sports coaches, the coaching style of leadership within the church differs significantly in a number of aspects. First, the ministry coaches are more laid-back. Second, they exercise less control from the sidelines. Third, they refrain from verbal abuse. Fourth, they do not operate in a high-pressure, competitive, winner-takes-all environment. Fifth, they do not hire and fire on the basis of current performance. Sixth, and most important, they must function as player-coaches and are thereby credible, vulnerable and accountable. The church is a voluntary society and a not-for-profit organization. As such it relies far more on intrinsic motivation, as there are few, if any, financial incentives.

FUNCTIONING AS A LEADER IN A COMMUNITY OF CHOICE

In the business world, employees are unlikely to withdraw their labor if there is high unemployment or if they are readily replaceable. Leaders of voluntary organizations do not have a similar hold on people. Consequently, in such "communities of choice," leadership qualities take on an even greater significance. Individuals, if they are to stay and continue to be involved, must own the organization's shared vision. The fact that they are volunteers means that if they choose to stay they are more likely to participate. The connective style of leadership creates the links between people. To do this, the leader must fulfill a servant role rather than use a rigid command-and-control approach. In order to keep volunteers, the leader must make sure that everyone feels valued and that their membership on the team is growth-enhancing rather than inhibiting.

Servant leadership is precisely what Jesus modeled in the upper room when he took off his outer clothing and washed the feet of his disciples (Jn 13:1-17). Servant leaders set position aside to do what is necessary at the time. Jesus' action was intended as an example for the disciples to emulate. It caused embarrassment for all the disciples, and in the case of the mercurial Peter it triggered complete indignation. "Now that I, your Lord and Teacher, have washed your feet," Jesus explained, "you also should wash one another's feet. I have set you an example that you should do as I have done for you" (vv. 14-15). Servant leadership sets the stage for a serving community.[7]

An invitation to become a member of a team should not be a guest pass to an exclusive club. Instead, team members serve each other as well as the wider community, no matter how menial the task. It is difficult for today's readers of John's Gospel to appreciate the revulsion the disciples felt, since, within their culture, foot washing was regarded as too menial for even Jewish household servants to perform. But leadership entails being prepared to undertake the most humble of tasks in the service of love. The servant leader is prepared to do anything (which must be clearly distinguished from being *pressured* into doing everything).

THE PREREQUISITE FOR TEAM BUILDING

The concept of team leadership arises naturally out of the New Testament's teaching on fellowship (*koinōnia*). Much deeper and wider than mere companionship, *koinōnia* is unique to the church of Jesus Christ. It is fellowship *in the gospel* (Phil 1:5) and includes all who have yielded their lives to Jesus Christ as Savior and Lord. It is fellowship *with the Father* (1 Jn 1:3). It is also fellowship *with the Spirit* (Phil 2:1), in that when we come to Christ, we receive the baptism in the Holy Spirit and are adopted into the family of God through the fellowship *with the Son* (1 Cor 1:9). We are able to "have fellowship with one another" (1 Jn 1:7) as a direct result of the redemptive work of the Trinity.

Precisely because fellowship is a unique quality of relationship, not only cementing the community but also activating it for ministry, we must watch out for the early warning signs of its erosion. Max De Pree identifies six early warning signs of the degeneration of a movement, which are applicable to the church. Teams fail to provide direction and maintain momentum within a movement when they begin to

- make trade-offs
- prefer comfort to ambiguity
- look for control rather than challenge
- trust job assignments rather than respecting individual gifts
- allow rules to dominate decision making
- become unable or unwilling to hold the group accountable[8]

The quality of our relationships is essential for cohesion and direction as a movement. There is a price to be paid for our working together as a team. Our identification with Christ means that we share in the power of his resurrection but also that we know what it means to share in his sufferings (Phil 3:10). This unique and profound relationship produces a depth of love and obedience toward God and one another. As the apostle John reminds believers in every age, "If we claim to have fellowship with him yet walk in the darkness, we lie and do not live by the truth. But if we walk in the light, as he is in the light, we have fellowship with one another, and the blood of Jesus, his Son, purifies us from all sin" (1 Jn 1:6-7).

No one discovers their true worth outside of community. Our identity is established, developed and affirmed through relationships. Contemporary Western Christians have to struggle to come to terms with the idea of *koinōnia* because it flies in the face of our individualistic and self-seeking cultural predisposition. Many leaders in the emerging church challenge this pervasive Western perspective. They believe individualism isolates the vulnerable and creates competitive and destructive environments in which the powerful gain at the expense of those who have little influence and who are regarded as expendable commodities.

Again, this corporate emphasis has profound implications for leadership. We must not overlook the fact that Jesus worked with a team from the very start of his ministry. And after Christ's ascension and the coming of the Holy Spirit at Pentecost, the disciples worked as a team to lead the Jerusalem church. When the church in Antioch commissioned its leaders, it sent out

Barnabas and Paul. Later, when Barnabas and Mark went to Cyprus, Paul took Silas as his companion and went to Lystra, where they were later joined by Timothy (Acts 16:1-5). Paul not only believed in team ministry for his itinerant church-planting ventures, but he also established teams of elders to lead these fledgling churches (see Acts 11:30; 14:23; Phil 1:1; 1 Tim 5:17).

Solo leadership, on the other hand, inhibits ministry development. Leaders who insist on operating as loners obviously do not develop team leadership in the congregations they serve. As a means of securing their own position, they prefer to keep others at a distance. Colleagues are turned into rivals. Like Paul, however, they ought to demonstrate the importance of working as a member of a team. By doing so, a church's leadership base is expanded, the church's leadership gifts are diversified, and the church body develops in a comprehensive and balanced manner (see Eph 4:11-13).

THE TRINITY AND THE TEAM CONCEPT

The human *koinōnia* I have so far described flows not only from the activity of God but also from the very nature of the Godhead. The early church struggled to comprehend their experience of God as Father, Son and Holy Spirit, which they came to express as Trinity (signifying tri-unity or three-in-oneness). God is not conceptualized in monistic terms, as in Judaism or Islam, but rather as a community of being. The relationship between the persons of the Godhead is something that we cannot fathom—it is unique and beyond our comprehension. But we do note that in Scripture no one person of the Trinity operates independently. The Father, Son and Holy Spirit are interrelated. In the seventh century John of Damascus spoke of the Trinity as *perichōrēsis*—a dance in which the Trinity operates with beauty and fluidity of movement.[9]

Though it is futile to attempt to delve into the precise character of the relationship between the persons of the Trinity, it does have profound implications for our understanding of human nature. Scripture makes it clear that we are made in the image of God. Interpreters influenced by a culture of individualism tend to interpret this in terms of the individual's tripartite nature: body, soul and spirit. Unfortunately, by doing this, we lose sight of the corporate emphasis in the biblical text. "Let *us* make man in *our* image, in *our* likeness," God called out. "So God created man in his own image, in the image of God he created him; male and female he created them" (Gen 1:26-27 emphasis added).

Note that the male and female together in their complementarity carry the image of God. Not "man" alone as gender, but "man" as genus: "male and female he created them."

Throughout his earthly ministry, Christ did not operate alone. He lived in communication with and obedience to his heavenly Father (Jn 10:30; 12:45; 14:9, cf. Jn 1:14). His entire ministry was conducted in the power of the Holy Spirit (Lk 3:21-22; 4:1, 14, 18; 10:21). In other words, Jesus operated out of his humanity; he was totally dependent on the Father and the Spirit. If he had operated on earth only in his divinity, his ministry could never become our ministry. Therefore, it is fitting that when Jesus appeared to his disciples in the upper room, he said, "Peace be with you! As the Father has sent me, I am sending you." And immediately thereafter, "he breathed on them and said, 'Receive the Holy Spirit'" (Jn 20:21-22). This incident is recorded only in John's Gospel and anticipates the day of Pentecost that was to come shortly. In both incidents, the corporate and inclusive nature of the experience is readily apparent.

George Cladis has expressed the church's mission as God's "desire to expand the loving fellowship of the Trinity to include human beings."[10] This is evident by Jesus' prayer in John 17. Jesus prays that "all of them [Christ followers] may be one, . . . just as you are in me and I am in you. May they also be in us so that the world may believe that you have sent me. I have given them the glory that you gave me, that they may be one as we are one" (Jn 17:21-22). The unity Jesus has in mind is much more profound than mere peaceful coexistence or mutual appreciation. Astonishingly, this unity is a reflection of the mutual indwelling experienced between the Son and his heavenly Father.

Rodney Whitacre comments on the word translated "just as," pointing out that it "signals not only comparison but cause." He explains that "both of these meanings are appropriate here, for this mutual indwelling of the Father and the Son is both the reason that all may be one and the pattern for such oneness. . . . This oneness includes both a unity of being and a distinctiveness of person."[11] Thus there is no true *koinōnia* without the manifest, unmistakable presence of God.

It is important to grasp this distinctive teaching in relation to team-based ministry. While we have much to learn from secular literature and the business world on the subject, a Christian understanding requires much more. The church should not be simply aping the world. It should be pointing in a different direction, revealing a better way.

On a practical note, in building a team from scratch it is advisable to begin with a small team of three or four people who have proved that they can work well together. This was the strategy that Jesus adopted in calling four friends, Peter, James, John and Andrew, to follow him. This number was later enlarged to twelve, and even later other unnamed followers joined their ranks (see Lk 10). There needs to be a period during which adjustments can be made in the course of dreaming together and of integrating the skills and experience brought by each team member.

During this adjustment period the team should seek the call of God on them as a group within a specific context. This is a time when each member can make a significant contribution in translating the mission that Jesus entrusted to his church into a vision of what the team is called to be and do. Each member should contribute to the development of the team's strategic goals. Above all, the adjustment period is a time of relationship building: each sharing his or her journey of faith, learning to appreciate each member's particular strengths and weaknesses, developing a corporate discipling process, making a commitment to the spiritual disciplines, and giving high priority to worship and intercession. The team must continue to renew its vision and not become overwhelmed with the challenges at hand. The sheer magnitude of the church's God-given mission forces us to think beyond the humanly possible, not as a flight of fancy but as a stimulus to faith.

THE COVENANT RELATIONSHIP

In *Leading the Team-Based Church* George Cladis describes team ministry in terms of covenanting, forging vision, creating culture, learning to collaborate, building trust, empowering one another and establishing a learning environment. The missional church consists of team-based communities that "covenant to be a fellowship together and live out the love of God—within the team and the broader community."[12]

By definition, every missional church needs to be team-based, recognizing that the gifts necessary for engaging in Christ's continuing mission require the cooperation of each person and the coordination of their individual contributions. Team members operate out of gratitude for all that the Lord accomplishes by his presence among them rather than out of a sense of obligation. Cladis also writes that the concept of covenant "paradoxically gives freedom to explore and discover while at the same time it binds people in love to a common agreement."[13] It provides strong bonds of mutual accountability in response to God's saving initiative and his persistent promptings.

The element that binds the team together is God's covenant, not a leader's personality. Cladis reminds leaders that their "task and responsibility are not to shape the group in their own image but to see that the team lives out its covenantal agreements with Christ and the congregation at large and that team members live out their covenantal agreements with one another." He continues, "In most cases, teams have relational problems not because of a single culprit acting intentionally but because of dysfunctional behavior that goes unrecognized and unaddressed."[14]

The covenant of one urban-renewal ministry, consisting of young adults living together and working as teams, includes a strong emphasis on relationships within the team. It entails becoming a model to young people living in the inner city by the character and compassion that the team members display. It means listening and serving them as well as interceding on their behalf both in prayer and advocacy. It also includes a desire to support local churches that are relevant and welcoming to these kids with special needs.

The covenant seeks to hold each person accountable in these areas.

A covenant should not be designed as a vehicle of control but as a focus, a direction and a challenge. Just as Israel needed to reaffirm its covenant relationship with God on a regular basis, teams need to ensure that their covenant remains in the foreground. They serve as reminders for present members and provide orientation to, and ensure "buy in" from, others who join the team.

A Firm Commitment to a Clear Mission

The team needs both cohesion and momentum to keep its members together. Therefore a clearly spelled-out mission statement is essential. A mission statement will ensure that everyone understands and shares the same fundamental call. Mission statements are not crafted out of thin air; the church's *missio Dei* is spelled out in the New Testament. It is to declare and demonstrate the good news of God's grace revealed in Jesus Christ. For this message to be received, its messengers must be believable. The unique and life-transforming power of this good news is what provides the essential motivation for others to follow.

No individual can adequately represent this message in a clear and comprehensive way. It takes an entire community of believers to communicate it convincingly. Each person in the church plays an important part by contributing his or her unique story and using his or her particular gifting from the Holy Spirit.

When a church is divided into ministry teams, each team brings "a specific sense of mission that is unique to their own activity and yet fits within and supports the larger vision of the whole congregation." When this is lacking, team-based churches lose focus, momentum and direction. Cladis remarks that "churches with ministry areas loosely held together and competing with one another need a strong common vision to unite them, otherwise there is lots of activity without much synergy."[15]

Unfortunately, many team-based churches, through laziness, insecurity or inexperience, shortcut the process of vision building by importing and adopting external vision statements. The team itself must build the vision. Sometimes this occurs through the God-given insight and initiative of a leader who brings a vision to the team members for their consideration and contribution. Alternatively, it might emerge through group exercises in prayer and planning, with each member contributing individual insights that eventually coalesce into a coherent pattern.

Many times the process of creating a vision or purpose statement is more important than the product. The final product, though, should be memorable and motivational. Leith Anderson has his own criteria for an effective mission statement. He asks, "Can the statement be memorized in three minutes or less? If it takes longer than three minutes to memorize, it probably won't be remembered. If it's not remembered, it probably won't make any difference. If it doesn't make any difference, it probably doesn't matter."[16]

CREATING AN INSTITUTIONAL CULTURE

Another critical element of team ministry, according to Cladis, is culture creation, which is to "develop the symbols, themes, activities, values, and structures that reinforce the faith and purpose of a given congregation."[17] Leaders play a key role in this task. Through character and behavior, leaders establish and promote the values they consider to be nonnegotiable. Institutional or communal culture develops around stories, when members have an opportunity to be heard. So leaders have an important role as storytellers and "story-encouragers."

In the case of long-established churches, leaders face a much stiffer challenge because the institutional culture is already deeply embedded. In a culture of predictable evolutionary change, all that might be needed is some tweaking to ensure that the church remains sufficiently alert and adaptable to the innovations taking place. However, the leadership may need to break old mindsets and habits in order to set a new direction. In such cases, they will have to create a new institutional culture within or alongside the old, which will eventually replace it.

Jim Collins identified four basic practices for culture creation: lead with questions, not answers; engage in dialogue, not coercion; conduct autopsies without blame; and build red-flag mechanisms that turn information into information that cannot be ignored.[18] By asking the right question we discern the nature of the problem or challenge. Follow-up questions identify the issues that need to be addressed in responding to the problem.

In the process of dialogue, each member of the team is able to put forward his or her ideas and test the insights with the collective wisdom of the group. The right of each person to express his or her opinion is respected. The group exercises patience and sensitivity toward any misgivings a group member might have. When events don't work out as planned, the group has the honesty and vulnerability to identify the mistakes made, and asks, "What would we do differently next time?" The red-flag mechanisms to which Collins refers are the warning signs that the team has identified that reveal when the team is in danger of losing direction and cohesion.

MAKING COLLABORATIVE CONNECTIONS

There is no genuine teamwork outside a climate of collaboration. Cladis reminds us that a team is "an extremely powerful unit of ministry" when it "learns how to discern the spiritual gifts of the individual team members and how to have members work together, pray hard, and share information and energy in order to move towards a sharply defined mission, vision, or cause."[19] In order to facilitate the collaboration that is needed for teamwork, each person must understand that they are appreciated for their distinctive contribution to the shared enterprise.

Paul affirms the connection between respective contributions and the project as a whole. "To each [individual]," he explained to the Corinthian church, "the manifestation of the Spirit is given for the common good" (1 Cor 12:7). Insisting on uniformity can often create an insurmountable barrier to collaboration. When certain people are affirmed and appreciated because they fit the mold, other individuals, who do not fit, may believe that they do not belong to the body as a whole (see 1 Cor 12:15-16). It leads to feelings of exclusion and resentment—and as Cladis explains, "teams that fizzle are made up of people who are confused, frustrated, abused and resentful."[20]

Those who are dismissive of the contribution of others stifle "every-member ministry." No one, the apostle Paul argued, is sufficiently omnicompetent that they are able to declare, "I don't need you" (1 Cor 12:21). In the business arena, Harland Cleveland insists, it is often the case that "the most narrowly specialized staff member is likely to be the stubbornest staff holdout on what to do next." He adds, "Gloom and reluctance are the hallmarks of expertise."[21]

Though important, collaboration must never be turned into a primary value. Collaboration is not an end in itself; it is a means to fulfill a vision and achieve a mission, a means in which everyone contributes and each person is valued for the input they provide. If leaders emphasize collaboration over, say, connectivity, they will tend to overvalue consensus, building teams that outlive their usefulness and are determined at all costs not to rock the boat. Connective leaders, on the other hand, strive for synergy. They are constantly stitching together multiple, short-term alliances.[22] According to Jean Lipman-Blumen, connective leaders are those who

- join their vision to the dreams of others
- connect and combine rather than divide and conquer
- strive to overcome mutual problems rather than common enemies
- create a sense of community that embraces diversity
- establish coalitions of committed leaders and constituents to achieve common purposes
- encourage active constituents to assume responsibilities at every level
- join with other leaders, even former adversaries, as colleagues, not as competitors
- nurture potential leaders, including possible successors
- renew and build broad-based democratic institutions instead of creating dynasties and oligarchies

- demonstrate authenticity through consistent dedication to goals that transcend their own egos

- demand serious sacrifice first from themselves and only then from others[23]

Tomorrow's leaders must have a keen understanding of interpersonal dynamics. Connective leaders not only facilitate initial contacts, they also help to strengthen relationships in times of tension and misunderstanding. Strong friendship links are not forged until people have survived at least one disagreement that has led to reconciliation.

MAKING SENSE

Leaders make sense of what is happening within the group. "Successful sense-making is more likely when people stay in motion, have a direction, look closely, update often, and converse candidly."[24] Karl Weick's distinction between decision making and sense-making is significant for younger leaders who have to think on their feet (or their knees), given the challenges they face. He quotes a comment by Paul Gleason, a renowned firefighter: "If I make a decision, it is a possession, I take pride in it, I tend to defend it and not listen to those who question it. If I make sense, then this is more dynamic and I listen and I can change it. A decision is something you polish. Sense-making is a direction for the next period."[25] Making sense is a necessary first step to deciding how to respond appropriately.

Finally, making sense must be translated into mutual trust in order for the team to function both with discernment and commitment. This must start with a trustworthy leader; namely, a man or woman whose word can be trusted. Trustworthy leaders keep the promises they make, and instead of operating out of pretense they admit what they do not know or understand. Cladis makes the important point that "in a world that thrives on betrayal and deceit, a culture of trust . . . is a wonderful source of healing and ministry in the church and the world."[26] People will forgive leaders who get it wrong, but they will not forgive denial or abdication.

LET'S DO IT!

In confusing times when leaders are perplexed about the best course of action to take, the prevailing attitude must be "Let's try it anyway and see what happens." This type of perspective creates the space and climate in which learning can take place. As the leaders try to imagine the unforeseen, this optimism needs to be tempered by discerning reflection. Yet, in the midst of rapid change, leaders must overcome the tendency toward procrastination. Instead, they must learn to think on their feet, on the move and with creativity.

Creative thinking must be combined with a willingness to experiment. Those with ideas need to be given the authority to implement them. Empowered teams enable members to learn and grow as they pray, plan, evaluate, play and celebrate together. Teams "reinforce the concept that there is no such thing as a passive Christian."[27]

SUMMARY

In this chapter I have challenged the unbiblical notion of leadership as one omnicompetent individual uniquely called to exercise ministry in the church. The church needs to reinstate the team concept of leadership, which embraces the gifts of the many people needed to lead the church into a postmodern and post-Christendom future. By giving priority to team building, the church can move beyond the prevailing culture of hierarchy and control to that of networking and empowerment.

Team-based leadership models a process designed to be replicated throughout the congregation. Christ followers grow in relationship with others as they provide mutual encouragement, hold each other accountable and appreciate the gifts that each brings to the group. This fosters the group's edification and fulfills its call to some specific ministry of the church. Teams of people networked together as part of a larger fellowship that shares an overarching call to mission will more readily function as the body that Christ envisioned.

6

Leadership Traits

The traits, activities, attitudes and characteristics of emerging leaders identified in this chapter (and the two that follow) are the distinctive features I became aware of in the course of interacting with and observing leaders in action. These younger leaders provide a corrective to the limitations and aberrations of the modernity mindset, especially in redefining leadership.

Yet in addition to the positive traits that enable them to function more effectively in the present cultural climate, emerging leaders also carry baggage heaped on them by that context. Some are reluctant to take initiative and to accept responsibility. At times they appear too casual and aimless in their readiness to live one day at a time. Some of them display not only detachment from the institutional church but anger toward it. Furthermore they may be naively idealistic regarding the fresh expressions of church that they wish to create. Some have reacted so strongly to the old models of leadership that they have attempted to create leaderless churches. Over time these churches either transitioned to more healthy models of leadership or simply disintegrated through conflict and subsequent attrition.

When assembling a composite list characterizing the most effective or most successful emerging leaders, we must be very careful not to create a nonexistent superperson. No single individual is gifted with every one of these traits; thus no one should feel overwhelmed or discouraged by comparing themselves to this list. The qualities listed are best evidenced throughout an entire leadership team rather than through any one individual.

The impressive individual leaders in the Bible and church history were all vulnerable in one way or another. Some of them experienced drawbacks and others even suffered disaster as a consequence of either giving in to a particular weakness or failing to find strength and support in other people. In the course of this chapter, we will examine the lives of a number of biblical characters from whom we can learn valuable lessons about leadership traits.

CHARACTER SHAPED BY GOD

I will begin our analysis of leadership traits by focusing on character. This intentionally draws our attention away from charisma. In the eyes of many, charisma is the *sine qua non* of leadership. Americans often assume that charisma—popularly understood as a commanding personality or personal presence—and leadership go hand-in-hand. At the outset I must emphasize that charisma is no substitute for character. Indeed, leaders who have charisma but lack character are a danger to others and often bring disaster on themselves.

Addressing the issue of leadership in the church, the New Testament places character first and foremost. It also posits a direct relationship between character and self-discipline. In the selection of overseers in the local church, Paul instructs Timothy to look for people whose lives are "above reproach." Paul adds that an overseer should be "the husband of but one wife, temperate, self-controlled, respectable, . . . not given to drunkenness, not violent but gentle, not quarrelsome, not a lover of money." Paul's requirements for deacons are no less stringent. They are to be "men worthy of respect, sincere, not indulging in much wine, and not pursuing dishonest gain." Moreover, one cannot passively assume that candidates have these qualities; they have to be investigated (1 Tim 3:1-3, 8, 10). For Paul, holiness and self-discipline are crucial for leadership. He exhorts Timothy to train himself to be godly (1 Tim 4:7). As Robert Murray McCheyne, the great nineteenth-century Scottish pastor and Bible teacher, is reputed to have declared, "My personal holiness is my people's greatest need."

Paul provides a similar list for Titus, who is to appoint elders throughout Crete. An "elder," Paul explains,

> must be well thought of for his good life. He must be faithful to his wife, and his children must be believers who are not wild or rebellious. An elder must live a blameless life because he is God's minister. He must not be arrogant or quick-tempered; he must not be a heavy drinker, violent, or greedy for money. He must enjoy having guests in his home and must love all that is good. He must live wisely and be fair. He must live a devout and disciplined life. He must have a strong and steadfast belief in the trustworthy message he was taught; then he will be able to encourage others with right teaching and show those who oppose it where they are wrong. (Tit 1:6-9 NLT)

This emphasis on godly character is especially important given the Cretans' reputation for laziness and dishonesty (Tit 1:12), not to mention the threat of the "many rebellious people, mere talkers and deceivers, especially those of the circumcision group" who had infiltrated the fellowship (Tit 1:10).

Those who are called to guide and guard the people of God also need to be competent, but competence is undermined by character failure. The Old Testament speaks of King David as having a balance of the two. David "shepherded [the people of Israel] with integrity of heart; / with skillful hands he led them" (Ps 78:72). Church leaders also have to model this balance for those whom they lead. Preachers are often said to cynically say, "Do as I say, not as I do." This is a far cry from the position taken by Paul, who exhorted the followers of Christ in Corinth to "follow my example, as I follow the example of Christ" (1 Cor 11:1).[1] Peter also reminded the leaders of the early church that they had to be examples to their respective flocks, demonstrating both eagerness to serve and, following Jesus' own words, an unwillingness to lord it over other believers (1 Pet 5:1-4).

Peter and Paul were not setting themselves on a pedestal. Theirs was not a claim of perfection or infallibility. Indeed, leaders in the Old and New Testaments were often all too aware of their weaknesses, limitations and vulnerability. Thankfully, the Bible does not idealize its heroes. The faults and failings of leaders are faithfully recorded alongside their amazing exploits and demonstrations of humble service. David, for example, could be just as capricious as he was generous. The most sordid period of his life was characterized by sexual lust, adultery and finally, in the vain attempt to hide his sin, complicity in murder (2 Sam 11:1—12:10). A terrible episode, yes, but in light of David's confession and repentance and God's forgiveness, it makes the powerful point that failure need not be final.[2] David's story in particular demonstrates why any analysis of leadership cannot ignore or deny the human factor, and it also shows why humility is a necessary prerequisite for any leader. As Aubrey Malphurs reminds us: "You can't become a leader of people without confronting and dealing with your ego."[3]

As church leaders model godly character with humility, believers come to a better knowledge of how they are supposed to treat one another, and how Christlike character is related to authenticity. Going back to the example of Titus, it was not enough that the believers in Crete *knew* that they were saved, but it was imperative that they *demonstrated* to others and to themselves that they were authentic.

I am grateful to Pastor Norman Copeland of Ward African-American Episcopal Church for drawing my attention to a key passage in Titus that emphasizes this point. The church's slogan for the year, which was prominently displayed on a banner behind the pulpit, was "Living Saved—Titus 2:11-14." The text that accompanied the slogan states,

> For the grace of God that brings salvation has appeared to all men. It teaches us to say "No" to ungodliness and worldly passions, and to live self-controlled, upright and godly lives in this present age, while we wait for the blessed hope—the glorious appearing of our great God and Savior, Jesus Christ, who gave himself for us to redeem us from

all wickedness and to purify for himself a people that are his very own, eager to do what is good.

The church's corporate character provides the mark of its authenticity. In Galatians, Paul uses a nine-item list to describe godly character, or what he calls the "fruit of the Spirit": "love, joy, peace, patience, kindness, goodness, faithfulness, gentleness and self-control" (Gal 5:22-23). These provide a character description of Christ himself. No single individual is likely to demonstrate the entire range with impressive consistency. It is Paul's desire that the church evidence these qualities collectively. Church leaders who recognize how important godly character is to the health, authenticity and witness of their congregation need to monitor their personal lives constantly as well as the fellowship they serve in order to ensure that the fruit is evident and abundant.

CALLED BY GOD

The concept of calling is essential to the life of discipleship. The first disciples were confronted by the invitation and challenge that Jesus gave to follow in his steps. The call of Christ is not a once in a lifetime experience, but rather represents the ongoing response of the disciple. Os Guinness, in his modern classic *The Call,* describes the Christian life: "a life lived listening to the decisive call of God is a life lived before one audience that trumps all others—the Audience of One." If this is true for every follower of Christ, it is especially significant for those in leadership, for "God's calling is the key to igniting a passion for the deepest growth and highest heroism in life."[4]

However, some leaders are so obsessed with their own sense of calling that they marginalize those around them or simply use them to serve their own ends. This runs contrary to the pattern of the New Testament, in which disciples are called, not in isolation, but as part of a community of the called. "The call of Jesus is personal but not purely individual; Jesus summons his followers not only to an individual calling but also to a corporate calling."[5] It is this corporate understanding that will provide safeguards against the reverse side of calling. Guinness identifies three temptations that represent this "reverse side" that every leader must address: conceit, envy and greed.

God's calling applies to the totality of God's people. It is not restricted to leaders. This is an important point not just for followers to grasp but also for leaders who themselves have a strong sense of calling. The myth of the "restricted call" has crippled the church's mission in the world. Traditionally, ordained ministry or the mission field, more broadly labeled "full-time service," has been regarded as the "highest calling." Over time this has led to two distinct classes of Christians: the clergy, those ordained to the pastorate, and the laity, the majority from which the few were selected.

Clergy means "called" (*klēros*), with the unspoken implication that the laity is not chosen or called by the Lord. Subsequently, the church is built around the call and gifting of this elite group surrounded by a marginalized laity. Such a separation breeds, on the one hand, resentment and struggles for power and influence and, on the other, passivity and the avoidance of responsibility over spiritual issues that are regarded as the domain of the clergy.

This marginalization of the laity from "the ministry" continued even during the rediscovery of "every member ministry" in the thirty years between 1970 and 2000. During that time, shelves of books were published which argued that spiritual gifts were distributed throughout the entire church body, and not restricted to a chosen few. Pastors preached sermons on gifting and distributed "gift identification questionnaires" so that church members could identify their gifts and contribute to the diverse ministries within the body of Christ. Unfortunately, in many cases the emphasis was placed on those gifts that directly assisted the pastor and helped the church's internal life (i.e., gifts that made programs function more effectively or that diversified the number of people involved). We largely ignored those spiritual gifts needed for the church's ministry to the world. Our focus was not the kingdom but the church—the church's growth, rather than its impact on society.

The New Testament provides a necessary corrective, emphasizing that all who are called to salvation are also called to service in the world and the church (Rom 8:30; Gal 5:13; 1 Pet 2:9). As we come to appreciate the comprehensive nature of God's call, we must recognize that laypeople are not amateur contributors within the structures of the institutional church. They must not be regarded as volunteers who support and run clergy-controlled programs. The term *laity* (*laos*) has to be restored to its original meaning—the people of God called to a priestly and apostolic ministry (2 Cor 6:16; Tit 2:14; 1 Pet 2:9). We are all members of the laity, including those who are ordained as pastors. We have all been sent by our ascended Lord into the world to represent his present reign, herald his anticipated coming and invite people to join us in following him. In this view of the church, the people of God become culture-creating teams dispersed throughout society as salt, yeast and light.

One consequence of an absence of a personal sense of call from God by church members is their focus on the need for personal fulfillment in order to find some sense of purpose for their lives. However, looking within oneself for self-realization has a serious downside. James Emery White comments, "When personal fulfillment is allowed to take the place of calling, our lives become little more than exercises in self-indulgence. Ironically, we were created such that our deepest fulfillment is found *as* we submit to God's calling on our life. The reason is simple: we are first and foremost to Someone, not to something or to somewhere."[6]

In order for the entire church to be motivated by a sense of divine call, it is imperative for its leaders to share this deep conviction, demonstrating their own personal call *and* God's call to the whole congregation. In fact, church leaders cannot merely share it; they must embody it to an extraordinary degree. For some, this will require a gigantic shift away from a controlling style of leadership to one of affirmation and empowerment. Leaders are sustained for the long haul by a sense of call that provides an antidote to discouragement and "to the deadly sin of sloth."[7]

Furthermore, every leader knows that leadership seldom consists of moving from one exhausting test and exhilarating triumph to the next. Most days consist of dealing with an unending succession of mundane matters.

But, Os Guinness reminds leaders, "calling transforms life so that even the commonplace and menial are invested with the splendor of the ordinary."[8]

CONTEXTUALLY APPROPRIATE

Successful leaders are prone to translate their effectiveness and success into a formula. Using hindsight, they take what was largely a case of trial and error and craft it into an orderly and seemingly reproducible sequence. However, many of these same leaders might be ill-prepared to start a new ministry from scratch. If they were to take such a drastic step, they might discover that the formula they have franchised is less useful the second time around! Many times, significant breakthroughs in ministry have occurred as a result of the right person being in the right place at the right time.

There are moments in the work of God in which God sovereignly brings together a "divine convergence." Of course, this should not justify a laissez-faire approach to ministry. God has given us the ability to imagine, conceptualize, plan and take initiatives. Ninety percent of what we learn occurs through trial and error. Brian McLaren argues that many of the individuals highlighted in his work became successful "through bold innovation and creative synthesis, not through unthinking imitation." And, McLaren insists, trial and error is a key part of the overall process. These leaders, he adds, "earned their success the old-fashioned way—through pain, tears, endurance, mistakes and prayer."[9]

The church should be extracautious about franchised formulas, since churches that are committed to bringing about change are shaped by the context in which they are birthed. The church does not exist in some idealized form outside of culture but rather expresses the gospel of God's reign as it engages its particular cultural context. The church also must not be shaped by a blind instinct for self-preservation in the erroneous belief that it has to do all in its power to save itself from its cultural surroundings. Rather, it is shaped by the call of God to mission. As the church finds its identity in culture-engaging mission, it finds its strength and creativity.

A missional church has a strong core of committed people, but it also has porous boundaries. Regarding this, Margaret Wheatley and Myron Kellner-Rogers write:

> Rather than being self-protective, boundaries become the place of meeting and exchange. We usually think of these edges as the means of defining separateness: what's inside and what's outside. But in living systems, boundaries are something quite different. They are the place where new relationships take form, an important place of exchange and growth as one individual chooses to respond to another.[10]

Rather than being barriers of separation, boundaries should be considered frontiers of mission engagement and interaction. While the early church had to address docetism, a heretical school of thought that denied the humanity of Christ, in much of the Western world today, we have to address a docetic-like ecclesiology that resists incarnating its own missional presence. We are a church that insists on continuing to do what it has always done, either because of ignorance or out of sheer defiance of the marginalized position it occupies in today's postmodern society and the corresponding erosion of support and goodwill.

In addressing the issue of contextually appropriate leadership we must recognize the fact that different cultures are attached to particular leadership styles. In some contexts authoritarian leaders are the expected model, providing security through every person knowing their place in the hierarchy and what is expected of them. In other contexts deference is paid to education, professional qualifications and technical competence, while in others age commands respect. In still other situations, followers gather around a person who has vision and relational skills. Missional leaders must be aware of these various expectations, and must sensitively and respectfully address the issues in seeking to introduce a concept of shared leadership responsibility.

Furthermore, the model of leadership adopted will also be governed by circumstances. Working by consensus draws on the resources and insights of the entire group and ensures ownership. Its downside is that the process is often time-consuming. Clearly, when faced with an emergency—having to vacate a building in danger of collapse, for instance—an authoritarian voice commanding everyone to clear the building is essential. This style, however, represents the exception rather than the rule, with the leader quickly adjusting his or her leadership style as soon as the emergency has passed.

COURAGE FORGED BY FAITH

Courageous leaders stand up for their beliefs, challenge others, admit mistakes and even change behavior when necessary. They demonstrate resolve as they battle inner turmoil, inertia and external opposition. A person who has courage is also composed and demonstrates consistent and appropriate emotional reactions, particularly in tough crisis situations. Courageous leaders are committed regardless of external circumstances. Indeed, if leaders expect courage from others, their own commitment to it is essential.

A solid biblical example of courageous leadership is found in God's exhortation and reassurance to Joshua. For many years Joshua had served as Moses' faithful lieutenant. Now, at the crucial moment when Israel was about to end its years of wandering in the wilderness and march into the Promised Land, the responsibility of leadership fell on his shoulders. Israel faced a succession of opponents, and it was only a fledgling nation, whose identity had been shaped by God's covenant relationship. That relationship had been established through Abraham but forged under Moses' leadership and circumscribed by God at Sinai.

Joshua needed affirmation and encouragement from God. So, as God called him into leadership, God assured him, "As I was with Moses, so I will be with you; I will never leave you nor forsake you." Within the following four verses, God told Joshua three separate times that if he would "be strong and courageous," God would prosper him and make him successful (Josh 1:5-9; see also Josh 10:8). Centuries later, Jesus commissioned his disciples in the same manner.

Today's entrepreneurial church leaders need a similar strong sense of God's call and his enabling and continuing presence as he guides them in their decision making. If the church is to take the innovative steps required in order to become a missional presence in these uncertain times, leaders in the church need the boldness and resilience of Joshua and of the early church.

Max De Pree, writing out of his experience in business as well as his participation on the board of Fuller Theological Seminary during a period of the school's accelerated growth, has provided helpful insights when it comes to the issue of risk. Leaders face "risk factors" in every strategic decision they make. De Pree prods us out of our comfort zone, declaring that "to risk nothing is perhaps the greatest risk of all." He adds, "It is interesting to reflect on what it is we risk. Sometimes we risk the present, and we do so most often consciously. Most of the time we risk the future, and we usually do so unconsciously."[11]

There are no risk-free decisions. All decision making involves ambiguity and uncertainty as we abandon old orders to make way for the new. Nevertheless, risk taking results in a kind of learning that is unavailable elsewhere. De Pree asserts that "the more we take risks, the more natural it becomes."[12] As leaders courageously take risks, exercising faith and assuming responsibility, they and the people around them grow together.

COMPETENCE ARISING OUT OF GIFTING AND EXPERIENCE

Demonstrated competence is essential for building the trust that is critical for the construction and continued health of authentic, effective communities. Competence applies both to the specific skills and knowledge necessary to fulfill one's task as well as to the ability to establish and maintain personal relationships among those who are working together to accomplish the task.[13] Competence also includes the willingness and ability to accept responsibility as well as knowledge of one's own limitations.

Peter Drucker, the world's foremost management guru, has argued that competence often trumps education. For him the key questions are not knowledge-driven but are: "Do you really like pressure? Can you be steady when things are rough and confused? When you sit down with a person, . . . do you know what to say?"[14]

Writing nearly a decade ago, Drucker roundly criticized the educational system for this very thing. "In helping people learn how to be responsible," he asserted, "our educational system is more and more counterproductive. The longer you stay in school, the fewer decisions you have to make."[15]

In the years since Drucker wrote those words, accrediting agencies of schools in the United States have placed more and more emphasis on competency-based curricula and courses. This is problematic for formal ministry education because it is somewhat artificial to list competencies for seminary courses without practical ministry. Competencies are apparent only after students have had opportunities to demonstrate their proficiency in ministry. Students who are already engaged in ministry during their formal education have a distinct advantage since they bring their experience into the classroom and can immediately apply what they are learning to specific situations. Even in the classical disciplines of biblical interpretation, theology and church history, students consistently ask the "So what?" question—"How do these insights and this information apply in my current context?"

In light of the limitations of education divorced from experience and application, Drucker himself advocates the recognition of leaders on the basis of performance and good judgment rather than credentials.[16]

The development of problem-solving skills is crucial when it comes to new competencies. One clue to an aspiring leader's potential is how he or she views problems. If reactions to challenging issues are persistently negative or if those who wish to lead always see threats rather than opportunities, it may be a sign that that person should be disqualified from leadership. Such people may attempt to ignore problems in the hope that they will disappear. Kenneth Cloke and Joan Goldsmith identify a number of obstacles to problem solving:

- seeing problems as negative
- becoming addicted to the problem or the solution
- identifying the wrong problem
- solving the problem unilaterally
- failing to learn from the problem[17]

Team leadership is one solution to such obstacles. Effective leaders often draw on the combined resources of a team in order to address problems, challenges and opportunities. When handled in a positive and creative manner, this process can generate amazing energy within the group. In any problem-solving exercise, it is useful to explore a range of possibilities before deciding on a course of action. Sometimes, an "off-the-wall" idea contains the spark of genius. In a well-managed brainstorming session, a wide range of ideas can be raised without the fear that other team members will dismiss an idea out of hand and put down the individual who has made the suggestion.

Creative teams intentionally include individuals who think "outside the box." Their role is particularly significant during times of chaotic change. However, brainstorming and creativity can also lead teams off-track. Dr. Henry Cloud, a psychologist who ministers to entrepreneurial leaders, writes, "Leaders, by their very nature as creators and initiators, are poor managers. The generative aspects of who they are generates *messes*."[18] A highly creative team needs strong leadership. Without it the energy and passion that drive the team's problem solving can dissolve rapidly into incoherence.

A team approach is also helpful as the team comes to realize that its members have neither enough experience nor knowledge to tackle the problem at hand; thus it recognizes the need to co-opt new people with the necessary resources. Alternatively, a team might occasionally seek the counsel of an outside person or group. Finally, very complex problems may require the combined strengths and effort of a cluster of teams.

The Bible is filled with individuals who demonstrated remarkable competencies and became phenomenal problem-solvers. The biblical hall of fame includes Joseph, Moses, Joshua, Saul (during his early years), David and the apostle Paul. The competencies of leaders in the New Testament church emerged out of their own natural gifts as well as from the spiritual gifts bestowed by the ascended Lord.

Having emphasized the need for competencies appropriate to the challenge, we must recognize that in many situations experts may not be able to provide instant solutions, and we must guard against presuming to offer more than they can deliver—or allowing people to expect and demand from them what it is not in their power to perform. Both within the life of institutions as well as in their response to the challenges presented from without, there are issues that are so complex that there is no chance of an easy answer. It will require the combined resources of the team to begin to design an appropriate response. The team may have to acknowledge its need for outside wisdom and expertise. And when all is said and done, there are some problems for which there is no human answer. Leaders must be able to distinguish between a problem to be solved and a fact of life that has to be lived with. In the latter case the church needs to adopt a stance of "adaptive leadership," seeking to relieve anxiety and drawing on the inner strength of the entire membership to face the crisis in the hope that life is on the other side of death.

CREATIVITY EXPRESSING THE NATURE OF GOD

Having mentioned how important it is to encourage creativity, it is crucial that we understand its various ingredients. In the first place, creativity blossoms in an atmosphere of flexibility and freedom. It requires an environment where precedents and assumptions can be set aside and where there is a willingness to allow fresh thoughts. Second, a creative mind is one that is insatiably curious, being prepared to question and reexamine anything and everything without feeling threatened. Indeed, curiosity often helps a leader to see links between isolated pieces of information, and those links are the wellsprings of creativity.

Creativity is enhanced where there are clear and wide channels of communication. The clearer the lines of communication and the more numerous and accessible the channels, the more likely a release of creative energy is, because more people are made aware of the issues and their contribution is invited. It further helps if these channels are as interactive as possible. Leading-edge educational technology is built on this premise. In the world of personal electronic communication, chatrooms and blogs—providing forums that maximize personal interaction—are gaining more and more attention. Online courses are typically designed so that peers learn by interacting with one another. There is no life-impacting communication outside of community, whether that community is face-to-face or the virtual community of cyberspace. In our electronically networked world, it is not an either-or option but a both/and requirement.

Creativity also requires a pioneering spirit. Creative leaders don't procrastinate or seek safety by doing the least amount necessary to get by. Instead, they take strategic initiatives. It is important to note that a true pioneer is not necessarily the lone explorer. Often, he or she is the leader of the wagon train. As the old saying goes: "You aren't leading until someone is following." Creative people are not the ones whose idea dies with them; they are people who make a difference by including others in the realization of their dream and thereby leave a legacy.[19]

Creative, pioneering leaders need to bring people alongside them. The contributions and interactions of those who share the excitement often stimulate even greater creativity within a group. Moreover, changing situations, new challenges and unforeseen crises also act as catalysts of creativity. Creative leaders are those who are prepared to examine ideas from all angles and explore various options, paying particular attention to the elements that run contrary to accepted theories. Indeed, a creative genius is often a person who is able to identify the relationship between two apparently disconnected ideas or pieces of information.

Understandably, any discussion of creativity is bound to make some leaders question their own fitness to lead. The reality is that a leader does not have to be creative. But he or she does have to be adventurous and secure enough to recognize and accept good new ideas, believing in those who have them.

As the church in the West struggles to redefine its role and restructures itself in response to its mission, it will have to learn not to fear creativity. In fact, the Western church's disappearing influence and the related downward trend in giving may actually spark creative genius. With money in reserve, there is a strong temptation to procrastinate and do things the way that they have traditionally been done. But when investments fail, endowments are depleted and contributions begin to dry up, people may find themselves open to a new climate of creativity that dispels the prevailing gloom-laden sense of inevitability.

If the church discourages and crushes creativity, choosing self-protective strategies of retrenchment, it plans its own demise. My personal assessment of the church's prospects in the West, however, is one of guarded optimism. Much that is unsustainable or that has outlived its shelf life will continue to die. At the same time I find an increasing number of ground-level initiatives that are making significant local, regional and, in a few instances, even international contributions. While there are positive, creative signs, they are not yet sufficient in their number or impact to change the societal tide.

COMPASSION OF GOD EXPRESSED IN LOVE FOR OTHERS

Creativity is vital for the future health of the church, but in established congregations it must never be pursued at the expense of present membership. Leaders cannot ignore the decisions of their predecessors or the consequences of those policies and practices that went unquestioned before. When leaders are preoccupied with future scenarios, overlooking or discounting the memories of church members, creativity can quickly degenerate into insensitivity and ruthlessness. This is why creativity must be balanced with care and concern for the personal well-being of present members, valuing their contributions to ministry.

The failure to value the past and listen to the wisdom of the elders can have dire consequences. A classic biblical example of this is found in the story of the transition between King Solomon and his son Rehoboam. Solomon had been a highly creative and ambitious leader, yet one who was overly demanding. So the experienced elders counseled Rehoboam as the new monarch to "lighten up" the crushing taxes and labor demands that Solomon had placed on the people of Israel. The elders pleaded with Rehoboam to be a servant leader, assuring him that "if today you will be a servant to these people and serve them and give them a favorable answer, they will always be your servants" (1 Kings 12:7). Sadly, Rehoboam rejected their advice. Instead, he listened to the younger men around him, on whose loyalty he felt he could depend. It was they who had most to gain by Rehoboam's succession. In order to exert their own authority over those who had served Solomon, the younger leaders called for a much harder line:

> The young men who had grown up with him [Rehoboam] replied, "Tell these people who have said to you, 'Your father put a heavy yoke on us, but make our yoke lighter'—tell them, 'My little finger is thicker than my father's waist. My father laid on you a heavy yoke; I will make it even heavier. My father scourged you with whips; I will scourge you with scorpions.'" (1 Kings 12:10-11)

Rehoboam's insensitivity triggered the division of Israel. The northern tribes did not have the same sense of allegiance to the Davidic line. Consequently, they made Jeroboam their leader (1 Kings 12:12-19).

Peter Drucker is all too aware of the tendency of many entrepreneurs in the business world to act as monomaniacs: leaders who are fiercely independent and are so driven by their own vision and perceptions that they disregard the expertise and counsel of those around them.[20] Entrepreneurs may flourish for a time and their enterprises may yield an impressive performance, but they often do not leave a legacy. What they have spent years building collapses after they leave.

Sadly, the church is not without its examples of crumbled monuments, ministries that live off their memories and feed on their own reputations. "One of the most common problems," Henry Cloud insists, "is visionary leaders whose strength in casting vision is, in part, rooted in their own notions of grandiosity. They are able to create all the vision and excitement—but they lack the relational IQ to effectively build a long-term team that likes being part of that vision after the first few years."[21] Discerning younger leaders are acutely aware of this problem, which is why many insist on maintaining a low profile and operating in a highly relational manner.

A key element when it comes to care and respect is the ability to listen. We must not listen merely for appearance, with a predetermined course of action already established. Such hearings are little more than public relations exercises—a means to defuse potentially explosive situations by providing people with the opportunity to vent their feelings in a public forum. Genuine listening requires careful attention to people in order to achieve fresh understanding and to receive new insights. Furthermore, it is only through true listening that we come to know the views of other people and appreciate the concerns that lie beneath their objections.

One crucial part of the reconciliation process in South Africa that led up to the 1994 elections, which returned Nelson Mandela as president, was the small groups of leaders from the African National Congress and the Afrikaner-dominated government that met together. One strictly observed rule at those meetings was that each side had to listen to the other without interruption in order to reach that new depth of understanding and build trust.

Listening is just as important in the communication process as speaking. If we are to hear one another we must create a level playing field. Hierarchy can easily distort message transmission. It can inhibit the powerless or cause them to speak out of frustration and anger. If speakers anticipate danger or adverse consequences, they may be so intimidated that they decide that it is not worthwhile to speak their mind.

That said, the silence of listening does not mean that the listener maintains a passive stance. Nor does it represent a pause during which listeners are thinking of the next thing to say or awaiting the first opportunity to interrupt or score a point. True listening is empathetic. It weighs what is being said and tries to uncover the unspoken part of the message, which may be the message's most important aspect. Active listeners also ask for clarification. They admit their misunderstandings and mistaken assumptions. They affirm, and when the other person is vulnerable and honest about their own limitations and inconsistencies, they express appreciation. Cloke and Goldsmith identify the following elements in active listening:

- Encouraging: "Please tell me more."
- Soliciting: Seek advice and clarification.
- Normalizing: "Many people feel the way you do."
- Acknowledging and empathizing: "I can appreciate why you feel the way you do."
- Mirroring: Reflect back the emotions and body language.
- Reframing: Reframe "You" statements into "I" statements.
- Summarizing: Rephrase to test understanding.
- Validating: "I appreciate your willingness . . ."[22]

A caring leader is also a cautious leader who does not act recklessly but stops to ponder the possible consequences of any decision, especially when those decisions affect people's lives. This is especially important for church leaders at times when corporate mergers and downsizing have resulted in layoffs. Such painful experiences can make people ultrasensitive to the consequences of change in the church.

On the other hand, leaders cannot shy away from tough decisions when it comes to confrontation, whether it is over character issues, assumptions that have remained unchallenged for too long, or individuals whose behavior or performance has jeopardized the team's effectiveness. Leaders have to function as the guardians of vision and values as well as hold people accountable for the contribution they have covenanted to make. The downside of a strongly relational emphasis is the loss of authority and mutual accountability. Henry Cloud notes that in recent years we have seen the "disappearance of authority structure, which makes it harder to lead, because you're trying to do it in a culture that has no template for following authority."[23] Younger leaders in the emerging church may be more prone to walk away when they face disagreements within the team rather than work through their differences of opinion.

CONFIDENCE IN WALKING THE PATH OF FAITH

Hierarchies can distort communication and hurt creativity, but they can be dismantled only as a climate of trust is established. As trust is built up within a community, personal and corporate confidence is reinforced. Max De Pree reminds us that "trust grows when people see leaders translate their personal integrity into organizational fidelity."[24] Trust cannot be built in a day; it must be constructed on a foundation of truth telling and honored promises. And De Pree goes further, distinguishing between sincere and promiscuous promises. The latter is simple posturing and manipulation, quickly detected and dismissed by followers.[25] Broken and forgotten promises will quickly undermine trust and erode confidence.

Trust takes even more time to build and more patience and understanding when working among people who have already suffered the consequences of broken trust in their professional or personal lives. Followers must come to believe that their leader is truly a servant who has their best interests at heart.

Great leaders are ambitious for the people who follow them. They measure their effectiveness in leadership by the growth in the people who work at their side. We are in the people-growing business, both in terms of their character becoming more Christlike, and in their gifts being identified and deployed to achieve their full potential and to maximize their contribution to the total enterprise.

Trust is demonstrated by the extent to which we value and respect colleagues, especially those who differ from us in personality, in the skills they possess and in experiences in life. The biblical account of the stormy relationship between King Saul and the young David provides an example of how a relationship between two people in a hierarchical relationship can quickly degenerate. Young David came to the attention of Saul at a time when Israel was under a humiliating threat from Goliath, the champion of the Philistine army. The bravery shown by David the shepherd in responding to the challenge is legendary. He killed Goliath with his slingshot in full view of the opposing armies.

As long as David remained useful to Saul as a daring military campaigner and as a soothing harpist, he stood in good stead in the king's eyes. But the moment David became a threat, Saul developed a mounting jealousy that eventually led to paranoia. Saul's blind hatred caused him to make repeated efforts to take David's life.

SUMMARY

Among the traits of effective leaders, character is foundational; in its absence charisma is likely to lead to a leader's downfall. Integrity and competency belong together. In response to the hazards that missional leaders have to face, whether in redirecting a traditional church with a maintenance mindset or in establishing new faith communities, I emphasized the necessity of a clear and deep-rooted sense of the call of God. Otherwise, emerging leaders will not survive the inevitable challenges to their faith. The hazards of mission sometimes result in casualties, which must be minimized by responsible and caring attitudes on the part of all involved.

Unlike most traditional pastors, missional leaders must be prepared to operate outside of the church subculture. Becoming contextually sensitive to and having compassion for unchurched people takes a long-term commitment. These emerging leaders will need courage to stand firm when they face opposition, whether from inside or outside the church. They must be committed to lifelong learning in order to develop the competencies needed to maintain their creative edge.

7

Activities of Leadership

Leadership involves the exercise of a wide range of functions. Nevertheless, leaders are not able to do everything. Each leader has his or her own particular strengths and weaknesses. It is important for leaders to be aware of their limitations. Indeed, it is one of the fundamental reasons why leadership, particularly church leadership, should be exercised as a team, with one member recognized as the overall leader. While the following range of activities applies to leaders of established traditional churches, our particular focus will remain on emerging leaders operating as members of a leadership team. We will view each of the activities in relation to the particular challenges that leaders face in establishing new faith communities, or in bringing about deep change to help churches transition from a Constantinian mindset to a missional one.

SEEING THE BROAD PICTURE

In a team it is important for the lead person to see the whole picture, to integrate and not lose sight of the mission in the midst of the everyday activities that take place. At the same time a team leader must resist the temptation to micromanage. But because "the devil is in the details," team leaders often succumb to this temptation. Micromanagement can easily undermine trust and result in a loss of the team's direction. While it is crucial that team leaders are assured that the details are being handled competently, it is important that they don't become personally involved in everything.

Nonetheless, there are some activities that the overall leader cannot delegate to others, especially issues foundational to the shaping of a corporate culture that incorporate both the values and the vision of the faith community. The leader must rekindle the vision, keeping and interpreting it in the context of the ministry's challenges and strategic goals.

Emerging church leaders see the big picture in terms of their post-Constantinian and postmodern cultural contexts. Many develop what has become known as a retrofuture stance. They look at future trends both local and global as well as at the early church that operated from the margins of society. Like the early Christians, they do not have a stereotypical model of church to which they feel they must conform.

IDENTIFYING THE MISSION

In the current literature on leadership, there is a great deal of confusion between *mission* and *vision*. In leadership circles, "mission" is that which identifies an organization's central, abiding and nonnegotiable task. In this book I have presented our mission as obedience to the Great Commission. In chapter three we explored the nature and extent of this mission—the Great Commission is the task to which Jesus committed his church and trained his disciples.

In the New Testament, John's Gospel puts particular emphasis on the mission of the disciples as a continuation of Christ's own mission (Jn 17:18; 20:21). Consequently, the church should itself be driven by the vision that Jesus displayed. Leighton Ford identifies key components of that vision: Jesus was driven by a sense of destiny that arose from his relationship with his heavenly Father. He came to earth in obedience to the Father and undertook a ministry of both identification and salvation. He came to seek and to save that which was lost (Jn 4:34; 6:29; 9:4; 20:21). He came to call sinners to repentance, and his saving work meant that he had to lay down his life as a ransom for many (Mk 10:45). He came not only to announce God's reign, but also to inaugurate it. While John the Baptist announced God's kingdom as a threat to a complacent and corrupt Israel, Jesus announced it as good news for the poor, who would be among the first to respond.[1]

The church of Jesus Christ is both the sign and anticipation of the kingdom. As such it should demonstrate the same priorities that were evident in Jesus' own ministry. At the same time the church is always an ambiguous sign of the kingdom. It is composed of forgiven sinners in a lifelong process of learning what it means to become Christlike. If Jesus did only what he saw the Father doing, the church needs similar discernment, coupled with a humble, complete dependence on the ascended Lord and the Holy Spirit's guidance and empowerment.

INCUBATING THE VISION

Vision is the interpretation and application of mission into a specific context. In the church, vision sees, with an eye of faith, the ways that we can turn the Great Commission into a reality. Vision also motivates us, convicting us as Christians to accept our identity as God's agents of change and transformation. Whereas mission identifies what we are doing or should be attempting, vision is concerned with what we should become in order for that vision to be realized in our particular context. Vision arises out of a clear sense of purpose that asks, Why are we here?[2] And in responding to that question, the leader is ahead of, but not superior to, others in terms of clarity of vision.

The leader's role in developing vision is first and foremost to lead the faith community in seeking the mind of God. Vision is not simply the bright idea or a success-guaranteed statement that the leader introduces to the group. Authentic vision must be generated from above and from within. Because the emerging church places strong emphasis on the church as the body of Christ, in which every member has both location and function, each person is a potential channel through which the mind of God may be expressed. The leader welcomes the contribution of all, not only within the leadership team but throughout the group. Initially, this comes in the form of brainstorming sessions. Then comes the corporate discipline of discerning what the Lord is revealing through the membership. Once the vision is established, the leader must make it his or her inspiration. The leader is the principal advocate, constantly holding the vision before the congregation so that the members share it with clarity and conviction.

The church's vision is therefore not the product of personal agendas or fantasies. It flows out of the mission of Jesus. Leighton Ford offers a clear challenge on this account:

> Our vision must come from the same place as Jesus'. It must come from the Word of our God, and from Spirit-filled minds and imaginations, and from asking, "How does Jesus see my world and my life and the people around me?" Our task is not to dream up visions or to develop strategies, but to see Jesus' visions and understand what the Father's strategy is for our lives.[3]

For Jesus, that vision was encapsulated in the kingdom of God that he came to inaugurate on the earth. It represents a provisional reality and also its consummation in a future hope. Those are the two essential elements of a vision.

Though vision must be owned, shaped and articulated by the principal leader of a team, it emerges from within the very prayers and aspirations of a community of faith. A leader may involve him- or herself in a variety of ways during the actual process of vision casting. At the same time, it is important to realize that "good visions become clouded when leaders can't separate themselves from the issues or become afraid of the consequences the vision demands."[4] In other words, the vision is always larger than the leader. They "own" it in the sense of personal identification, but they do not own it as a personal possession. It belongs to God as the author and to the church as the instrument; its realization comes through the resources provided by the Holy Spirit. Every God-given vision demands more than we can give in our own strength or resources. It throws us on the grace of God and requires that we learn to live by faith.

While a leadership team is expected to clarify the key issues, priorities and expectations, the overall leader is responsible for ensuring that the end is kept in sight. Leaders embody the future that the group holds in view. They function as a prophetic sign of that reality. Jesus' closest disciples never questioned his authenticity precisely because they experienced his grace and truth. As Leighton Ford explains further, "Jesus' leadership was not a style he adopted, but a reality he expressed. So the question for us is not, Can I learn from Jesus certain techniques which will make me a more successful revolutionary or entrepreneur or counselor or evangelist? The question is, What ends did Jesus pursue?"[5]

LINKING VISION TO PASSION

Mission drives vision and, in so doing, provides a contextually appropriate direction, passion and patience for the long haul. Pastor Bill Hybels of Willow Creek Community Church is widely recognized as one of the most visionary leaders of the church in North America today, operating out of a clear sense of purpose. In his view, vision is "a picture of the future that produces passion,"[6] and he describes the essential elements of vision in the following way: It must be significant and broad enough to become a life's quest. It has to be stated with sufficient clarity so that it indicates when a course correction is necessary.

I count it a privilege to serve as one of three "visitors" to The Order of Mission (TOM) that started with the vision of the leadership team at St. Thomas' Church, Crookes, in the city of Sheffield, England. The Order of Mission has three "visitors" whose task is to keep the Order's leadership true to its original vision. The "visitors" meet with the Order's leadership on a regular basis to ensure accountability. Other missional churches might benefit from similar accountability structures. An essential aspect of that accountability is to ensure that the flame of passion does not flicker and die with the passage of time.

A true vision of the future is, like Hybels has said, "a picture that produces passion." Some leaders may be tempted to conjure up a vision for the sake of their own survival or because it is a current fad in the leadership literature. If this is the case, it will likely fade either with the first set of challenges or the moment that a leader is tempted by the offer of another position. Authentic vision has survivability, over time and during leadership transitions. Charles Swindoll writes, "Vision is spawned by faith, sustained by hope, sparked by imagination and strengthened by enthusiasm."[7]

Passion is essential if a leader is to communicate his or her vision in a contagious manner. Passion, however, is not simply enthusiasm. The latter is often short-lived.[8] A community's leadership team, as well as the community itself, wants to know the depth and strength of a leader's commitment. They do not wish to be abandoned in midcourse.

Not only must passion be contagious, but ownership of the vision must be equally contagious. Ownership must be cultivated and continually expanded among the present members of the community as well as among new people who join it. If that form of communication is neglected, then vision becomes fragmented or begins to fade.

INITIATING STRATEGIC ACTION

Strategic action is not about programs. It is about initiatives designed to implement essential elements of a vision, instill values, and activate the gifts and abilities that are needed for its realization. "Strategic thinking is the ability to think and plan with long-term insight, in the light of current developments, and to identify consequent deliverable key areas of action."[9] Yet such thinking must not be set in concrete. It will need to be reviewed regularly in light of any unforeseen developments. In all strategic thinking our vision is always restricted and at times out of focus.

Leaders cannot simply sit back and wait for things to happen. They have to be prepared to take the lead, even if it means taking a plunge into storm-tossed waves and freezing water. Peter Drucker emphasizes this point when he writes that the present cultural and economic climate has created a situation where "we can no longer plan on the basis of forecasting and probabilities. Unique events have no probabilities."[10] He observes in relation to the business world that "innovations seldom create changes, they simply exploit changes that have already happened."[11]

One key component of leadership is timing. The first thirty years of Jesus' life were spent in obscurity, whereas his years of active ministry were crowded into a period of less than three years. Jesus waited until the completion of his own cousin's ministry before beginning his own. John the Baptizer called people to repentance and baptism. The culmination of John's ministry was Jesus' baptism, by which the Son of God identified with sinful humankind. Jesus' own ministry did not go into high gear until after his cousin had been imprisoned and beheaded.

Many leaders also go through a period of training in relative obscurity. For most of us, this entails a time of breaking as God makes us aware of our weakness and limitations. Though tough, painful and unnerving, this period often safeguards us from the prideful attitude of thinking that ministry arises from our own innate abilities. Then, when the designated time arrives, the broken leader has a clearer sense of destiny. It is vital to remember, however, that destiny should be realized only in company with others. The Lord is the sole leader of his church. He distributes callings and gifts throughout his body. Therefore, leaders must be careful to act in concert with one another rather than as independent entrepreneurs.

In order to compensate for a sense of vulnerability and loneliness, many leaders are hungry for friends. However, the presence of friends can be a mixed blessing if relationships become too cozy and self-serving. A connecting leader does not confine his or her network to personal friends. Instead, he or she brings together a wider and more diverse group of people, sometimes including even individuals with tension-creating viewpoints. Connecting leadership works by building friendship networks. These leaders have a lot of diverse friendships.

There were long-standing friendships among the twelve disciples, but the New Testament also indicates that there were significant differences among them in terms of temperament, trade and political allegiances. Malcolm Gladwell, in observing the kind of people who bring about significant change, noted that those who make connections know everyone and bring people's worlds together. The people who are your established friends will not open up a new world to you—but an acquaintance more likely will.[12]

Steve Nicholson, the national director of church planting for The Vineyard, USA, cautions against recruiting friends for your leadership team. He strongly advises that decisions should be made on the basis of the functions that individuals on the team will fulfill. If they happen to be friends, or become friends in the process, that is a bonus.[13] He is concerned that working on the basis of friendship may mean that better-qualified people are excluded and that friends may be retained in positions where they are ineffective to avoid damaging the friendship.

EXERCISING IMAGINATION

It is the "imagineers" who are the culture creators. The creative input of imagineers is often unpredictable. Imagination has to be translated into the doable, otherwise it will simply be a kite-flying activity with the tethered kite eventually coming down to earth. Other members of the team have the task of making sure that the imagineer does not float off into the stratosphere.

Children are a constant challenge to the adult world in the use of imagination. To the extent that education replaces imagination and teachers insist upon rationality and analysis as the only means of "knowing," the childhood capacity for imagination undergoes erosion. Far too many unimaginative, procedure-driven managers are found among older generations of leaders. By contrast, leaders at the forefront of emerging churches are people endowed with captivating imaginations and entrepreneurship. Perhaps it is precisely those who have not lost their childhood gift who are proving to be the most farsighted and innovative.

Yet we must not lose sight of the fact that imaginative or visionary leaders also require managers for the realization of the vision. The contribution of the manager is to develop sequential steps for the realization of strategic goals, and also to work out appropriate responses to unforeseen opportunities or crises.

I write this on the day following a visit to Sheffield to meet Mike Breen, who was an Anglican rector in the city. In a run-down industrial area of Sheffield, St. Thomas' Church purchased the premises of an electrical engineering company that was being liquidated. When the property suddenly became available, St. Thomas' immediately saw its potential as a ministry center for worship, local-ministry initiatives and also as a base for The Order of Mission.

Within six weeks of occupancy, the church had removed all of the electrical machinery from the four large factory buildings and was in business as the Philadelphia Site. When Mike showed my wife and me around, he never described it in terms of what we actually saw, but in terms of this community's vision for the site. The place hummed with activity and was filled with young people fired by the church's vision.

There is a surge of creative thinking evident among younger leaders. Thankfully, these genial mavericks are increasingly coming to the attention of senior leaders in traditional denominations, especially among those who recognize that they are heading toward a bleak future if long-term trends continue. Their youthful curiosity and openness are hopeful signs. However, for such upward penetration to take place, the situation typically has to be very desperate, which is probably why it is more apparent in the United Kingdom than in the United States at the present time.

INSPIRING THE TEAM

Leaders who struggle with low morale and are weighed down by defeatism are typically in no position to inspire a team. They project their low or negative expectations by their attitudes and actions. However, inspiration is also sometimes triggered by desperation. Leaders who have become overconfident may need to come to the end of their own resources in order to begin a process of personal spiritual renewal or restoration. God takes the initiative in giving them insight and energy when the leaders are at their lowest point.

Enthusiasm needs to be distinguished from inspiration. *Enthusiasm* is often limited to a single individual, and therefore it fails to ignite passion in other people. People may respond to an enthusiast with cynicism or a mad dash to safer ground. *Inspiration,* on the other hand, is contagious. It can be compared to the spread of an epidemic. "Epidemics," Malcolm Gladwell explains, "are sensitive to the conditions and circumstances of the times and places in which they occur."[14] They begin in one location with a handful of people, but then they spread rapidly by physical contact or close proximity. The church needs more leaders with contagious inspiration who energize other people.

Inspirational leaders motivate others through their own modeling of commitment and confidence. Such leaders characteristically value and respect those around them and are typically committed to the personal and professional development of those working under or alongside them. They habitually give opportunity for others to learn and grow. "Transforming leaders," according to Leighton Ford, "are those who are able to divest themselves of their power and invest it in their followers in such a way that others are empowered, while the leaders themselves end with the greatest power of all, the power of seeing themselves reproduced in others."[15]

But inspiration isn't everything. In order to maintain their inspirational role and at the same time avoid emotional and physical burnout, leaders have to pace themselves. Sooner or later many are overwhelmed by the constant demands of ministry. No matter how many issues they face, there are always more coming. It is vital that leaders understand that their work is rarely ever "done." Leaders need to recognize those moments when "enough is enough," and realize that they are not God's answer to every problem that confronts them.

Leaders should also be careful not to give the impression that they are indispensable. When leaders are tempted to "play God," they set themselves up not only for failure but also for self-destruction. Jesus calls his followers, including leaders, to wear his yoke. It may appear heavy, but as he said, we will discover it surprisingly light because he is bearing it with us (Mt 11:28-30).

Finally, leaders have to be committed for the long haul, especially when they are starting new ventures in particularly challenging environments. In cases like this, their inspiration has to be refueled, perhaps through the stimuli of colleagues, consultations with other leaders, reading and meditation on Scripture as well as regular times of listening to God.

INCLUDING THE WILLING

It is sobering to discover how few people have a sense of ownership of their church's vision or are even aware of its mission. This state of affairs may arise out of (1) controlling leadership, (2) the leader's lack of credibility, or (3) the church's loss of momentum and direction.

Inspiring leaders are "embracers" and "includers." They do not consider ability and enthusiasm in others as a threat to their own position because they understand that their vision is not exclusively theirs, but God's. Committed to providing access and opportunity, such leaders are, in Leighton Ford's words, "kingdom-seekers and not empire-builders."[16]

Missional leadership has to be connective and transformational. Connective leaders are more than transactional leaders. The latter are skilled at negotiating differences and creating short-term alliances based on consensus and compromise. While they may be skilled at negotiating, their approach is not as good at producing synergy as that of the connective leader. Transformational leaders connect and combine rather than divide and conquer. They join their vision with the dreams of others. Instead of a focus on common enemies, transformational leaders strive to overcome mutual problems. And in the end they create communities that do not merely clone the like-minded but embrace diversity—provided there is prior agreement on mission, vision and values.

Because it is usually futile to invest time trying to motivate the disinterested, leaders should spend more time identifying those who want to get involved. Good leaders take the time to empower the willing. Jesus called those who had sought him out at the instigation of John the Baptist. Their initial following indicated their willingness to make such a commitment.

Jesus empowered others by giving of himself. He shared his life with his followers on a day-to-day basis. The Twelve comprised a community with a goal to express the reign of God under the rule of Christ. They shared time with one another, usually in company with Jesus (Mk 3:14). They learned together, observing and listening to Jesus. The more they taught, the sharper their awareness became of what they didn't know. They took risks together and learned from their failures (Lk 9:40-43). Jesus instilled into his disciples, especially during the days leading to his crucifixion, the promise that they would enjoy a shared future. After his ascension, Jesus continued to give himself to his disciples through the initial baptism and the continuous infilling of the Holy Spirit.[17]

INTERPRETING THE CONFUSION

As leaders navigate stormy seas and unknown rocky shores, most try to establish their position and make constant, just-in-time course corrections. Making sense of the mess that surrounds us and lies ahead becomes their daily preoccupation. A good meteorologist presents the current weather as well as the broader trends of high and low pressure areas moving into a region. Likewise, church leaders can ill afford laziness or ignorance of obtainable facts that relate to their local contexts.

Mission leaders should find some affinity with meteorologists. They face a complex set of circumstances, both in terms of the individual issues they have to include, as well as their assessments of the broader significance of local conditions. However, they cannot simply rely on feelings and instinct. Just as weather forecasters cannot ignore data and rely on twinges in their bunions to do their work, so those in leadership must pay attention to scraps of information gathered from multiple sources in order to build up an accurate picture of the spiritual climate. They watch the news programs, read about current events, talk to people in the community—school teachers, city planners, police, newspaper reporters, realtors—who know what events and trends will make a significant impact.

The arrival of the information age has had a profound effect on leadership, with information assimilation replacing positional authority.[18] Leaders must learn to integrate information and insights from multiple sources and interpret them in the light of Scripture. One vital component that requires time and attention, both individually and collectively, is hearing directly from God. Prophets are people who have learned to listen attentively.

Churches and networks that are highly experimental in nature also need accountability structures that invite outside assessors to provide counsel, raise questions, sound alarms, keep the movement true to its vision and ensure integrity among the leaders. Such "visitors" need to make regularly scheduled visits and unannounced appearances. Such churches and networks also need a team of prayer partners to intercede for wisdom, integrity, direction, strength and protection among the leaders.

If a leader is to make sense of confusion, he or she needs intuition and the ability to integrate any insights gained after the necessary inquiry. Intuition has been described as "knowing without knowing *how* you know" and is an elusive component of highly creative leaders.

Wherever there is confusion, there is also the potential for conflict. Leighton Ford has identified three different types of conflict with which leaders have to deal.[19] He refers to "supra-conflict," "contra-conflict" and "intra-conflict."

By supra-conflict, Ford means conflict with Satan and the supernatural. He believes that spiritual warfare arises wherever there is a significant work advancing the reign of God.

Contra-conflict occurs between religious leaders. This can be caused by jealousy or the loss of power and control, or it can arise out of a genuine concern for the direction of a particular movement. Because of the potential for contra-conflict, clear and multiple channels of communication need to be opened up and maintained during times of change. Since so many initiatives have been rising from the ground level of existing denominations rather than from their pinnacles, leaders of new movements need to ensure that they keep their denominations fully apprised. Denominational leaders do not like surprises, nor do they like to be brought into a problem belatedly in order to clear up a mess.

Intra-conflict refers to tensions among an inner group of disciples. We see this in James and John's asking for the seats of authority on Jesus' immediate left and right (Mt 20:20-28).

Leaders also have to work through transforming conflict when an entire movement is faced with such significant changes that it raises the anxiety level and tempts everyone to fight or flight. During these times, leaders need to explore alternative scenarios patiently. They must also recognize that people need time for emotional adjustment as well as intellectual persuasion—often more time for the former than for the latter.

IMPROVISING WITH LIMITED RESOURCES

Most new movements do not have access to significant gifts and grants. Neither do they have endowments to rely on. According to Charles Handy, leaders of new movements have to be "new alchemists," that is, those who are "able to make something out of nothing."[20] Many of these new movements have as much financial security and career prospects as did Jesus' first disciples. When they began to follow Jesus, the disciples had no idea where their journey together would lead. Many younger leaders are increasingly demonstrating this level of practical faith.

Conservative leaders do not typically move until they have financial guarantees, but entrepreneurial leaders move ahead one stage at a time, relying on the Lord to supply their needs on a daily basis. This is not to imply that God underwrites all reckless initiatives; spiritual discernment is important. Leaders need to be sensitive to any checks that God may place on their enthusiasm or challenges he sends their way.

Managers of initiatives that require large amounts of capital before they can begin are likely to continually beg for resources. Capital-intensive enterprises necessitate severe spending controls, which in turn require appropriate bureaucracies to establish and maintain such controls. New movements, on the other hand, often operate so that they are reproducible despite any economic restraints. This minimizes their vulnerability to economic fluctuations.

This type of financial policy is also significant for the church because it can be an incarnational expression of mission in economically deprived urban areas. The church in the West must learn to operate with modest budgets and meager resources in order to appropriately express God's mission. Otherwise, the church will have to confine itself to affluent, upper-middle-class suburbia, while subsidizing missions to areas where conditions of social and economic deprivation prevail.

SUMMARY

We have explored the activities that characterize younger leaders who re-envision the church as a mission-shaped and mission-driven movement. Older leaders can learn from the younger leaders' cultural awareness, clarity of vision, passion for the translation of the gospel into language that those who have no biblical memory can understand, and insistence that the faith community must live out its faith claims, personally and corporately, by engaging with the broader culture.

Younger leaders, for their part, frequently express their longing for mentors who can contribute wisdom from their years of ministry and who understand the pitfalls in the path of newer, entrepreneurial movements. But they want mentors who can listen with discernment and patience. These younger leaders desire accountability, not only among their peers but from spiritual directors who will not shrink from exploring every aspect of personal life, spiritual development and ministry commitments. When there is no such accountability, younger leaders, like their elders, are more likely to burn out emotionally and physically, or fall into sexual sin as a means of escape from ministry burdens they can no longer bear.

8

Leadership Attitudes

Sometimes new movements arise out of anger and frustration in reaction to the ponderous nature of existing institutions. For the most part, though, younger church leaders are not characterized by attitudes of rebellion and defiance. Many fully appreciate the tradition that formed them, expressing a cultural trend described by some as "retrofuture."[1] Their passion for mission has provoked them to reinterpret their own traditions as they try to recapture the radicalism that was present among the founders of many older movements and traditional denominations.

Once a movement loses its purpose and direction, its tendency is to stall and fragment into warring factions. Margaret Wheatley and Myron Kellner-Rogers insist that this is why self-reflection is such a critical aspect in the life of a community or movement:

> "Who are we?" "What matters?" . . . When we don't answer these questions as a community, when we have no agreements about why we belong together, the institutions we create to serve us become battlegrounds that serve no one. All energy goes into warring agendas, new regulations, and stronger protective measures against those we dislike and fear. We look for ourselves in these institutions and can't find anyone we recognize. We grow demanding and less satisfied. Our institutions dissipate into incoherence and incompetence.[2]

Church leaders should play a vital role in encouraging a critical, honest yet positive organizational self-reflection. Additionally, churches that see disciple making as a key part of their missional presence are typically headed by leaders with attitudes that both build confidence and foster commitment over the long haul. Since attitudes are contagious within an organization—creating either a corporate atmosphere of well-being or one of discouragement and suspicion—their importance cannot be underestimated. This chapter describes some of the attitudes that characterize emerging church leaders.

PASSION: COMMITMENT TO THE FAITH COMMUNITY AND ITS MISSION

Emerging leaders not only help their respective faith communities apply the church's mission with vision, they also share one particular characteristic—passion. They are passionate people, and this passion is not only shared by their leadership teams but is also found throughout their entire network. It is palpable, contagious and attractive. In fact, new people are often drawn into these communities because the enthusiasm, the joy and the overflow of life directly affect their lives.

But passionate people, driven by a sense of mission, can also become overbearing, even to the point of ruthlessness. They sometimes use and discard people for a mission and a vision that, to them, has become all-important. In the business world this destructive style of leadership is frequently pursued in the interest of management by objectives. That management strategy represents the imposition of performance goals that are often perceived as unrealistic, unreasonable and crushingly demanding. "A good goal is my goal; a bad goal is your goal" became an oft-quoted saying among the unfortunates who labored under such ruthless demands.

Passionate leaders exercise power through their energy and inspiration. But such power must be handled with great care. In the emerging churches, leadership is not defined as power *on* people (through the leaders' capacity to influence and make things happen). Neither is it power *over* people (through their ability to organize and to coordinate people and activities).

Instead, the focus in emerging churches is better described as power *with* people, which is the strength created when a group pulls together. Emerging leaders demonstrate a power *for* people, acting as their advocates and representatives. In these ways, leaders exercise power for the sake of others, empowering them through the leaders' influence.[3] Through honoring individuals and building relationships, emerging church leaders are demonstrating their passion for people, not merely for purpose.

INDEPENDENCE: RESISTING THE PRESSURES TO CONFORM

Emerging leaders reject mindless or play-safe conformity, which they recognize can cause the demise of any movement. In their work on communities, Margaret Wheatley and Myron Kellner-Rogers address the deadly impact of conformity.

> Instead of honoring the individual as a unique contributor to the capability of the community as is common among indigenous peoples, instead of recognizing the community's need for diverse gifts, society requires the individual to conform, to obey, to serve the "greater good" of the community. . . . The price that communities pay for this conformity is exhausting and, for its members, it is literally deadly.[4]

Institutions typically exert pressure to conform as a means of ensuring their inherited identity and reinforcing the power of their leaders. Conformity is the psychological cement that provides security through familiarity. Unfortunately, conformity also undermines initiative and creativity. When pressured to conform, individuals often adopt attitudes that do not match their personalities and assume roles that do not represent their gifts and experiences.

Churches exert pressure to conform to inherited traditions, a particular sequence in the worship service, style of music and preaching. They impose demands through the expectations they place on pastors in terms of their priorities in ministry: the committees they attend, the organizations they lead and the people they visit.

In *A Peacock in the Land of Penguins,* Barbara Hateley and Warren H. Schmidt tell an amusing and perceptive story about the consequences of conformity: A penguin colony admires the more colorful birds, but in order to move up in their penguin organization, all birds have to become as penguin-like as possible. The organization recruits, trains and controls with that end in view.

Some of the birds
who wanted to move up
in the pecking order
became very good
at taking on the penguin look
and penguin behaviors.

But even *they*
found they never quite
made it
into key positions.

The penguin organization recruited all manner and color of birds, but once they arrived and settled in,

Their hearts were filled
with frustration,
disappointment
and sadness.

They had come to the Land of Penguins
with such high hopes
and great expectations.

They had come to contribute
and be successful.
But what they got instead
was quiet criticism
stifling conformity, and subtle rejection.[5]

Eventually, all the birds left the organization. Some of them left of their own accord, while the elders forced others out. In the end, all were sad, disappointed and confused.

Many churches have been abandoned by those under thirty-five because they refused to conform to the church's subculture. This rejection was not simply personal rebelliousness but came from frustration that the church had become a barrier to reaching out to their own generation with the gospel. They felt undervalued and disempowered, and left in search of a more liberating environment where they could be themselves and relate to those like them.

CREATIVITY: EXPLORING INNOVATIVE APPROACHES

As it adjusts to post-Christendom, the church faces radical changes in its own self-understanding. This is not the time for conformity but rather for creative thinking and innovation organized around an inspiring and inclusive vision. Moreover, since innovation can only flourish in a permission-giving and empowering environment, many church leaders may find that they have to break with precedent in order to create that type of atmosphere. Freedom is a prerequisite of imaginative and creative thought.

Innovation can also be scary and risky. Innovators are gifted with the power of imagination, but all of those vivid mental pictures must be translated into reality. Invariably, innovators are restless people. An innovator's vision is constantly unfolding and evolving. It becomes clearer as he or she alternates between conceptualization and actualization, but its realization is almost always partial and imperfect. Nevertheless, Bill Easum counsels leaders, "Never stifle an innovating moment—even if you're not sure if it is the right thing to do," and "listen to your instincts, not your critics."[6]

Venturing into unknown territory launches us on a steep learning curve. In the process, mistakes will be made, and alternative approaches will be developed and used or discarded. This process requires nerve, resolve and an irrepressible sense of humor. Innovative leaders cannot afford to take themselves too seriously.

CURIOSITY: INSATIABLE APPETITE FOR KNOWLEDGE AND UNDERSTANDING

Another characteristic of emerging church leadership is insatiable curiosity. Being innovators, many emerging leaders have a continual need to gain fresh insights and learn new skills.[7] They are constantly asking "Why?" and "So what?" as they seek to establish how they should respond to what they have learned. Their interests are broad, enabling them to acquire knowledge and wisdom from a wide range of sources. They are lateral thinkers, gifted in seeing relationships and connections where others don't. Whereas linear thinkers tend to be locked in to a logical sequence, lateral thinkers range free as they seek knowledge and wisdom from a wide range of disciplines. Searching for insights and solutions, they think innovatively. They are adept at drawing lines between the dots. This is an especially significant gift given a cultural moment defined by complexity and chaos. Many emerging church leaders in today's postmodern context recognize that everything is related to everything else; consequently one must learn to approach challenges laterally.

A curious leader not only is open to new ideas but is someone who demonstrates a genuine interest in what other people think. Noncurious people are often insecure. They tend to distance themselves or shut themselves off from others. Curious leaders are relational. They constantly interact with those around them, welcoming the input of others. They are prompt to seek the advice of those they think might have a contribution to make. Often, they have a visionary streak. Instead of simply moving a project ahead in a logical sequence of steps, they make leaps of imagination. Last, curious leaders do not mistake trends with destiny. Instead of fatalism, they believe that we are able to shape our futures.

Unfortunately, curious people are also easily distracted and typically unfocused. In order to avoid predicaments, leaders who are curious must remain highly focused in order to assimilate and relate information gained. In other words, new knowledge must be integrated into the larger picture rather than become a diversion and distraction.

Anxiety is the most common "virus" that, if allowed to prevail, will destroy curiosity and creativity. There is a significant distinction between the curious person who is stimulated by genuine interest and the compulsive person driven by anxiety. Worry may nag people into finding out all they can, but in the process it will destroy the creativity needed to assimilate and reconfigure the new information. The mountain of facts and opinions can crush leaders.

People who are constant worriers take too much upon themselves. Such leaders become so anxious to produce results that they begin to assume their own indispensability. When they begin to cast themselves in the role of kingdom builders, they begin to play God. "Sometimes we think that God's work depends so much on us that we become feverish, compulsive and overly involved—workaholics of the kingdom rather than disciples of the King. This kind of hyper-activism does not come from the obedience of faith but from the anxiety of unbelief."[8]

HOPE: SUSTAINED BY FAITH IN A GOD-ASSURED FUTURE

Curious and creative church leaders are stimulated by hope. They demonstrate a quality of "unwarranted optimism."[9] The combination of curiosity and innovation requires nerve as well as faith in God's guidance and provision. Indeed, the Scriptures repeatedly establish the strong link between faith and hope. The epistle to the Hebrews reminds us that "faith is being sure of what we hope for and certain of what we do not see" (Heb 11:1). Hope is not the ungrounded belief of Mr. Micawber, that irresponsible debtor in *David Copperfield* who repeatedly asserts that "something is bound to turn up." Unwarranted optimism is not the same thing as irresponsibility or avoidance. Hope is born of faith, whereas fantasy is generated in the fog of denial and delusion. The hope sustaining church leaders is firmly grounded on the promise that Jesus will build his church, and the gates of hell will not prevail against it (Mt 16:18).

Hope also creates a space for creativity, a place where innovative choices can be made in the midst of challenges and confusion. Unless it is stimulated by and grounded in faith, hope quickly evaporates. Max De Pree observes, "Of all the virtues hope is the most fragile, fleeting and the least concrete."[10]

For encouragement, every leader needs the supportive presence of other people. During those times when leaders become weary and discouraged with the burden of leadership, they need the support of people with a mix of temperaments, especially of those with a positive outlook. Wise leaders recognize that they need the ministry of others. They cannot be constantly giving out and setting the pace.

Faith, hope and love are God's gifts to us. But they are not one-time gifts that we can presume are our lifetime possessions. They need to be sustained by an ongoing, trusting relationship with the Lord. Jesus made it clear to his disciples that fruitfulness in life and ministry depends on abiding in him (Jn 15:4). This is a richer and more biblical goal than success and achievement because fruitfulness is the true test of the genuineness of a servant. It flows from a leader who is in relationship with Jesus and is obedient to his commands.

Fruitfulness is about reproduction and multiplication. It holds together quality and quantity, thereby demonstrating the authenticity of the church's ministry and mission. Fruitfulness carries with it a surer legacy than success. Success often comes and goes with a particular individual, but fruitfulness contains the seeds for further, exponential reproduction.

However, it is crucial that leaders understand that faith and hope are not qualities that blossom during sunny days filled with unimpeded progress and ease. Jesus warned his disciples that abiding in Christ entails painful pruning, a process of paring back to essentials that brings even greater fruitfulness (Jn 15:1-2). Abiding is not an enforced relationship. It is not one of mere convenience or personal gain. Rather, it is a relationship characterized by the strong bonds of love for the Lord and for one another, each of which entails self-surrender (Jn 15:10, 12-17). We are encouraged to be "joyful in hope, patient in affliction, faithful in prayer" (Rom 12:12). There is no love without pain. But the pain we experience is the birth pangs of joy.

INCLUSION: CONSTANTLY SEEKING THE PARTICIPATION OF THE TOTAL MEMBERSHIP

Leaders are not just connected to and responsible for their immediate colleagues or an elite group; they're also connected to the entire faith community entrusted to their care. This includes the youngest to the oldest, the most limited, the most gifted and the most recent arrival. Such a perspective stems from two theological convictions: (1) people are made in the image of God, and (2) leaders are called to be shepherds of an entire flock. Every member of the body of Christ is of intrinsic worth and has a specific place and function. Taking this into consideration, a pastoral leader has a distinct call to ensure the spiritual well-being of a community of God's people. Consequently, pastoral leaders cannot confine themselves to their preferred area of ministry. They have to be generalists, interested in people in every life stage and condition.

People feel included when they are listened to, their concerns are addressed and their worth is recognized. Vision is shared among the church members to the extent that each person feels included and valued. Ideally, in the emerging church there are no passive consumers because all are involved. As one emerging church leader commented about his community, "There is nothing to consume in this church." It is intentionally small enough for everyone to be actively and creatively involved in the corporate worship experience as well as the mission activities.

But this inclusive and generalist approach does not imply that a leader is at everyone's beck and call. The attempt to placate every disgruntled individual drains leaders to the point that they lose their vision and tempts them to abdicate their responsibilities. Passive consumers usually turn into disgruntled critics. By listening, addressing concerns and recognizing worth, leaders can move people from disgruntled, consumer-oriented criticism to joyful, dedicated involvement and ownership.

Inclusion and full participation are much easier to achieve in smaller churches. The smaller the church, the harder it is for people to get lost in the crowd or slink into anonymity. The larger the church, the greater the emphasis on small groups and team building needs to be in order for people to be genuinely included and valued. However, exhortations or directives from above are not the best way to achieve this. A more effective approach is to create an environment in which people can discover their talents and gifts in relationship with people they like and trust. They become surrounded by friends who share their passions and concerns for ministry.

Once people have established their primary association with the church (attendance at worship services), it is very difficult to lead them to the next level of commitment. Assuming that leaders believe that membership is about full inclusion, they need to encourage every member to become involved in small groups that teach life skills and provide opportunities for ministry. In this way, ministry becomes one of the essential outcomes of the corporate worship experience. Worship is no longer conceived of in the restrictive sense of a sixty-to-ninety-minute interlude in the day, but as an expression of our self-offering to God in all of our activities week-by-week and day-by-day.

Churches that have successfully developed this structure place serious emphasis on offering biblical teaching in the context of the celebration event that brings together all of the small groups and ministry teams. Members of these groups come together eager for teaching that is both comprehensive and life related.

Participation ensures inclusion. Ministry is developed and diversified when individuals are valued and their uniqueness is recognized. Ministry opportunities do not flow primarily from seminars or programs but from relationships. In a healthy group the diversity of gifts becomes apparent when needs arise among the members and the group identifies wider ministry opportunities.

Inclusion, however, is hampered by two attitudes found in the church in Corinth. First, some individuals excluded themselves because they felt they were not as gifted as others in the church, especially those in the limelight. Second, some were made to feel insignificant by arrogant, self-sufficient individuals who rejected the contributions of those around them (1 Cor 12:14-26). Leaders have to encourage individuals with an inferiority complex and deflate those who have an inflated opinion of their own abilities and importance.

Inclusion takes into account not only the personality and giftedness of each person but also their life experiences, professional skills and passion. Church leaders should understand that each person is called and commissioned by God to make his or her distinctive contribution within the context of the total enterprise. At the same time, they should also be aware that some people might be disruptive and use their own agendas to subvert the mission of the church. These individuals have to be confronted and challenged. The early church exercised discipline in cases of immorality, when people took advantage of the generosity of church members in order to live lazy lives, and when people propagated false doctrine and challenged the authority of the leadership. Inclusion still requires boundaries. Without them, fellowship is torn apart and movements lose direction.

INTERDEPENDENCE: BUILDING AUTHENTIC RELATIONSHIPS

The inclusive stance of leaders is based on an attitude of appreciation, wanting the very best for other people and desiring to see them become Christlike in character. Good leaders see the potential in people rather than the problems. In plain language, emerging leaders like people because they thrive on relationships. The presence of people energizes rather than drains them. Furthermore, they are constantly establishing connections between people and then stepping out of the way to watch what happens. They are not threatened by the creative energy generated as people come together.

Leaders play a crucial role in relationship building. And once established, those relationships must be constantly and carefully maintained. Fellowship and ministry flows from relationships. Once they are damaged or destroyed, the church will fall apart. Consequently, leaders must embody the values they would encourage in others. Max De Pree writes, "Leaders are walking and talking manuals of behavior." They ensure that everyone has a right to be heard, serving as "guardians of equal access." They affirm that everyone "has the right to pursue potential and to be taken seriously." Leaders create a corporate culture characterized by "civility, good manners, sensitivity and forgiveness."[11]

FORGIVENESS: A POSITIVE RESPONSE TO FAILURE

People who have had little previous involvement with the church will have little understanding of what it means to follow Christ. Consequently, they will have to make significant lifestyle adjustments as they learn the implications of living in obedience to Jesus.

The church in Corinth is an example of the challenge of helping people to clean up their lives and reorder their priorities. New converts came into the church fellowship from a pagan environment. Paul reminded them of the power of the gospel and the way that they needed to live as Christ followers.

> Do you not know that the wicked will not inherit the kingdom of God? Do not be deceived: Neither the sexually immoral nor idolaters nor adulterers nor male prostitutes nor homosexual offenders nor thieves nor the greedy nor drunkards nor slanderers nor swindlers will inherit the kingdom of God. And that is what some of you were. But you were washed, you were sanctified, you were justified in the name of the Lord Jesus Christ and by the Spirit of our God. (1 Cor 6:9-11)

People stumble and fall, and have to be picked up and dusted off. A church engaged in the context of post-Christendom and neopaganism has to emphasize restoration in conjunction with salvation. And such an attitude cannot be confined merely to the problems faced by new believers. We all stand in need of grace in order to persevere in our pilgrimage and renew our commitment as disciples of Jesus Christ.

One further point needs to be taken into consideration. New believers who have come from highly dysfunctional lifestyles tend to be overly idealistic about the church fellowship that has played such a significant part in their transformation. At first, many view the church through rose-tinted spectacles, but then, whether gradually or suddenly, they become disappointed and feel let down after becoming painfully aware of some inconsistency. Early on in their walk with Christ, new believers need to be taught that the church has many blemishes and that we are called to exercise forgiveness while holding one another accountable. We need the grace of

Christ in order to not harbor resentment and harden our attitudes toward one another. We are all at different stages in our spiritual journey, and no disciple of Jesus is a finished product. We are works in progress.

The church does not restrict membership to the socially compatible. It embraces people of all ages, personalities and backgrounds. Its diverse makeup bears testimony to the reconciling power of the gospel. This unity was powerfully demonstrated in the early church as Jews and non-Jews were brought together in the same fellowship. But such inclusiveness also introduces tensions. In some parts of the world the greatest challenge is tribal barriers, whereas in others it is racial tension, economic disparity or generational differences.[12]

Inclusiveness is not achieved through conformity but by patiently and generously working with diverse peoples. Leaders play a significant role in this process, both as interpreters and reconcilers. Creating unity within diversity requires patience and fortitude. Leaders must be prompt to intervene when necessary, and in the face of misunderstanding and misapprehension they have to demonstrate long-term stamina. They must develop the ability to see issues from the other person's point of view. This last point is crucial, especially in new communities of believers. When members of a community do not share a common history, it is much more likely that they will misinterpret and criticize each other's visceral responses.

Newly established churches and smaller fellowship groups committed to the Great Commission demonstrate a dynamism that brings its own special tensions. Without a long history that cements institutional loyalty, these institutions are inherently unstable during their early years. People can be quick to leave when they encounter personal difficulties or ministry challenges. Early joiners, though initially enthusiastic, are often early leavers. Consequently, in forming a core team for the new outreach, potential members need to be vetted carefully in order to weed out the unstable enthusiasts. Their surge of enthusiasm at the outset must be matched by their strength of commitment in the long run.

New church ventures come with a sense of adventure, but team struggles with limited resources and unanticipated setbacks create tension. Tempers are likely to become frayed at times, especially when a team is composed of highly creative people. Disagreements must not be allowed to undermine mutual trust and respect. Tensions should be creative rather than destructive. But for this to happen, each member must be prepared to admit that he or she is wrong and ask forgiveness for being opinionated and impatient. During times of tension the team members must learn to ride the storm without creating waves. Leaders attune their ears to the way people speak about those around them, which provides a thermometer indicating the warmth or coldness of their relationships.

HUMILITY: DEMONSTRATED BEFORE GOD AND THE COMMUNITY THEY SERVE

Leaders of emerging, mission-shaped churches are made acutely aware of their dependence on God. They do not undertake their role on account of the status it bestows. Unlike an established, well-attended church with a reputation to uphold, new or reconfigured churches bear no such burden. Their leaders have embarked on a high-risk operation, and they know that unless they follow the Lord's leading and rely on the resources only God can supply, the venture is likely to fail and become a target of ridicule. In many cases this vulnerability keeps them dependent and humble before God.

New models of church are established on a "learn as you go" basis. There are no blueprints to follow, and clones can't be reproduced. Leaders are forced to learn through trial and error, and therefore should not presume to know everything in advance. Sooner or later an image of omnicompetence and foresight will be made to look foolish. Hence, many emerging church leaders are genuinely humble. When people come with questions, these leaders are likely to confess that they don't know the answer, but they quickly add, "Let's try to find out."

The majority of mission-shaped churches are low-budget operations, and most do not have the resources or the inclination to own their own property. They rent or lease functional and modest premises. Their leaders typically avoid status symbols that identify well-established and prestigious positions. However, this absence of status reflects more than their churches' finances. It represents a lifestyle characterized by humility and simplicity. These leaders work *with* people, not *over* them. They will do all in their power to resist the separation created by leaders who assume a superior status.

Typically, emerging church leaders have no interest in creating a dynasty. They do not think hierarchically but relationally. Power, control and hierarchical dynasties have no place in networking organizations that are decentered and fluid. The rapid changes and complex interrelationships that are characteristic of the information age and globalization require a different kind of leadership. In his extensive research into companies that remained market leaders over an extended period, Jim Collins identified the distinctive qualities of their senior leaders. He observed that these leaders

> embody a paradoxical mix of personal humility and professional will. They are ambitious . . . for their company, not for themselves. . . . They set up their successors for even greater success in the next generation. They display a compelling modesty. They are infected with an incurable need to produce sustained *results*. . . . [They] display a workmanlike diligence—more plow horse than show horse. . . . [And they] attribute success to factors other than themselves.[13]

This list of qualities applies equally well to leaders of emerging churches.

Humility is evidenced by words but is also accompanied by appropriate body language that demonstrates accessibility, approachability and empathy. Access should not be apportioned in accordance with rank. Each person should be treated with dignity and patience, and without condescension. "Leaders," Max De Pree argues, "belong to their followers."[14] The attitudes that leaders display reflect their character. They either encourage and empower or discourage, marginalize and demean. Leaders of many of the emerging churches are ambitious for the people God has entrusted to them. They want to see them grow in Christlikeness and in ministry effectiveness.

SUMMARY

Leaders project their attitudes on the people they lead. Pessimistic, problem-focused leaders engender defeatism. They paralyze rather than motivate. We have identified those positive attitudes that characterize emerging leaders and generate and sustain the momentum necessary for a missional church. Leaders are passionate people. They are the new generation of nonconformists; they refuse to be bound by precedents, and they think about church and mission in fresh ways. They demonstrate an insatiable curiosity and know that they face a steep learning curve. Consequently, failure is acknowledged as part of the learning process. Nevertheless, they approach the future in hope. They believe that in Christ the best is yet to come and want all around them to share in that future.

Emerging leaders recognize that the church is constructed by fostering relationships. Their hope is coupled with humility in the realization that mission is built more on the miracles of God's grace and his sovereign initiatives than on human achievement. Humility allows them to laugh at their own limitations and keeps them dependent on God.

9

Facing the Cost of Leadership

Some individuals aspire to leadership out of a sense of adventure, while others do so for the satisfaction of being recognized and followed. For still others, being a leader strokes their ego. They imagine the power and privilege that a position of leadership brings. Jesus corrects any such misguided notions. He continuously reminds his disciples that leadership is about service and sacrifice.

At one point James and John, the sons of Zebedee, try to maneuver themselves into the most prestigious positions in Jesus' future kingdom. They ask to be seated on his right and left (Mk 10:35-45). Their notion of the kingdom that Jesus came to establish on earth is altogether different from what Jesus has in mind. Jesus explains to them that they don't know what they are asking: "Can you drink the cup I drink or be baptized with the baptism I am baptized with?" (Mk 10:38). In their all-too-ready response, their misunderstanding is made clear. They think Jesus is referring to a cup of celebration, when in fact he is referring to the cup of suffering. While James and John want greatness by asserting themselves and lording it over others, Jesus achieves greatness by becoming a servant and giving his life. In choosing the pathway of the servant he was given the name above every name.

Here we see the sharp contrast between Jesus' understanding and that of his disciples. While they thought of leadership in terms of benefit to themselves, Jesus thought of the cost he had chosen to pay. Jesus identified with humankind to the extent of paying the penalty and carrying the burden of the sins of the world.

In God's kingdom, successful leaders are not those who scramble to the top. Rather, they serve from below. Jesus sets the supreme example. He is all too aware of the unseemly squabbling for position among his closest followers:

> You know that those who are regarded as rulers of the Gentiles lord it over them, and their high officials exercise authority over them. Not so with you. Instead, whoever wants to become great among you must be your servant, and whoever wants to be first must be slave of all. For even the Son of Man did not come to be served, but to serve, and to give his life as a ransom for many. (Mk 10:42-45)

Leadership among Jesus' disciples is different from that experienced by the Israelites under Roman occupation. True leadership is not characterized by domination and subjugation.

Leadership is often more about scars than stars. We must never forget that Jesus, when he appears to his disciples on Easter, identifies himself by his nail-pierced hands and the wound in his side (Jn 20:20, 26-29). We can neither ignore nor avoid his example. Toward the end of his long life, the apostle John reminds his readers: "This is how we know what love is: Jesus Christ laid down his life for us. And we ought to lay down our lives for our brothers" (1 Jn 3:16). In Hebrews 11 we are presented with God's leadership "hall of fame"—a group of people whose lives are characterized by sacrificial service. Their sufferings included being tortured, flogged, jeered, chained, imprisoned, stoned, sawed in two and put to death by the sword.

PREPARED TO TAKE RISKS

When leaders embark on new ventures with inadequate human and financial resources—success seemingly out of reach—they are taking a huge risk, and a number of problems can be anticipated. One arises from the fallibility of human leaders. Is a leader responding to God's direction or simply following his or her own inclinations? Do the steps being taken represent an act of faith or of folly?

Other potential problem areas include timing, location, team building and simply taking an unwise course of action. A high percentage of new initiatives flounder. Many leaders, though they may ultimately prove to be effective in starting new faith communities or leading new movements, experience frustration and sometimes utter failure in their initial attempts. Some have also suffered by becoming the target of criticism and ridicule.

Leaders must be prepared to carry a burden of personal failure. Additionally, when new ventures flounder, leaders carry a heavy responsibility for those whom they feel they have let down. This is true even though they know people are responsible for their own decisions. Leaders must ensure that people are following the Lord's leading rather than succumbing to peer pressure or a cult of personality.

Some leaders are attracted to Christian service because of the working environment. It seems to be a safe haven from the pressures of the secular world. Unfortunately, such people are less likely to be risk takers and are less prepared to pay the price of leadership. Often they possess a conservatism reinforced by years of security and continuity found in a traditional church culture. While everything else in life changes at an alarming rate, the church for them has remained a familiar place, an anchor in a storm-tossed world.

Although this attitude is far more commonplace among the older church members, it is also found among some aspiring younger leaders whom I have encountered in seminaries. Such insecure leaders often become staunch defenders of the status quo and strident advocates of a new conservatism. Their deep-seated aversion to risk taking and innovation is reinforced when their education occurs in an environment that buttresses their long-standing beliefs. Sadly, when they lead their own churches and watch their congregations age and dwindle in number, they continue to maintain a ghetto mindset.

SHOWING PATIENCE AND PERSEVERANCE

Although we are primarily concerned with emerging churches that are breaking the traditional "maintenance" mold in order to engage contemporary culture, we must not overlook the thousands of long-established yet struggling churches. Most of these are located in deprived urban environments and rural areas that are being depopulated. God has not abandoned these communities of believing people. They, as much as the innovative new communities and networks of emerging churches, require a new generation of leaders.

God is also calling younger leaders to revitalize older congregations. And these leaders need to be identified, trained and equipped. Without patience and perseverance, leaders assigned to such tough situations can inflict incredible pain on these communities of faithful Christ followers. Indeed, many struggling congregations experience a succession of leaders, which causes them to feel abandoned and alienated.

Mark Lau Branson has developed a particular interest in and personal commitment to small, struggling, multicultural urban churches.[1] He believes that inner-city churches should not be left to grow old and die. Rather they need to draw renewed strength from their history of being the church in the midst of hardship and discouragement. They should resist feeling intimidated by the stories of successful suburban churches.

Patience and understanding in the context of leadership should not be viewed as a handholding ministry to a dying patient. They are not comfort givers resigned to the seeming hopelessness of the situation. In that case the comfort giver is in danger of dying with the patient. Perseverance goes hand-in-hand with patience, arising out of the unshakable belief that God has a future for each community of faith. The church's condition is not terminal. It may have to die in the sense of having to let go of some aspects and traditions from the past. But this kind of dying leads to resurrection, not extinction.

In a culture that demands instant gratification and results, the qualities of patience and perseverance have to be reinforced. They are indispensable for every spiritual challenge and are as true for leaders of new faith communities and movements as they are for those leading old, struggling churches. The new challenges are different than the old, though they are no less daunting. One of the highest price tags on leadership is being prepared to stick with it for the long haul, over the roughest terrain and steepest hills. Younger leaders need the wisdom that flows from the enduring faith of older generations whose testimony of endurance can prepare them for what lies ahead.

Facing Resistance to Change and New Ideas

At first glance, younger leaders in the emerging church do not seem to face as much resistance to new ideas or change as do their predecessors. But appearances are deceptive, for potential resistance is likely to lurk beneath the surface and often appears within a surprisingly short space of time. This should not be surprising, for most people who participate in an emerging church come with their own history. Each person in an emerging church has a story to tell.

As we go through life, some of us find ourselves reacting against our past, while others try to preserve its cherished elements. Most experience both aspects. A method like Mark Branson's "appreciative inquiry" helps to identify those experiences that have shaped us into the people we are today. Appreciative inquiry is a church consultation approach that encourages members of the church to tell their own stories, relating what drew them to the church in the first place and what it is they value and celebrate about the congregation as they look back over the years they have been members. It gives people a context with which they can anticipate and interpret each other's responses and insights. It also helps members to reveal the defense mechanisms that they build to protect the areas of sensitive scar tissue in their lives.

Resistances to new ideas and to changes in policy often emerge sooner than anyone in a new community anticipates. As new circumstances arise or a second wave of individuals eager to become more involved appears, a community can find its initial concepts challenged. New voices begin to question what have become the group's cultural norms. Typically, this produces a threat that alarms the group's core members. When that happens, many leaders respond with a knee-jerk protectionism, especially since the group's founders have paid a high price in (1) developing the community's ideals, (2) being brave enough to challenge accepted wisdom and practices, and (3) taking the initial risks while facing potential criticism.

This sensitivity to criticism is heightened when the founding pastor or leader of a movement departs or dies, leaving others to carry on the legacy. Sometimes such sensitivity reaches the point that any questioning of the former leader's decisions is regarded as the betrayal of a sacred memory. When a community or movement is more than ten years old, new pastors should expect to pay a price in terms of resistance or intransigence because in that amount of time institutional norms become increasingly entrenched. It is sobering to reflect that the most conservative institutions in the church today began as radical movements at their inception. Yesterday's radical leaders become today's conservatives who are seldom prepared to pay the high price of innovation a second time around.

SURVIVING CRITICISM

In any context criticism is an inevitable price of leadership. Leaders are the most visible targets for all who are frustrated or disgruntled. This problem becomes especially sharp as an institution becomes more and more dysfunctional. Leaders become scapegoats. They are made the fall guys for institutions looking to deny corporate responsibility or divert attention away from corporate malfeasance.

Warranted or not, a leader cannot escape criticism. Moreover, it does little good for a leader to try to prevent criticism and to attempt to increase his or her popularity; those who do overlook the fact that popularity also carries a high price tag. Leaders who cultivate personal popularity sooner or later discover they have developed a fragile and highly perishable commodity. Leaders have to be prepared to make unpopular and controversial decisions if the movement is to survive and flourish. When popularity becomes the touchstone of leadership, the leader has no way of surviving criticism. Such leaders end up altering their course in response to every prevailing wind of popular opinion.

Leaders survive criticism only when they are convinced of the rightness of a course of action. Max De Pree says a leader's task is to define reality whether or not people are ready to face the facts. Having defined that reality, the leader must initiate a process by which that reality can be addressed. This doesn't mean that leaders are infallible. Wise leaders surround themselves with independent thinkers who freely challenge their leader's ideas, offer alternatives and are prepared to enter into intense dialogues and disagreements. Through such discourse creative ideas and solutions are forged.

Leaders should address legitimate criticism in a positive way, recognizing both its genuineness and concern. On the other hand, destructive criticism needs to be countered, and its underlying motivation exposed. When leaders feel so threatened that they are no longer prepared to listen to dissenting voices, a climate of criticism prevails. Often, such critics are quickly dismissed as lacking in faith or branded as "subversives." Leaders must make room for the possibility and affirm the value of a "loyal opposition" who raise awkward questions and provide positive critique.

Criticism can become so widespread that it leads to outright rejection. J. Oswald Sanders, a former leader of China Inland Mission, comments, "Often the crowd does not recognize a leader until he has gone, and then they build a monument for him with the stones they threw at him in life."[2] Sometimes rejection is deserved, especially when leaders make unreasonable demands or lack credibility. On the other hand, rejection may arise when the pathway of discipleship has been faithfully proclaimed but its recipients are not prepared to pay the price. Jesus knew enormous popularity and also wholesale rejection: "Even in his own land and among his own people, he was not accepted" (Jn 1:11 NLT). Christ's followers cannot expect to be treated differently.

Enduring Loneliness

There is a loneliness that arises from the calling of a leader. It is the loneliness of visionaries who see beyond their contemporaries and whose ideas fly in the face of beliefs that are unquestioningly accepted by those around them.

It is the loneliness of having to make decisions that affect the lives of other people. It is the loneliness of the preacher who carries a burden to deliver a word from God that he or she knows will expose disobedience or faltering faith. It is the loneliness that comes when leaders find themselves deserted, not only by their followers but also by their closest friends.

King David cried out to God in the midst of such painful experiences. He looked to the Lord's protection from not only his enemies but even his closest friends (see Ps 3—7; 10—13; 17; 22). Jesus knew an even more intense loneliness when his disciples slept while he was in spiritual agony in Gethsemane (Mk 14:32-42). Later, the apostle Paul felt abandoned in Asia. "You know," he reminded Timothy, "that everyone in the province of Asia has deserted me, including Phygelus and Hermogenes" (2 Tim 1:15). At such times leaders have to draw on their spiritual resources. Loneliness is best countered while working with a team. Leaders who need an adrenaline rush from their adoring followers are destined for a fall.

Some leaders experience a loneliness of their own making. Out of arrogance or an innate insecurity they remain aloof from others. Such leaders do not want anyone to get too close to them because they fear that their weaknesses will be detected and perhaps exploited. In their minds, leaders must project an image of perfection or at least confident self-sufficiency. Saints don't keep people at a distance; celebrities do. Saintly leaders are transparent because they know they are nothing apart from the grace of God, consequently, they have nothing to hide.

DEALING WITH COMPETING PRIORITIES

Leith Anderson has identified a number of factors common to contemporary urban life that, when taken collectively, have made leadership among the people of God both complex and frustrating.[3] He notes that many people have to work longer hours in more competitive environments and yet have a continuing sense of uncertainty about their jobs. This means that time is at a premium. Not only do most people work longer hours, they also work on a more flexible schedule. Consequently, they do not know very far in advance when they will have any available time. Moreover, an increasing percentage of the workforce has to work on weekends. In Los Angeles about 20 percent of the working population are at their jobs on Sundays. This is a far cry from the days when churches were able to depend on an army of volunteer women who worked from their homes and could set their own schedules. Today there are many other competing priorities that affect volunteerism: children in competitive sports, weekend travel and affluence, which creates more choices.

When people live in such an increasingly stressful and uncertain environment, they bring their troubles into the church. Does church exacerbate an already high stress level or allow people to unwind in an environment of affirmation and fulfillment? A *Time*/CNN poll revealed that most people want to slow down and live a more relaxed life. "People want to find a more even balance between the demands of their personal and organizational life."[4]

Leith Anderson reminds church leaders that busy people are not necessarily less committed but are trying to balance priorities.[5] Leaders need to help those who are most pressured build priorities that reflect the values of the reign of God. Leaders may have to challenge people to consider reordering their priorities. But they must not make unrealistic demands. Cherished church programs may need to be redefined or pruned in the interests of building supportive relationships. Churches, by their own example, need to show people how to set proper priorities.

SUFFERING REVERSALS

Seldom does any work of God move forward without difficulty, opposition and setbacks. As we listen to the stories of successful leaders, we must pay attention to the pains they have also endured. We need to take heed of the dark episodes that are a necessary prelude to happy outcomes.

Setbacks are trials of faith. Just as intense heat is necessary to convert brittle iron into high-tensile steel, setbacks are necessary for the strengthening of faith. Such experiences bring us to the end of our own resources and throw us afresh on the grace of God. We have to exercise faith that the Lord will see us through, believing that all things work together for good to those who love God (Rom 8:28). Such hard periods ensure that we give God the glory rather than our own, unaided human endeavors.

With any new initiative, leaders face a new learning curve. Fresh insights emerge and new skills are developed when leaders are prepared to experiment—and make mistakes. New routes may turn out to be dead ends, but by venturing forth, leaders learn to recognize and avoid future dead ends. In the meantime many innovations are developed in the journey.

CHANGING IN RESPONSE TO GROWTH

Leaders develop their own style as their church or movement grows. However, there are predictable points at which leadership styles need to change in order for the growth to be maintained. Failure to anticipate these times of transition can stall the movement or cause it to fragment.

A strongly relational style of leadership can be maintained only with a limited number of people. Some Gen-X leaders are so committed to direct personal interaction that the churches they lead will inevitably remain small. This is intentional on their part. Consequently, church growth occurs only through establishing a network of small churches, much like the churches of the New Testament. In such situations, an emerging pastor maintains close relationships with his or her church members and mentors the leaders of the other churches in the network.

Alternatively, if a particular church grows beyond the sixty-five-member mark, its leader must increasingly loosen personal ties and encourage the formation of subgroups that provide the relational bonding. The leader will then maintain personal relationships with the leadership team, but not with the total membership. Either way, leaders must be prepared to change their leadership style and release individuals with whom they have worked closely during the formative days. Leaders sometimes become so wedded to their particular style that they need outside consultants to help them make the necessary transition.

THE PRESSURE OF MAKING DECISIONS

Although the stress of leadership cannot be avoided, it can be managed. First, leaders must take control of their own schedules, maintaining a reasonable workload. The pressure can become intolerable when leaders have to make too many decisions within a short space of time. One secret is to limit the decisions that must be made. Once the crucial issues have been identified, a leader can make a relatively small number of decisions; the rest should naturally fall into place. Second, leaders need to share the decision-making and implementation process in mutually affirming relationships with built-in accountability structures. Decision making should always be a corporate process. Leaders who insist on making decisions in isolation make themselves overly vulnerable and end up shouldering unnecessary burdens. Third, leaders need to resist the urge to micromanage. They must instead delegate time-consuming duties and bestow authority commensurate with the responsibility.

A church is an integrated system. Consequently, decisions affecting one area might have unintended consequences for another. Thus an integrated approach to decision making needs to be established. Individual decisions must be implemented in step with other decisions and with an eye toward timing and sequence.

MAKING DO WITH LIMITED RESOURCES

Charles Handy describes entrepreneurial leaders as "new alchemists." These are leaders who are able to make something out of nothing. For the most part, leaders within the emerging church do not have the financial backing of traditional denominations and established institutions. They are, at least initially, operating with very low budgets. Most do not aspire to become leaders of megachurches. They insist that the communities they are establishing must be reproducible and not dependent on a large capital outlay.

Many emerging church leaders are working two jobs. They have few financial resources. Their churches do not have big financial contributors to meet their budgets. Their congregations are likely to be meeting in rented facilities. Significantly, they do not regard their limited finances as inhibiting growth. Rather, it forces them to find new ways of expanding their networks. For many in the emerging church, learning to make do cheerfully has become a way of life. Many of these leaders point to the early centuries of the Christian movement, a period when churches multiplied successfully without great financial resources or social privileges.

Learning to make do with severely limited resources not only applies to finances but also to the few people available to contribute their time and talents. Consequently, they have to learn to do more with less.

RECRUITING CONSTANTLY

Effective leaders are people who are ambitious for those around them. They realize that there are times when people should move on in order to develop their skills and apply their entrepreneurial experience to other initiatives. Wise leaders also expect and plan for a high turnover in leadership. They know that, especially when working with a younger leadership team in a new enterprise, a significant percentage of leaders commit for just a short period of time, often less than three years.

All of this means that leaders are faced with the ongoing burden of recruitment. They have to identify people with the vision and skills necessary to develop new ministries and train them to be replacements. This constant demand is often quite wearing emotionally. It also requires a significant investment of time. Leaders must be prepared to give of themselves, pouring out their life experience into the lives of tomorrow's leaders. When the apostle Paul shared the gospel in Thessalonica, he not only communicated his message but also gave of his very self, which itself was an essential part of gospel communication. "We loved you so much that we were delighted to share with you not only the gospel of God," Paul explained, "but our lives as well, because you had become so dear to us" (1 Thess 2:8).

When trained people quit, they take their skills and experience with them. So it is essential for them to invest in the future by training their own assistants before they leave. The apostle Paul provides a biblical example in his training and sending out of Timothy.

PHYSICAL AND EMOTIONAL WEARINESS

It takes longer to recover from emotional exhaustion than it does from a bout of physical weakness. After a good night's sleep or a long walk, people typically feel physically refreshed. Emotional exhaustion, on the other hand, requires time away in which to unwind and regain emotional equilibrium. Leadership in evangelism, discipling and church planting is especially taxing; it involves facing spiritual opposition, sometimes on a daily basis. Close, regular contact with needy people who are looking for help can also prove spiritually draining.

The apostle Paul experienced emotional weariness, physical weakness and intimidation in Corinth, a city with an international reputation for loose and violent living. He tells us that he arrived there in fear and trembling (1 Cor 2:2-3), but that the Lord reassured him by saying: "'Do not be afraid; keep on speaking, do not be silent. For I am with you, and no one is going to attack and harm you, because I have many people in this city.' So Paul stayed for a year and a half, teaching them the word of God" (Acts 18:9-11). Out of this experience Paul was able to testify to the believers he left in that city that "we do not lose heart. Though outwardly we are wasting away, yet inwardly we are being renewed day by day. For our light and momentary troubles are achieving for us an eternal glory that far outweighs them all. So we fix our eyes not on what is seen, but on what is unseen. For what is seen is temporary, but what is unseen is eternal" (2 Cor 4:16-18).

Many of the major cities of the Western world present similar challenges. The demands, dangers, and rough and tumble of spiritual warfare are likely to produce casualties. Leaders need to develop survival strategies. They need to be spiritually equipped and missiologically astute, making them streetwise to discern and interpret what is going on around them. The street must become as much the classroom as the seminary or training center.

One organization called Servant Partners is actually training young leaders for church planting and church assistance and service in the urban centers of the United States as well as the megacities of the developing world.[6] Rudy Carrasco at the Harambee Center in Pasadena, California, also has a passion for training young, indigenous, urban leadership in the United States.[7] He describes the Harambee program in the following terms.

PHILOSOPHICALLY: Our vision is to develop children and youth from our community (who are predominantly African-American and Latino) into adult Christian leaders who are contributors to society, practitioners of holistic Christian community development and agents of racial reconciliation. All of our activities are influenced by this philosophy. Our focus is our neighborhood in Northwest Pasadena, but we also seek to serve, train and uphold peer ministries nationwide in their pursuit of indigenous leadership development.

PROGRAMS: We have an Afterschool program, a junior staff (teen) program, summer programs, a private Christian school, and an emerging concept that I've dubbed (for now) the Harambee Institute. In the Afterschool program we do basic activities like homework assistance, good news club, supervised recreation, arts and crafts, and classes in vocal music, karate, tap dance, and computer learning. All are infused with the above-stated philosophy.

With our junior staff, we take a group of teens and, in a focused way, teach them job skills, engage them in college prep, and lead them in weekly Bible study, and all the while they are drawing a stipend. A select few take a spring break mission/service trip every April. The majority of our junior staff teens go to college.

Our private Christian school, Harambee Preparatory School, is an excellent private education infused with holistic Christian community development values.

Our emerging Harambee Center has a wide range of influence. We consistently receive visitors from churches, parachurch ministries, universities, seminaries, and denominations who seek to learn from our model and appropriate aspects of it into their own work. I also write on Harambee's ministry in national publications as well as secular newspapers, and speak nationwide at conferences and schools, and advise policymakers from The White House on down—all of this related to our Harambee model.

We have an internship program that draws volunteers for the summer or a year at a time. At present we have two interns from Denmark and one from northern California.

This model is emerging because I'm taking steps to formalize our teaching of Christian community development and the Harambee model.[8]

SHARING RISKS

The cost of leadership is borne not only by leaders but by all who follow in their steps. We all bear the consequences of each other's actions. The costs of discipleship need to be spelled out to prospective followers, who must be given the opportunity to embrace them willingly. This applies not only to colleagues but also to family members.

There are no hidden costs with Jesus. He lays them out in the starkest terms, cautioning his disciples that those who follow him must be prepared to take up the cross daily (Lk 9:23). A disciple in the first century would have felt the sledgehammer impact of such a statement much more than we do today. We have never watched a condemned criminal carry the instrument of his own execution. To a would-be disciple who was motivated by the material benefits of discipleship, Jesus replied that he himself had nowhere to lay his head.

The costs of leadership may include turning one's back on a lucrative profession in the business world or stepping away from the security of an established church with its negotiated salary and benefits package. It may entail leading people into a financially risky undertaking and to an uncertain future. It may mean leaving the comforts of suburbia for a high crime area in an inner-city neighborhood.

J. Oswald Sanders reminds leaders that the cost of every great achievement is not paid in a lump sum. "It is bought on the time-payment plan, a further installment each new day. Fresh drafts are constantly being made, and when the payment ceases the leadership wanes."[9] We have to be prepared to pay in regular installments throughout our lifetime. If we find ourselves unprepared to make the next installment, we must be prepared to step aside.

As we face the cost of leadership, we do so with the realization that its price demands our all. Yet, at the same time, we cannot forget that in the process, we submit ourselves to our heavenly Father who gave his only Son, who in turn gave his all for our salvation. We will also discover that in giving our all, we will find true freedom and fulfillment. Faith, hope and love are the qualities that will remain with us when all else has passed away (1 Cor 13:13). These gifts of the Holy Spirit strengthen us to persevere. They help us see beyond our present circumstances, keeping in mind that Christ personally guaranteed that he would be present with us as we step out in obedience to his leading. Leith Anderson counsels us to do the following on a regular basis.

- Look at the kingdom, not just your corner.

- See beyond our circumstances to the presence of Christ with us.

- Focus on successes, not problems.

- Beware of exaggerating problems and empowering failures.

- Keep a list of blessings and successes.

- Look at reality with all of its imperfections, not just exceptions.

- Reconfirm your call rather than be swayed by complaints.[10]

Whatever the price we are called to pay, the amount is insignificant in comparison with the price that God has paid on our behalf.

Nevertheless, leaders need to establish adequate safeguards to protect themselves from paying an inflated price imposed by the demands of others. Their demands (and also those which we impose upon ourselves because of our false sense of self-importance and indispensability) go beyond what God requires of us. God's demands are in line with the gifts he has bestowed and the physical and emotional strength he has endowed us with. When we feel constantly worn down by relentless demands and are being diverted into activities for which we do not have the necessary gifts and do not sense God's call, then we should learn to say no. Furthermore, if there are people standing aloof who are better qualified than we are, then we should step aside and challenge them to get involved. If we are truly following the example of Jesus, our prior allegiance is to our heavenly Father, to do as he directs and not to succumb to the unreasonable demands that people place on us.

Summary

Throughout this chapter I have emphasized the high cost of leadership, especially in relation to the emerging church in its missional setting. It entails showing love in the face of criticism and having a tender heart as well as a thick skin. It includes the loneliness that faces any leader but especially one who is in a pioneering situation and surrounded by young people. Leaders must resist being overwhelmed by the challenges and opportunities that they have few resources to respond to. They often have to be content with small things while nurturing a big vision, having the faith to believe that small beginnings can lead to significant developments. Leaders also share the risks and vulnerability of everyone around them. They have no safe place where they can withdraw.

10

Leadership Emergence and Development

In our post-Christendom, postmodern culture we need a new kind of leader. We give a high priority to identifying and resourcing a new generation of leaders in the Western church. This requires new thinking and new strategies. It means that we have to break free from old molds; or, to use Jesus' own imagery, continuing to pour new wine into old wineskins or sewing patches of new, unshrunk cloth onto old clothing is an exercise in futility (Mt 9:16-17). It may require radical steps, but it does not imply a wholesale jettisoning of the past. We are talking about the need for new wineskins, not their replacement by plastic containers! Nevertheless, the present missional context necessitates a critical reappraisal of the Western church and its leadership.

IDENTIFYING NEW LEADERS FOR CHANGING TIMES

The changes currently taking place in the Western church's relationship with its culture are likely to be long term. Furthermore, it is highly unlikely that we will return to the conditions that prevailed for so many centuries under the Christendom paradigm. So it would be a grave mistake to assume that the emerging church movement is a mere fad that will quickly disappear, or that its leaders will eventually conform to traditional expectations.

Assuming that today's world needs a new kind of leader, we must develop different ways of identifying, selecting and training prospective candidates. Moreover, those who are already in a formal ministerial training process need to be prepared more adequately for the challenges that await them. This means training leaders as missionaries who are able to operate in a crosscultural setting, frequently from the margins of society.

In 2004 the Church of England's Department of Mission and Public Affairs released a report titled *Mission-Shaped Church*. Its first recommendation, listed under the heading "Leadership and Training," alerted theological colleges of the need to make the training of missional leaders a denominational priority. "The initial training of all ministers, lay and ordained, within the Church of England," the report asserts, "should include a focus on cross-cultural evangelism, church planting and fresh expressions of church. This should be a significant feature of Continuing Ministerial Education (CME) from ordination through to years three and four." Many denominations in the United States need to formulate a similarly proactive approach rather than maintain the status quo in the hope that their situation will eventually turn around.

Fortunately, a number of groups *are* seeking to alert and resource the church. The Gospel and Our Culture network provides a newsletter and a series of books dealing with the theme of the missional church in the North American context. And Leadership Network organizes conferences and a growing series of books dealing with various aspects of the emerging church.

This reappraisal of educational philosophy is not confined to the church. Business leaders and educators alike are similarly rethinking the role of education for the workplace. For instance, Warren Bennis asks:

> Are we providing an education that will provide the cognitive, emotional, interpersonal, and leadership competencies that will be required for sustained success in the New Economy? . . . Are we giving our students a passion for continual learning, a refined, discerning ear for the moral and ethical consequences of their actions, and for an understanding of the purposes of work and human organizations?[1]

The high dropout and casualty rates in local church ministry should alert seminaries and Bible colleges to the reality that recent graduates are particularly vulnerable to enemy fire. They also face the unrealistic expectations placed on them by declining congregations who expect them to inject hope and effect a turnaround. The situation is further exacerbated by the fact that many newly ordained pastors emerge from their training with a distorted or naive view of ministry and mission in today's challenging cultural climate. Like World War I army recruits facing trench warfare for the first time, they complain, "No one ever told me it would be like this."

THE DILEMMA FACING SEMINARIES

Seminaries are not completely to blame for this state of affairs, for they have to meet the academic requirements both of the denomination and the academy. Consequently, the principal basis of student assessment for accredited seminaries is academic ability rather than the authenticity and clarity of the students' sense of call or their suitability for ministry in terms of personality, giftedness and competence. Contrary to what most people believe, seminaries actually play a small role when it comes to helping students confirm their call to ministry or in assessing their students' suitability for future ministry.

This is especially true in the case of multidenominational seminaries whose students represent a wide range of church traditions. In addition, their student bodies are made up of an increasing percentage of nondenominational students, who may not be subject to selection criteria, and of self-appointed independent church planters.

The primary reference point of graduate schools, of which seminaries are one type, is to meet the academic requirements of accrediting agencies. At the present time there is considerable pressure from accrediting agencies to establish competencies in regard to programs and courses. This has its benefits. It is fairly easy to measure competencies in the classic seminary disciplines: biblical languages, biblical exegesis, church history and philosophy. However, the task becomes much more problematic when applied to ministry-focused courses. Many students have little or no prior experience in ministry or have become detached from their local church during their years of education and training. Furthermore, with the pressure of their seminary course load, their "secular" work to cover living expenses and their family responsibilities, they have little time to relate their coursework to ministry involvement.

For the majority of students, newly acquired knowledge outpaces their experience and wisdom. Since seminaries typically teach theory in isolation from the practice of ministry, students often graduate without the insights and skills they need to engage the world outside the confines of the church.

But the solution is not as easy as simply adding additional ministry coursework. When seminaries require more adequate practical training for ministry, the options are often unmanageable because of timing or the student's situation. Ministry training becomes a mere add-on to the established curriculum. The typical three- or four-year course for the Master of Divinity degree is already crammed full with the classical disciplines. With rising costs, inadequate grants and the need to work increased hours to pay for their education, students have little time to relate their training to ministry experience. Many who would most benefit from ministry-related courses simply can't afford to take them.

Under present conditions it is extremely difficult for seminaries to move to a place where they can provide ministry formation for many of their students. While this may be theoretically possible for those students who already occupy part-time staff positions in churches, the course content may not always take their situations into account. Or when the content is out of sync with the real-life issues they are facing, it fails to provide adequate opportunities for integration and application.

Robert Banks has explored the relationship between theory and practice in some detail. He argues for a more dialectical approach in seminary education. The two must be constantly related instead of theory being examined in isolation from actual situations. Theory simply does not provide students with the skills for problem solving; it must be front-ended with problem-settings that provide the basis for theoretical exploration.[2]

FACILITATING MISSIONAL ENGAGEMENT

Such debates have been going on for some time, but they are now being given fresh urgency. Now is the time for action, before the situation further deteriorates. Banks proposes a missional model of theological education in the following terms:

> The "missional" model of theological education places the main empha-
> sis on *mission,* on hands-on *partnership* in ministry based on interpreting
> the tradition and reflecting on practice with a strong spiritual and com-
> munal dimension. On this view theological education is primarily
> though not exclusively concerned with actual *service*—informed and
> transforming—of the *kingdom* and therefore primarily focuses on ac-
> quiring cognitive, spiritual-moral, and practical *obedience.*[3]

The primary focus of a theological school must be to "make disciples." These in turn will make new disciples as they move out into apostolic ministry to engage cultural networks to introduce people to Christ and establish new communities of disciples.

Through each of these "tribal" networks, communities of Christ followers will face the challenge of becoming a transformational influence on their culture. In order to implement such a vision theological courses cannot consist primarily of the internal debates that have taken place in history or are being waged at the present time among theologians. Rather, the classic disciplines will need to be taught from a missional rather than a Constantinian perspective, addressing contemporary issues and popular culture.

Rather than focusing on internal debates, theological education must relate to the questions raised in popular culture. We need to move beyond *theology of mission* as a separate discipline to a *missional theology* that affects the seminary curriculum as a whole.

IDENTIFYING TOMORROW'S LEADERS

How do we identify the next generation of church leaders and provide them with appropriate resources? Should it differ from current practices? Can a new generation of leaders be prepared in sufficient numbers?

At the present time, most denominations cannot meet the demand for leaders because their seminaries don't have adequate numbers preparing for ministry. Even with the recruitment of second-career candidates for ministry, and with calling on retired clergy, denominations are falling behind. One consequence is that an aging leadership contributes to the aging of the congregation.

The majority of people entering seminaries have already been socialized in churches that are in maintenance mode. Too many are attracted to the recognition and the security that the church's present structures and ethos provide. They are not the kind of creative thinkers and risk takers that the new missional challenges require. This realization has stimulated the Church of England to discover new ways to identify and train its leaders:

> The Ministry Division of the Archbishops' Council should actively seek to encourage the identification, selection and training of pioneer church planters, for both lay and ordained ministries. . . . Specific selection criteria should be established. Patterns of training should be appropriate to the skills, gifting and experiences of those being trained. Those involved in selection need to be adequately equipped to identify and affirm pioneers and mission entrepreneurs.[4]

The recommendation is comprehensive in scope and highlights the key issues that any church or movement must address if it is to facilitate the emergence of appropriate leadership. It raises the question, How will they emerge? and answers this in relation to present ministry performance versus a future ministry potential that is based largely on academic assessment.

Training needs to be designed according to the individual's learning style, personal gifting and calling. It must maintain the interrelationship between theory, practice, reflection and assessment. Outcomes have to be measured in terms of personal formation, not simply on the amount of information assimilated. Formation, in this case, means knowledge, experience and understanding.

Where will tomorrow's leaders come from? We must avoid looking only to academic elites, those who are recommended by "flagship" churches, or those in midlife crisis seeking new direction or more security. When churches and seminaries use such criteria they often overlook potential leaders who are emerging at the ground level and outside normal structures.

VALUING FRONTLINE EFFECTIVENESS

Whenever an organization reaches a critical phase in its life and finds itself undergoing a period of uncertainty and rapid transition, the most significant leaders are those breaking new ground and pioneering new situations. Though they may appear to be operating on the fringe, the fringe may turn out to be a breakthrough frontier. Nevertheless, such individuals are easily overlooked or even rejected.

It is instructive to consider the kind of people God chose as leaders. Abraham and Sarah were an unlikely couple from Chaldea. Joseph, the youngest of twelve brothers, was scoffed at by his older siblings. In spite of his intervention on their behalf, Moses was rejected by his own people. Because of his age, David was discounted by his family as a possible royal candidate. In the New Testament the Twelve, whom Jesus selected as apostles, were trades people with little formal education. They were not priests, scribes or Pharisees.[5]

WHO, THEN WHAT

Jim Collins concludes, from his own research into successful companies, that the first question to address when launching a new enterprise is "Who?" It is more important to "get the right people on board before figuring out where to go." So the "What?" question comes later. The team's makeup is just as important as the leader's vision. For "the 'genius with a thousand helpers' model . . . fails when the genius departs."[6] In other words, the skill of the leader lies in selecting the right team and in building healthy and creative relationships within the group.

Collins also stresses the importance of having people who can identify opportunities rather than those who only get bogged down with problems. "Put your best people to address the biggest opportunities not the biggest problems," Collins explains. "Good-to-great management teams consist of people who debate vigorously in search of the best answers, yet who unify behind decisions, regardless of parochial interests."[7]

PROVIDING A MISSION PERSPECTIVE

If the Western church is to develop a missional perspective, it must recognize that it does not merely have a mission; it is the product of mission. It represents the fruit of mission, which in turn translates into becoming an agent of mission. Leadership training has to move beyond the pastoral care of the flock to an equal or greater emphasis of ministry to the world.

The leaders of FORGE, a church-planting initiative in Australia, insist that "the church needs to recover the apostolic, prophetic and evangelistic modes to be an authentic missional church."[8] For the church to be apostolic, it must operate on the early church's example, giving priority to church planting through evangelistic outreach. It must keep a "kingdom perspective" that entails a holistic approach to mission, encompassing all of life and addressing broader cultural issues. The church, if it wishes to survive and flourish, cannot define mission in terms that it finds most comfortable and compatible, but instead must identify with God's own discomfiting and daring mission in the world (*missio Dei*).

Jesus has commissioned and equipped his church to continue his mission with his priorities and his resources. Our approaches should be as culture specific as were Jesus' own initiatives. His was a bottom-up approach. It began modestly, as grains of mustard seed, but it had great potential for reproduction and expansion, even in a hostile climate and in the face of opposition and persecution. The secret of its expansion lies in his followers' experience of Jesus' continuing presence in the local churches' midst by his Holy Spirit, the priority the apostles placed on evangelization and the establishing of new churches, and the church's cultural engagement and indigenous presence. Their leadership was raised up primarily from within those local churches.

Effective mission strategies must be based on careful and discerning cultural analysis. Such analysis requires the perspective of both insiders and outsiders. The former are able to understand their cultural context instinctively because they have been shaped by it. At the same time, the latter provide objective criteria that can be used to identify those elements that threaten to restrict, subvert and distort the gospel, and consequently limit its impact.

RECOGNIZING INDIGENOUS LEADERSHIP POTENTIAL

The Church of England's *Mission-Shaped Church* report described incarnation not only as being *with* people but also accepting them *how* they are. It emphasized that "the critical factor will be our ability to identify and train emerging leaders in context."[9] The critical factor relates to whether the church will able to sustain a missional impact in society. If crosscultural churches are to be established, indigenous communities must identify and develop their own leadership.

According to the report, the Church of England should develop procedures and provisionally acknowledge the work and gifting of existing and future lay leaders who are already in church plants and other expressions of church. A process needs to be put in place that provides in-service training and education as an integral part of the discernment process to authorize those already in ministry. This would be an alternative to the established pattern of providing training after a candidate for ministry has entered the discernment process.[10]

When extractionist policies were pursued in the past, it usually resulted in people being trained *out* of a situation instead of being better equipped to return to their ministry. The training environment altered them to the point that they were no longer effective when they returned to the cultural settings in the place where God had originally placed them. Learning from these past mistakes, the report recommended that "a pattern of training, mentoring and apprenticeship 'on the job' should be developed, rather than outside or apart from the mission situation where the leader (or potential leader) is exercising their ministry."[11]

Bob Hopkins insists that an exponential church-planting model needs to be developed in response to current (and urgent) missionary opportunities. In this model, training takes place within the mission context. By contrast, the present leadership training system is so elitist, slow and expensive that it constitutes a bottleneck rather than a fountain source of leaders. In order to implement such a vision, these bottlenecks have to be broken and opportunities for training made accessible to emerging leaders.

The development of a truly missional concept of leadership training requires closer contact between seminaries and theological colleges and churches and mission agencies. To begin, "resource church models"[12] need to be identified so that seminaries, with their professional expertise, can help churches craft training modules while also providing them with an academically rigorous curriculum. Seminary teachers could hold classes in such resource churches, teaching alongside church-based mentors who can address the "So what?" questions raised by the ministry's context. Robert Banks has provided a list of practical suggestions as to how courses that cover classical theological disciplines could be applied in such a manner.[13]

In order to encourage indigenous leadership, the church has to recognize that standards of effectiveness are often context specific. Grassroots leaders should never be discounted simply because they do not meet the expectations and requirements of the academic institution. The academic qualifications that are demanded and social norms that are applied often have little relevance to the competencies required in contexts in which local people, respected by their communities, are already exercising effective leadership. Leadership potential will flourish when that potential is recognized and as training opportunities are made available that combine local knowledge with exposure to outside Christian educators. The instructors need crosscultural sensitivity and the ability to apply appropriate learning evaluation criteria.

Bill Hybels, a significant missional leader within his own cultural context and a mentor to other pastors, has developed a list of pertinent questions that provide a helpful leadership checkup. He identifies the following questions for mission leaders to consider in assessing their own sense of call and to sustain them over the long haul.

- Is my calling sure?
- Is my vision clear?
- Is my passion hot?
- Am I developing my gifts?
- Is my character submitted to Christ?
- Is my pride subdued?
- Am I overcoming fear?
- Are interior issues undermining my leadership?
- Is my pace sustainable?
- Is my love for God and people increasing?[14]

These questions are especially important in the case of leaders emerging outside official structures, since they are more prone to underestimate their potential and even disqualify themselves from further progress. Leadership thrives as expectations are raised. Jean Lipman-Blumen describes the three-part role of those who provide encouragement. First comes *entrusting*. As we trust those with whom we work, their confidence increases and their performance improves. Trust, however, must be linked to *enabling*, that is, providing the support that is needed to maximize the possibility of success. This also means that an encourager has to be prepared to accept reasonable risks, exercise patience and recognize that inner strength needs time to grow and develop. In fact, Lipman-Blumen underlines the "value of the good near miss" in the learning process. Finally, achievement also *ennobles* and leads to transcendence as the individual and the entire leadership team rise to a new level.[15]

STIMULATING THE IMAGINATION

In times of cultural transition, church planting is often more about the creation of new forms of church rather than the wholesale cloning of existing "successes" that are the products of another time and place. The authors of *Mission-Shaped Church* argue that "the planting process is the engagement of church and gospel with a new mission context, and it is this that should determine the fresh expression of church."[16] The development of fresh expressions is especially difficult for those leaders who have been nurtured in and feel deep affection for a particular cultural expression of church. It is how church is supposed to be, isn't it? But the people they are attempting to reach with the good news of Christ may not be convinced.

Missional thinking requires a lot of conceptual exploration that ranges outside the parameters of rarely questioned assumptions. As leaders exercise their minds they will begin to discover that "intelligence" takes a number of forms. For instance, *imagination* is a form of intelligence that is often overlooked in a culture in which the overriding emphasis is on *reason.*

The authors of the FORGE statement, which describes their commitment to rethinking leadership selection and training in the Australian context, believe that the next generation of leaders is most likely to emerge in the context of "environments where the missional imagination of God's people is awakened, nurtured and developed." For this reason FORGE insists that missional leaders should be trained within a context that provides them with the stimuli and challenges to think creatively and, moreover, a context that allows them to live with the consequences of their ideas. "Imagination is the basis of vision, innovation and creativity."[17]

"Interns are stimulated to think in pioneering and innovative ways of engaging in mission and building Christian community."[18] Within the FORGE program potential church planters begin with a two-week residential intensive seminar establishing a missional ecclesiology. This exploration stimulates their imagination at the outset. They then further develop their thinking by involvement in a church-planting project with the support of team members and under the supervision of a mentor. They are not conditioned by the expectations of having to clone an existing model but rather are invited to apply missional thinking to the unique ministry situation in which they operate. They develop a culture-specific vision that is not simply a projection from past experience or borrowed from elsewhere. It is produced through imaginative reflection and the development of new configurations.

One of the gifts of the Spirit prophesied by Joel and reiterated on the day of Pentecost is that "your sons and daughters will prophesy, / your old men will dream dreams, / your young men will see visions" (Joel 2:28; Acts 2:17). Visionaries are not bound by the past. Instead, they are able to discern new things that God has in store since God has revealed them. Neither dreams nor visions are the product of a rational process. Education for leaders, then, requires that we pay attention to young visionaries who are not bound by the past and also to old dreamers who long for a new day.

FORMATION BY PARTICIPATION

Again, preparation for ministry needs to be reconceived as engagement in ministry. If mission is the mother of theology, then our theological development best takes place within a mission environment, in churches and agencies that are involved in the cultures encountered in the communities they serve. This is a dramatic shift of focus from a preoccupation with internal agendas that reflect the domestic interests and tensions of the church. As the FORGE document emphasizes in its "Educational Philosophy" section, "People cannot learn mission removed from the context of mission." People need a context within which they can explore and exercise their imagination alongside other team members, thereby generating collective wisdom and ideas. They also need opportunities to learn from their mistakes, face their unrealized expectations and celebrate serendipitous moments. The Order of Mission training scheme in Sheffield and the Australian FORGE program state, "We try to place the intern in a position where they are 'at risk' or out of their comfort zone and therefore most inclined to learn. We then bring the learning to them when they need it most,"[19] integrating theological education with ministry experience on the streets, in the workplace and locations where people socialize.

Charles Handy notes, "'Education is experience understood in tranquility.' Too often, in the past, the experience and the understanding have been unconnected."[20] The learning environment for church leaders must be taken out of the safe environment of the classroom, or more accurately, an environment where the academically minded shine but those with a different learning style feel intimidated. Granted, an action-reflection model may frighten the academically gifted, but it is worth the risk, since academic ability does not always translate into ministry competence.

Leaders will grow in a more holistic manner, intellectually and experientially, when their learning context challenges performance and creates risk. It is important to note that the same challenging environment will also bring hidden personality issues to light as the emerging leaders work through stressful situations. These can then be dealt with in an appropriate and timely manner rather than ignored or left undetected, only to be manifested later with serious consequences.

GAINING KNOWLEDGE, WISDOM AND UNDERSTANDING

The action-reflection learning model ensures that students live with the consequences of their decisions. Our limitations, mistakes and quirks all contribute to the total learning experience. Kenneth Cloke and Joan Goldsmith comment, "Actually, it is *precisely* our flaws, complexities, and diversities that make us empathetic, interesting, and adaptable. Our mistakes, glitches, and blemishes are enormous sources of creativity that can help us locate fresh solutions to seemingly intractable problems."[21] They provide the raw material that causes us to reexamine our assumptions, goals and plans.

Too much of traditional education is focused on assessing a person's knowledge, correcting misunderstandings and filling the gaps. Unfortunately, there is little emphasis on life transformation. Does education make a difference in a student's life? Does he or she emerge from it more mature and competent? Cloke and Goldsmith point out:

> There is a fundamental difference between altering, improving, or correcting something and transforming it or turning it around. Turnaround and transformation are nonlinear, unpredictable, and discontinuous. They occur through choices, leaps of committed action, deep listening, subconscious perceptions, and instantaneous flashes of insight. They take place at a right angle from accepted truth, to what is, to who we think we are.[22]

Transformation is most likely to occur as individuals take on new responsibilities and work within the context of a team. Teamwork helps people acquire new levels of understanding and new skills that are typically not gained by working in isolation. Teams provide reliable feedback and mentoring or coaching by more experienced people.

When new leaders are apprenticed to pioneering leaders and practitioners, life-transforming learning often takes place. Failure can also be transforming. Painful experiences break down a person's pride, self-assurance and preconceptions, freeing him or her to think in new ways. Last, transformation can happen in the afterglow of celebrating success that marks a significant turning point.

For the Christian community, transformation renews confidence in the presence of the Lord, who works in ways beyond our comprehension and deserving. Transformation results in greater achievement, a dramatic change in morale, the blossoming of gifts and an enriched experience of sharing with others. Such outpourings of the grace of God bring blessings to the community that are returned to God in gratitude.

If, as Max De Pree argues, workplaces should be "places of realized potential,"[23] the church should be even more so. The church is not only a human institution but also the body of Christ, in which every member has a location and a function. It is where people are meant to grow through communal relationships and covenant commitments. The church, even more than the workplace, is meant to create a transformational learning environment as it "opens itself to change, to contrary opinion, to the mystery of potential, to involvement, to unsettling ideas."[24]

"Places of realized potential," De Pree explains, "offer people the opportunity to learn and to grow" by providing the gift of challenging work that is difficult, risky and meaningful. It is also a place that is prepared to shed its obsolete baggage. "It is a place where people understand the significance of abandonment," and a place that "heals people with trust and with caring and with forgiveness."[25] Learning takes place to the degree that creating a critical mass for change breaks the grip of habit.[26] This moves people out of the realm of theoretical possibilities and into the arena in which new paradigms that have the potential to change a corporate culture are fought for in a sharp exchange of ideas.

Our thinking concerning the education and training of students for church leadership needs to move from mechanistic models to organic ones. A good gardener uses a combination of theoretical knowledge, an understanding of local soil and weather conditions, and an instinctive and uncanny sense of timing, all of which leads to taking a calculated risk. God has designed and chosen to work through complex organic structures rather than through predictable machines. Bill Easum comments, "The universe is more like a giant garden that flourishes through chaos than a giant clock that is left to wind down."[27]

Networking Among Participating Churches, Agencies and Seminaries

At the present time there are a number of coalitions uniting seminaries, Bible colleges, churches and agencies in leadership training programs. In the recognition that they can no longer work independently if they are to respond to current missional challenges, each affirms the strengths of the other. One such program is endeavoring to provide blanket coverage throughout England, offering master's level programs to people already engaged in ministry. It is envisaged that some fifty churches will host the courses. These centers are strategically located so that no student is more than one hour's driving time from one of them. Those with practical experience in ministry teach the classes, and the degree program is fully accredited. My own institution, Fuller Seminary, offers its own online master's degree program in which students learn in cohort groups. A growing number of seminaries are developing master's of divinity programs with a one-year residency requirement and the remainder of the courses available either online or in intensive-study formats. There are also a growing number of accredited training centers for urban ministry that are emerging in major cities. Others believe that accreditation is culturally inappropriate for the leaders they are seeking to resource and encourage.

In Australia, "FORGE is a network for specialising in missions-to-the-first-world training, which is undertaken in modules and based on an action-reflection internship-training model."[28] It consists of a network of theological colleges, churches and agencies that collaborate to develop leadership-training opportunities. They each bring their distinctive contributions: colleges provide accredited courses while churches and agencies set up training venues and internships.

Internships are designed for a single academic year and require about twenty hours a week. They are combined with three intensive courses spread throughout the year, each requiring a five-day live-in experience. The first course introduces the missional church paradigm within the Australian context. The second explores the inner life of the intern (spirituality, sustainability and discipleship). The third provides insights and skills for developing pioneering leadership. The leadership component is the last because it draws on the experience and realized potential of the intern. These three intensive courses are part of ten, four-hour interactive seminars, each lasting a month, covering a range of topics relevant to the student. The leaders of FORGE are very careful to state that they do not seek to replace traditional theological education; rather, they wish to supplement it.

St. Thomas' Church in Sheffield, a church that combines Anglican and Baptist traditions, has launched a one-year training program to (1) provide biblical literacy, (2) help leaders internalize the classic spiritual disciplines, (3) offer personal mentoring, and (4) give leaders ministry experience through outreach initiatives in and around the city. Students in the program support themselves financially through part-time work. Many live in the homes of parishioners, which keeps costs down and, more importantly, provides the context of a Christian family in which students can receive added mentoring and spiritual formation.

St. Thomas' has trained over two hundred students in this program. Some of them have continued with St. Thomas' while others have used their skills to form and lead new communities of faith. Twice yearly the church hosts a national, and now increasingly international, gathering of church planters. Those attending celebrate what God has done, and they seek answers to many of the specific issues they currently face. This church has now grown to over two thousand people and has become the largest church of any denomination in north England. However, it has no interest in becoming a megachurch (à la North America). Its primary desire and plan is to create an ever-growing network of disciples who are learning "life skills" in small group settings. Many of these groups even meet as regional clusters.

In April 2003, The Order of Mission (TOM), whose home base is St. Thomas' Church, was launched by the then archbishop of York, David Hope. He also serves as TOM's senior visitor. Members of the Order take vows of simplicity, purity and accountability. They also observe the discipline of the ancient monastic hours of prayer, but they do so in a contemporary manner. TOM members do not live in a monastic community but are in the workplace. While the majority are not able to share in the church's daily prayer times, they are still able to access the intercessions for the day by means of text-messaging, which is far more widespread in the United Kingdom than in the United States. TOM's training program has also established links with theological colleges to expand their training program. A second year of training is now in place.

These networks work together to provide and share academic resources, mission venues, insights and experiences. Many of them work across denominational lines and with a variety of agencies. In today's era of post-denominationalism, such coalitions are likely to increase.

Personal Coaching and Mentoring

Personal coaching and mentoring enhances both spiritual and professional formation. Such mentoring is provided on an individual basis or within small groups. Peter Senge has identified the roles that the mentor fulfills to help individuals in their ministry development.

- *facilitator:* helps people identify their gifts and passion, understand their personality type and relate their gifts to calling and ministry

- *appraiser:* provides candid feedback on performance and reputation; clarifies standards and expectations; listens to people's self-assessment, frustrations and hopes; relates performance to goals; suggests specific actions to improve

- *forecaster:* points out emerging trends and new developments, provides new opportunities, indicates new directions, understands cultural and spiritual realities

- *advisor:* identifies possibilities in relation to the individual's gifts, experience and performance; points out obstacles; provides support

- *enabler:* develops detailed plans, arranges useful contacts, establishes networks, identifies resources[29]

Mentoring is still somewhat of a novel concept in the church. The vast majority of leaders have had little experience in such a relationship. This is very strange considering the New Testament's emphasis on mentoring relationships: Jesus and the Twelve, and the apostle Paul and his traveling team (which included John Mark and Timothy). Indeed, before the emergence of seminaries, the standard preparation for ministry was to be apprenticed to a pastor or scholar.

Currently, we suffer from a dearth of qualified mentors. The training of mentors is a priority. We who serve as trainers and educators need to help churches realize the strategic importance of a mentoring ministry. A mentor's primary function is not to teach content but rather to provide feedback. Mentors need enhanced listening skills. The conversation between mentor and apprentice seeks to be constructive rather than critical; it proposes a course of action rather than imposes one's own viewpoint. It is a trusting relationship that allows both parties to be honest and frank with one another. In addition, mentoring provides strategic opportunities for service for older leaders and senior members of the congregation. It keeps them in a learning mode rather than a reactive one.

The argument presented in this chapter for an emphasis on the practice of ministry in seminary curricula and for the integration of theology and mission should not be interpreted as the dumbing-down of education. Training has to be of high quality and must embrace a wider range of understanding that can be translated into specific skills. Writing in relation to the FORGE project, the leaders affirm that

> growth of the intellect is essential to missional leadership development. If we are to meaningfully engage our cultural setting we must first understand and interpret it. This requires significant intellectual development and skills. However, we believe that there are other ways beyond the system of the academy with which to develop an intellectual grasp of theology and ministry. We aim to engender a deep love of learning in all that we do.[30]

LEADERS WHO LEAVE A LEGACY

The most significant test of leadership is not present performance but the legacy that the leaders leave behind them. Has the leader left the movement healthier, not just larger? Has the mission stayed true to the original vision? Has that vision been revisited and reinterpreted in light of changing conditions? Are its new leaders creative and prepared to take risks? Does a movement export leaders with proven track records? Do those leaders demonstrate their creativity and competence by starting new movements? Are they prepared to leave the stimulus and security of the past to follow a new God-given vision? Os Guinness emphasizes the importance of the leader's sense of call from God in order to sustain a lifetime of faithful and effective ministry: "Calling is central to the challenge and privilege of finishing well in life."[31]

Max De Pree distinguishes between strategic planning and action that is required to leave a legacy. "A strategic plan is a long-term commitment to something we intend to do. A legacy results from the facts of our behavior that remain in the minds of others, the cumulative informal record of how close we came to the person we intended to be. For me, what you plan to do differs enormously from what you leave behind."[32]

In biblical terminology this is the difference between success and fruitfulness. Unlike fruitfulness, success does not guarantee a legacy. "What we do will always be a consequence of who we have become." A legacy is deeper and more enduring and should have a more substantial place in the lives of organizations. It is not just about meeting goals. By focusing on legacy we raise character issues, set standards and attempt to live up to them.

In summary: in order to identify and facilitate the next generation of leadership, we must provide training that (1) is accessible (location and time), (2) is appropriate in terms of the topics addressed and the manner in which courses are taught, (3) demonstrates connectedness between theory and the practice of ministry, and (4) is affordable for younger leaders. The selection process needs to be more proactive, identifying the people on the ground who are showing the most potential in ministry. Such people have a desire to learn and be guided by the best resources available. Similar to the sporting world, the church needs "talent scouts" who can come alongside emergent leaders early in their ministry and provide them with mentoring and training opportunities.

A leader who leaves a legacy lives on in the actions of many people.[33] Jesus is the supreme example of this, and the church provides two thousand years of evidence.

Notes

Introduction: Where Have All the Leaders Gone?

[1]Warren Bennis, quoted in Kenneth Cloke and Joan Goldsmith, *The Art of Waking People Up* (San Francisco: Jossey-Bass, 2001), p. xi.

[2]See Lyle E. Schaller, *The New Reformation* (Nashville: Abingdon, 1995); and his *Tattered Trust* (Nashville: Abingdon, 1996); George Gallup Jr. and D. Michael Lindsey, *Surveying the Religious Landscape* (Harrisburg, Penn.: Morehouse Press, 2000).

[3]See Wade Clark Roof, *Spiritual Marketplace* (Princeton, N.J.: Princeton University Press, 1999).

[4]For the United States see Gallup and Lindsey, *Surveying the Religious Landscape*, pp. 17-19; for the United Kingdom see Peter Brierley, *The Tide Is Running Out* (London: Christian Research, 2000), pp. 95-96, and *Coming Up Trumps!* (Milton Keynes, Bucks, U.K.: Authentic Media/ Christian Research, 2004), p. 39.

[5]Quoted by Warren Bennis, "The Future Has No Shelf Life," in *The Future of Leadership,* ed. Warren Bennis, Gretchen M. Spreitzer and Thomas G. Cummings (San Francisco: Jossey-Bass, 2001), p. 12.

Chapter One: Redefining Leadership

[1]Kenneth Cloke and Joan Goldsmith, *The Art of Waking People Up* (San Francisco: Jossey-Bass, 2001), p. 4.

[2]Ibid.

[3]J. Robert Clinton, *Leadership Emergence Theory* (Pasadena, Calif.: Barnabas, 1989).

[4]James M. Kouzes and Barry Z. Posner, *The Leadership Challenge,* 3rd ed. (San Francisco: Jossey-Bass, 2002), p. xxiv.

[5]Steven M. Bernstein and Anthony F. Smith, "The Puzzles of Leadership," in *The Leader of the Future,* ed. Frances Hesselbein, Marshall Goldsmith and Richard Beckhard (San Francisco: Jossey-Bass, 1996), p. 282.

[6]Robert Banks and Bernice M. Ledbetter, *Reviewing Leadership* (Grand Rapids: Baker, 2004), pp. 16, 17.

[7]Walter Wright, *Relational Leadership* (Carlisle, U.K.: Paternoster, 2000), p. 2.

[8]Ibid.

[9]Shirley Roels, *Moving Beyond Servant Leadership,* Leadership Briefing (Pasadena, Calif.: De Pree Leadership Center, 1999), p. 3.

[10]Roger K. Greenleaf, *Servant Leadership* (New York: Paulist Press, 1977), p. 45.

[11]James C. Collins and Jerry I. Porras, *Built to Last* (New York: HarperCollins, 1997), p. 94.

[12]See Peter M. Senge, "Leading Learning Organizations: The Bold, the Powerful, and the Invisible," in *The Leader of the Future,* ed. Frances Hesselbein, Marshall Goldsmith and Richard Beckhard (San Francisco: Jossey-Bass, 1996), pp. 46-56; and chap. 7 of Bill Hybels, *Courageous Leadership* (Grand Rapids: Zondervan, 2002).

[13]Jean Lipman-Blumen, *Connective Leadership* (New York: Oxford University Press, 1996), p. 30.

[14]Ibid.

[15]Ibid., p. 32.

[16]Leith Anderson, *Leadership That Works* (Minneapolis: Bethany House, 1999), p. 44.

[17]Senge, "Leading Learning Organizations," p. 45.

[18]Warren Bennis, "Leading from the Grass Roots," in *The Leader of the Future,* ed. Frances Hesselbein, Marshall Goldsmith and Richard Beckhard (San Francisco: Jossey-Bass, 1996), p. 24.

[19]Ibid., p. 6.

[20]Peter Brierley bears out this observation on the basis of his research. In a personal e-mail he writes, "Your comment that churches making a significant impact among under 35-year-olds needing folk in the 70+ category was proved by our research from the 1998 English Church Attendance Survey in a report we wrote in collaboration with Springboard called Growing Churches in the 1990s. We found exactly what you said—42 percent of churches grew when 25 percent of their attenders were 65+, the highest percentage of any age mix."

[21]Bill Easum, *Leadership on the OtherSide* (Nashville: Abingdon, 2000), p. 32.

[22]Charles Handy, "The New Language of Organizing and Its Implications for Leaders," in *The Leader of the Future,* ed. Frances Hesselbein, Marshall Goldsmith and Richard Beckhard (San Francisco: Jossey-Bass, 1996), p. 7.

[23]George Gallup Jr., "Secularism and Religion: Trends in Contemporary America," *Emerging Trends* 9, no. 10 (1987): 3.

[24]Frances Hesselbein, *Hesselbein on Leadership* (San Francisco: Jossey-Bass, 2002), pp. 33-34.

[25]See Robert Lewis, *The Church of Irresistible Influence* (Grand Rapids: Zondervan, 2001).

Chapter Two: Why Leadership Styles Must Change

[1]Charles Handy, "A World of Fleas and Elephants," in *The Future of Leadership,* ed. Warren Bennis, Gretchen M. Spreitzer and Thomas G. Cummings (San Francisco: Jossey-Bass, 2001), pp. 29-30.

[2]See Steve Bruce, *Religion in the Modern World* (Oxford: Oxford University Press, 1996).

[3]See Alister McGrath, *The Twilight of Atheism* (New York: Doubleday, 2004).

[4]John G. Stackhouse Jr., *Humble Apologetics* (New York: Oxford University Press, 2002), p. 12.

[5]See Eddie Gibbs, *In Name Only* (Wheaton, Ill.: Victor, 1994).

[6]Jonathan Rauch, "Let It Be," *Atlantic Monthly* 291, no. 4 (2003): 34. Rauch may just be misinterpreting the response of his friends who resolved not to react in the judgmental manner he anticipated.

[7]Different authors give slightly different age brackets and labels, e.g., Mike Regele, *Death of the Church* (Grand Rapids: Zondervan, 1995), pp. 113-24; George Barna, *The Second Coming of the Church* (Nashville: Word, 1998), p. 72.

[8]Charles Handy, *The Age of Paradox* (Boston: Harvard Business School Press, 1994), p. 37.

[9]Andrew Grove, *Only the Paranoid Survive* (New York: Doubleday, 1996), pp. 3-7.

[10]See Wade Clark Roof, *Spiritual Marketplace* (Princeton, N.J.: Princeton University Press, 1999), pp. 62-65.

[11]Robert Webber, *Ancient-Future Evangelism* (Grand Rapids: Baker, 2003).

[12]Dominic Crossan, *The Dark Interval* (Niles, Ill.: Argus, 1975), p. 44.

[13]Frances Hesselbein, *Hesselbein on Leadership* (San Francisco: Jossey-Bass, 2002), p. 3.

[14]Ibid., p. 8.

[15]Harlan Cleveland, *Nobody in Charge* (San Francisco: Jossey-Bass, 2002), p. 119.

[16]Ibid., p. 122.

[17]Ibid.

[18]Ibid., pp. 119-23.

[19]Ibid., p. 8.

[20]Ibid., p. 11.

[21]Spencer Johnson, *Who Moved My Cheese?* (New York: G. P. Putnam's Sons, 2002), p. 46.

Chapter Three: Leaders Passionate About the Great Commission

[1]David Bosch, *Transforming Mission* (Maryknoll, N.Y.: Orbis, 1991), p. 57.

[2]See Donald A. Hagner, *Matthew 1-13,* Word Biblical Commentary (Dallas: Word, 1993), 33a:lxv.

[3]Ibid., 33a:58.

[4]Bosch, *Transforming Mission*, p. 58.

[5]Ibid., p. 74.

[6]See ibid., p. 64.

[7]Craig S. Keener, *Matthew,* IVP New Testament Commentary (Downers Grove, Ill.: InterVarsity Press, 1997), 1:399.

[8]From the longer ending of Mark that is not found in the oldest manuscripts.

[9]David J. Bosch, "The Structure of Mission: An Exposition of Matthew 28:18-20," in *Exploring Church Growth*, ed. Wilbert R. Shenk (Grand Rapids: Eerdmans, 1983), p. 219.

[10]Bosch, *Transforming Mission*, p. 57.

[11]See Greg Ogden, *Transforming Discipleship* (Downers Grove, Ill.: InterVarsity Press, 2003), p. 48.

[12]See Donald A. McGavran, *The Bridges of God* (London: World Dominion Press, 1955).

[13]See Claude E. Paine and Hamilton Beazley, *Reclaiming the Great Commission* (San Francisco: Jossey-Bass, 2000).

[14]See Eddie Gibbs, *In Name Only* (Wheaton, Ill.: Victor, 1994).

[15]Ogden, *Transforming Discipleship,* p. 43.

[16]Eugene H. Peterson, *A Long Obedience in the Same Direction*, 2nd ed. (Downers Grove, Ill.: InterVarsity Press, 1980), p. 17.

[17]Hagner, *Matthew 1-13*, 33a:885.

[18]Keener, *Matthew*, 1:402.

[19]Harry Boer, *Pentecost and Missions* (Grand Rapids: Eerdmans, 1961).

[20]Bosch, *Transforming Mission*, p. 75.

[21]*Mission-Shaped Church: Church Planting and Fresh Expressions of Church in a Changing Context* (London: Church House, 2004) is the report presented by the working group of the Church of England's Mission and Public Affairs Council to the General Synod 2004.

[22]See Lesslie Newbigin, *Foolishness to the Greeks* (Grand Rapids: Eerdmans, 1986).

[23]Andrew Walls, "Western Society Presents a Missionary Challenge," in *Missiological Education for the Twenty-First Century*, ed. Dudley J. Woodberry et al. (Maryknoll, N.Y.: Orbis, 1996).

[24]See *Mission-Shaped Church: Church Planting and Fresh Expressions of Church in a Changing Context*, p. 20.

[25]See ibid., pp. 81-82; and "Empirical Indicators of a 'Missional Church,'" *The Gospel and Our Culture* 10, no. 3 (1998): 5-7.

[26]See George Lings and Bob Hopkins, *Mission-Shaped Church: The Inside and Outside View*, Encounters on the Edge 22 (Sheffield, U.K.: Sheffield Centre, 2004), p. 18.

[27]See *Mission-Shaped Church: Church Planting and Fresh Expressions of Church in a Changing Context*, p. 32.

[28]Lings and Hopkins, *Mission-Shaped Church: The Inside and Outside View*, p. 17.

Chapter Four: What's Different?

[1]Peter Drucker, *Managing in a Time of Great Change* (Oxford: Butterworth-Heinemann, 1995), p. 67.

[2]Jean Lipman-Blumen, *Connective Leadership* (New York: Oxford University Press, 1996), p. 6.

[3]Ibid.

[4]Eddie Gibbs, *ChurchNext* (Downers Grove, Ill.: InterVarsity Press, 2000), p. 32.

[5]Harlan Cleveland, *Nobody in Charge* (San Francisco: Jossey-Bass, 2002), p. 119.

[6]Ibid., pp. 121, 122.

[7]Bill Easum, *Leadership on the OtherSide* (Nashville: Abingdon, 2000), p. 53.

[8]See Mike Regele, *Death of the Church* (Grand Rapids: Zondervan, 1995), pp. 47-52.

[9]See Gerd Theissen, ed., *Social Reality and the Early Christians*, trans. Margaret Kohl (Minneapolis: Fortress Press, 1992).

[10]Wayne Meeks, *The First Urban Christians* (New Haven, Conn.: Yale University Press, 1983), pp. 29-30, 75-77; and Rodney Stark, *The Rise of Christianity* (San Francisco: HarperSanFrancisco, 1997), pp. 29-33.

[11]Cleveland, *Nobody in Charge*, p. 44.

[12]Gifford Pinchot, "Building Community in the Workplace," in *The Community of the Future*, ed. Frances Hesselbein et al. (San Francisco: Jossey-Bass, 1998), p. 129.

[13]Lipman-Blumen, *Connective Leadership*, p. 10.

[14]We must distinguish between a conservatism that is faithful to the biblical text and one that seeks security in a previous age of the church, a particular tradition or even a culturally con-

ditioned interpretation of the biblical text. For these reasons I have become increasingly uneasy with the label "conservative." I believe that all Christians who seek to be biblically faithful are radicals who constantly reexamine their beliefs in the light of Scripture.

[15]See Robert Banks and Bernice M. Ledbetter, *Reviewing Leadership* (Grand Rapids: Baker, 2004), pp. 35-42.

[16]Thomas Stewart, "Trust Me on This—Organizational Support for Trust in a World Without Hierarchies," in *The Future of Leadership,* ed. Warren Bennis, Gretchen M. Spreitzer and Thomas G. Cummings (San Francisco: Jossey-Bass, 2001), p. 68.

[17]Ibid.

[18]Margaret J. Wheatley and Myron Kellner-Rogers, "The Paradox and Promise of Community," in *The Community of the Future,* ed. Frances Hesselbein et al. (San Francisco: Jossey-Bass, 1998), p. 12.

[19]Ibid., p. 11.

[20]William Bridges, "Leading the De-Jobbed Organization," in *The Leader of the Future,* ed. Frances Hesselbein, Marshall Goldsmith and Richard Beckhard (San Francisco: Jossey-Bass, 1996), p. 16.

[21]Ibid., p. 21.

[22]James M. Kouzes and Barry Z. Posner, *Credibility* (San Francisco: Jossey-Bass, 2003), p. 157.

[23]Cleveland, *Nobody in Charge,* pp. 36-41.

[24]Tom Beaudoin, *Virtual Faith* (San Francisco: Jossey-Bass, 1998), p. 57. For further information see Andrew Careaga, *eMinistry* (Grand Rapids: Kregel, 2001).

[25]Howard Rheingold, "Virtual Communities," in *The Community of the Future,* ed. Frances Hesselbein et al. (San Francisco: Jossey-Bass, 1998), pp. 117-19.

[26]Ibid., pp. 119-20.

[27]Ibid., pp. 121-22.

[28]Easum, *Leadership on the OtherSide,* pp. 100-103.

[29]Wayne Cordeiro, *Doing Church as a Team* (Honolulu: New Hope, 1998), pp. 163-69.

[30]Ibid., pp. 74-76.

[31]Suzanne W. Morse, "Five Building Blocks for Successful Leadership," in *The Community of the Future,* ed. Frances Hesselbein et al. (San Francisco: Jossey-Bass, 1998), p. 234.

Chapter Five: Team Building

[1]See Patrick M. Lencioni, *The Five Dysfunctions of a Team* (San Francisco: Jossey-Bass, 2002).

[2]Edgar H. Schein, "Leadership and Organizational Culture," in *The Leader of the Future,* ed. Frances Hesselbein, Marshall Goldsmith and Richard Beckhard (San Francisco: Jossey-Bass, 1996), p. 68.

[3]Ibid., pp. 67, 68.

[4]See Eddie Gibbs, *Way to Serve* (Leicester, U.K.: Inter-Varsity Press, 2003), pp. 123-41.

[5]Schein, "Leadership and Organizational Culture," p. 68.

[6]Peter Drucker, *Managing in a Time of Great Change* (Oxford: Butterworth-Heinemann, 1995), pp. 86-90.

[7]See Gibbs, *Way to Serve,* pp. 118-22.

[8]Max De Pree, *Leading Without Power* (San Francisco: Jossey-Bass, 1997), pp. 29-31.

[9]See George Cladis, *Leading the Team-Based Church* (San Francisco: Jossey-Bass, 1999), pp. 4, 92-94.

[10]Ibid., p. 10.

[11]Rodney A. Whitacre, *John*, IVP New Testament Commentary (Downers Grove, Ill.: InterVarsity Press, 1999), 4:417-18.

[12]Cladis, *Leading the Team-Based Church*, p. 10.

[13]Ibid., p. 11.

[14]Ibid., pp. 37, 39.

[15]Ibid., pp. 48, 49.

[16]Leith Anderson, *Leadership That Works* (Minneapolis: Bethany House, 1999), p. 194.

[17]Cladis, *Leading the Team-Based Church*, p. 66.

[18]Jim Collins, *Good to Great* (New York: HarperBusiness, 2001), pp. 74-80.

[19]Cladis, *Leading the Team-Based Church*, p. 88.

[20]Ibid.

[21]Harlan Cleveland, *Nobody in Charge* (San Francisco: Jossey-Bass, 2002), p. 163.

[22]See Jean Lipman-Blumen, *Connective Leadership* (New York: Oxford University Press, 1996), p. 23.

[23]Ibid., p. 17.

[24]Karl Weick, "Leadership as the Legitimation of Doubt," in *The Future of Leadership,* ed. Warren Bennis, Gretchen M. Spreitzer and Thomas G. Cummings (San Francisco: Jossey-Bass, 2001), p. 96.

[25]Ibid., p. 95.

[26]Cladis, *Leading the Team-Based Church*, pp. 14, 15.

[27]Ibid., p. 15.

Chapter Six: Leadership Traits

[1]See also 1 Cor 4:16; Phil 3:7; 1 Thess 1:6; 2 Thess 3:7, 9.

[2]Eddie Gibbs, *Way to Serve* (Leicester, U.K.: Inter-Varsity Press, 2003), pp. 99-102.

[3]Aubrey Malphurs, *Being Leaders* (Grand Rapids: Baker, 2003), p. 36.

[4]Os Guinness, *The Call* (Nashville: W Publishing Group, 2003), pp. 70, 78.

[5]Ibid., p. 93.

[6]James Emery White, *Embracing the Mysterious God* (Downers Grove, Ill.: InterVarsity Press, 2003), p. 121.

[7]Guinness, *Call,* p. 139.

[8]Ibid., p. 185.

[9]Brian McLaren, *The Church on the Other Side* (Grand Rapids: Zondervan, 1998), p. 111.

[10]Margaret J. Wheatley and Myron Kellner-Rogers, "The Paradox and Promise of Community," in *The Community of the Future,* ed. Frances Hesselbein et al. (San Francisco: Jossey-Bass, 1998), p. 12.

[11]Max De Pree, *Leading Without Power* (San Francisco: Jossey-Bass, 1997), p. 139.

[12]Ibid., p. 146.

[13]For an elaboration of this point, identifying the six areas of leadership credibility, see Steven M. Bornstein and Anthony F. Smith, "The Puzzles of Leadership," in *The Leader of the Future,* ed.

Frances Hesselbein, Marshall Goldsmith and Richard Beckhard (San Francisco: Jossey-Bass, 1996), p. 284.

[14]Peter Drucker, *Managing in a Time of Great Change* (Oxford: Butterworth-Heinemann, 1995), p. 6.

[15]Ibid., p. 7.

[16]Ibid., pp. 7-8. In the final chapter we will explore some of the practical implications of these insights in regard to the selection and training of future leaders.

[17]Kenneth Cloke and Joan Goldsmith, *The Art of Waking People Up* (San Francisco: Jossey-Bass, 2001), pp. 182-85.

[18]Henry Cloud, "Leaders That Grow," interview by Jeff Bailey, *Cutting Edge* 8, no. 1 (2004): 5.

[19]See James M. Kouzes and Barry Z. Posner, "Seven Lessons for Leading the Voyage of the Future," in *The Leader of the Future,* ed. Frances Hesselbein, Marshall Goldsmith and Richard Beckhard (San Francisco: Jossey-Bass, 1996), p. 107.

[20]Drucker, *Managing in a Time of Great Change,* p. 8.

[21]Cloud, "Leaders That Grow," p. 5.

[22]Cloke and Goldsmith, *Art of Waking People Up,* pp. 163-66.

[23]Cloud, "Leaders That Grow," p. 5.

[24]De Pree, *Leading Without Power,* p. 127.

[25]Ibid., p. 129.

Chapter Seven: Activities of Leadership

[1]Leighton Ford, *Transforming Leadership* (Downers Grove, Ill.: InterVarsity Press, 1991), pp. 53, 54.

[2]See Peter Brierley, *Coming Up Trumps!* (Milton Keynes, Bucks, U.K.: Authentic Media/Christian Research, 2004), pp. 83-94.

[3]Ford, *Transforming Leadership,* p. 104.

[4]Max De Pree, *Leading Without Power* (San Francisco: Jossey-Bass, 1997), p. 117.

[5]Ford, *Transforming Leadership,* p. 76.

[6]Bill Hybels, *Courageous Leadership* (Grand Rapids: Zondervan, 2002), p. 32.

[7]Charles Swindoll, *Quest for Character* (Portland, Ore.: Multnomah Press, 1987), p. 98.

[8]Hybels, *Courageous Leadership,* p. 36.

[9]Brierley, *Coming Up Trumps!* p. 5.

[10]Peter Drucker, *Managing in a Time of Great Change* (Oxford: Butterworth-Heinemann, 1995), p. 35.

[11]Ibid., p. 36.

[12]See chap. 2 of Malcolm Gladwell, *The Tipping Point* (Boston: Little, Brown, 2000).

[13]Steve Nicholson, "How to Recruit a Church-Planting Team," *Cutting Edge* 8, no. 1 (2004): 16.

[14]Gladwell, *Tipping Point,* p. 139.

[15]Ford, *Transforming Leadership,* pp. 15-16.

[16]Ibid., p. 81.

[17]See ibid., chap. 11.

[18]Drucker, *Managing in a Time of Great Change,* p. 3.

[19]Ford, *Transforming Leadership,* pp. 254-58.

[20]Charles Handy, "A World of Fleas and Elephants," in *The Future of Leadership,* ed. Warren Bennis, Gretchen M. Spreitzer and Thomas G. Cummings (San Francisco: Jossey-Bass, 2001), p. 31.

Chapter Eight: Leadership Attitudes

[1]See Gerard Kelly, *Retrofuture* (Downers Grove, Ill.: InterVarsity Press, 1999).

[2]Margaret J. Wheatley and Myron Kellner-Rogers, "The Paradox and Promise of Community," in *The Community of the Future,* ed. Frances Hesselbein et al. (San Francisco: Jossey-Bass, 1998), p. 17.

[3]Evelyn Whitehead and James Whitehead, quoted in Catherine Nerney and Hal Taussig, *Reimaging Life Together in America* (Lanham, Md.: Sheed & Ward, 2002), p. 180.

[4]Wheatley and Kellner-Rogers, "Paradox and Promise," p. 13.

[5]Barbara Hateley and Warren H. Schmidt, *A Peacock in the Land of Penguins* (San Francisco: Berett-Keohler, 1995), pp. 5, 76, 77.

[6]Bill Easum, *Leadership on the OtherSide* (Nashville: Abingdon, 2000), p. 58.

[7]Ibid., pp. 59-60.

[8]Leighton Ford, *Transforming Leadership* (Downers Grove, Ill.: InterVarsity Press, 1991), p. 92.

[9]Harlan Cleveland, *Nobody in Charge* (San Francisco: Jossey-Bass, 2002), p. 8.

[10]Max De Pree, *Leading Without Power* (San Francisco: Jossey-Bass, 1997), p. 160.

[11]See ibid., pp. 62-64.

[12]See George Yancey, *One Body, One Spirit* (Downers Grove, Ill.: InterVarsity Press, 2003).

[13]Jim Collins, *Good to Great* (New York: HarperBusiness, 2001), p. 39.

[14]De Pree, *Leading Without Power,* p. 71.

Chapter Nine: Facing the Cost of Leadership

[1]Mark Lau Branson, *Appreciative Inquiry and Congregational Change* (Herndon, Va.: Alban Institute, 2004).

[2]J. Oswald Sanders, *Spiritual Leadership* (Chicago: Moody Press, 1967), p. 112.

[3]See chap. 5 of Leith Anderson, *Leadership That Works* (Minneapolis: Bethany House, 1999).

[4]James M. Kouzes and Barry Z. Posner, *Credibility* (San Francisco: Jossey-Bass, 2003), p. 93. See also Carl Honore, *In Praise of Slowness* (San Francisco: HarperSanFrancisco, 2004).

[5]Anderson, *Leadership That Works,* pp. 74-80.

[6]For more information on Servant Partners see <www.servantpartners.org>.

[7]For more information on the Harambee Center see <www.harambee.org>.

[8]E-mail to the author, December 3, 2004.

[9]Sanders, *Spiritual Leadership,* p. 104.

[10]Anderson, *Leadership That Works,* pp. 164-74.

Chapter Ten: Leadership Emergence and Development

[1]Warren Bennis, "The Future Has No Shelf Life," in *The Future of Leadership,* ed. Warren Bennis, Gretchen M. Spreitzer and Thomas G. Cummings (San Francisco: Jossey-Bass, 2001), p. 13. See also Peter Drucker, *Managing in a Time of Great Change* (Oxford: Butterworth-Heinemann, 1995), pp. 7, 13, 38, 42.

[2]Robert Banks, *Re-envisioning Theological Education* (Grand Rapids: Eerdmans, 1998), p. 139.

[3]Ibid., p. 144.

[4]*Mission-Shaped Church: Church Planting and Fresh Expressions of Church in a Changing Context* (London: Church House, 2004), p. 147.

[5]This does not, however, signify that God bypasses those with social standing and academic training. The apostle Paul is a case in point. See Acts 22:3; Phil 3:4-8.

[6]Jim Collins, *Good to Great* (New York: HarperBusiness, 2001), p. 63.

[7]Ibid.

[8]"Educational Philosophy," FORGE <www.forge.org.au/mambo/content/blogcategory/12/54>.

[9]*Mission-Shaped Church: Church Planting and Fresh Expressions of Church in a Changing Context,* pp. 12, 135.

[10]Ibid., p. 147.

[11]Ibid., p. 148.

[12]Ibid., p. 130.

[13]Banks, *Re-envisioning Theological Education,* pp. 176-81.

[14]Bill Hybels, *Courageous Leadership* (Grand Rapids: Zondervan, 2002), chap. 9.

[15]Jean Lipman-Blumen, *Connective Leadership* (New York: Oxford University Press, 1996), pp. 21-22.

[16]*Mission-Shaped Church: Church Planting and Fresh Expressions of Church in a Changing Context,* p. 21.

[17]"Mission Statement" and "Educational Philosophy," FORGE <www.forge.org.au/mambo/content/blogcategory/12/54>.

[18]"Educational Philosophy," FORGE <www.forge.org.au/mambo/content/blogcategory/12/54>.

[19]Ibid.

[20]Charles Handy, "A World of Fleas and Elephants," in *The Future of Leadership,* ed. Warren Bennis, Gretchen M. Spreitzer and Thomas G. Cummings (San Francisco: Jossey-Bass, 2001), p. 40.

[21]Kenneth Cloke and Joan Goldsmith, *The Art of Waking People Up* (San Francisco: Jossey-Bass, 2001), p. 31.

[22]Ibid., p. 33.

[23]Max De Pree, *Leading Without Power* (San Francisco: Jossey-Bass, 1997), chap. 1.

[24]Ibid., pp. 11-12, 14.

[25]Ibid., pp. 11-16.

[26]See Cloke and Goldsmith, *Art of Waking People Up,* p. 34.

[27]Bill Easum, *Leadership on the OtherSide* (Nashville: Abingdon, 2000), p. 20.

[28]"Forge Internships," FORGE <www.forge.org.au/mambo/content/blogcategory/13/62>.

[29]Adapted from Caela Farren and Beverly L. Kaye, "New Skills for New Leadership Roles," in *The Leader of the Future,* ed. Frances Hesselbein, Marshall Goldsmith and Richard Beckhard (San Francisco: Jossey-Bass, 1996), pp. 179-80.

[30]"Educational Philosophy," FORGE <www.forge.org.au/mambo/content/blogcategory/12/54>.

[31]Os Guinness, *The Call* (Nashville: W Publishing Group, 2003), p. 227.

[32]De Pree, *Leading Without Power,* p. 163.

[33]See ibid., pp. 166-77.

Bibliography

Anderson, Leith. *Leadership That Works*. Minneapolis: Bethany House, 1999.

Banks, Robert. *Re-envisioning Theological Education*. Grand Rapids: Eerdmans, 1998.

Banks, Robert, and Bernice M. Ledbetter. *Reviewing Leadership*. Grand Rapids: Baker, 2004.

Barna, George. *The Second Coming of the Church*. Nashville: Word, 1998.

Bennis, Warren, Gretchen M. Spreitzer and Thomas G. Cummings, eds. *The Future of Leadership*. San Francisco: Jossey-Bass, 2001.

Boer, Harry R. *Pentecost and Missions*. Grand Rapids: Eerdmans, 1961.

Branson, Mark Lau. *Appreciative Inquiry and Congregational Change*. Herndon, Va.: Alban Institute, 2004.

Brierley, Peter. *Coming Up Trumps! Four Ways into the Future*. Milton Keynes, Bucks, U.K.: Authentic Media/Christian Research, 2004.

———. *The Tide Is Running Out*. London: Christian Research, 2000.

Bruce, Steve. *Religion in the Modern World: From Cathedrals to Cults*. Oxford: Oxford University Press, 1996.

Careaga, Andrew. *eMinistry*. Grand Rapids: Kregel, 2001.

Cladis, George. *Leading the Team-Based Church*. San Francisco: Jossey-Bass, 1999.

Cleveland, Harlan. *Nobody in Charge*. San Francisco: Jossey-Bass, 2002.

Clinton, J. Robert. *Leadership Emergence Theory: A Self-Study Manual for Analyzing the Development of a Christian Leader*. Pasadena, Calif.: Barnabas, 1989.

Cloke, Kenneth, and Joan Goldsmith. *The Art of Waking People Up*. San Francisco: Jossey-Bass, 2001.

Collins, James C., and Jerry I. Porras. *Built to Last*. New York: HarperCollins, 1997.

Collins, Jim. *Good to Great*. New York: HarperBusiness, 2001.

Cordeiro, Wayne. *Doing Church as a Team*. Honolulu: New Hope, 1998.

Crossan, Dominic. *The Dark Interval: Towards a Theology of Story*. Niles, Ill.: Argus, 1975.

De Pree, Max. *Leading Without Power*. San Francisco: Jossey-Bass, 1997.

Drucker, Peter. *Managing in a Time of Great Change*. Oxford: Butterworth-Heinemann, 1995.

Easum, Bill. *Leadership on the OtherSide*. Nashville: Abingdon, 2000.

Ford, Leighton. *Transforming Leadership*. Downers Grove, Ill.: InterVarsity Press, 1991.

Gallup, George, Jr., and D. Michael Lindsey, *Surveying the Religious Landscape*. Harrisburg, Penn.: Morehouse Press, 2000.

Gibbs, Eddie. *ChurchNext*. Downers Grove, Ill.: InterVarsity Press, 2000.

————. *In Name Only*. Wheaton, Ill.: Victor, 1994.

————. *Way to Serve*. Leicester, U.K.: Inter-Varsity Press, 2003.

Gladwell, Malcolm. *The Tipping Point*. Boston: Little, Brown, 2000.

Greenleaf, Roger K. *Servant Leadership: A Journey into the Nature of Legitimate Power and Greatness*. New York: Paulist Press, 1977.

Grove, Andrew. *Only the Paranoid Survive*. New York: Doubleday, 1996.

Guinness, Os. *The Call*. Nashville: W Publishing Group, 2003.

Hagner, Donald A. *Matthew 1-13*. Word Biblical Commentary 33a. Dallas: Word, 1993.

Handy, Charles. *The Age of Paradox*. Boston: Harvard Business School Press, 1994.

Hateley, Barbara, and Warren H. Schmidt. *A Peacock in the Land of Penguins*. San Francisco: Berett-Keohler, 1995.

Hesselbein, Frances. *Hesselbein on Leadership*. San Francisco: Jossey-Bass, 2002.

Hesselbein, Frances, Marshall Goldsmith and Richard Beckhard, eds. *The Leader of the Future*. San Francisco: Jossey-Bass, 1996.

Hesselbein, Frances, et al., eds. *The Community of the Future*. San Francisco: Jossey-Bass, 1998.

Honore, Carl. *In Praise of Slowness: How a Worldwide Movement is Challenging the Cult of Speed*. San Francisco: HarperSanFrancisco, 2004.

Hybels, Bill. *Courageous Leadership*. Grand Rapids: Zondervan, 2002.

Johnson, Spencer. *Who Moved My Cheese? An A-mazing Way to Deal with Change in Your Work and in Your Life*. New York: G. P. Putnam's Sons, 2002.

Keener, Craig S. *Matthew.* IVP New Testament Commentary 1. Downers Grove, Ill.: InterVarsity Press, 1997.

Kouzes, James M., and Barry Z. Posner. *Credibility: How Leaders Gain and Lose It, Why People Demand It.* San Francisco: Jossey-Bass, 2003.

——. *The Leadership Challenge.* 3rd ed. San Francisco: Jossey-Bass, 2002.

Lencioni, Patrick. *The Five Dysfunctions of a Team.* San Francisco: Jossey-Bass, 2002.

Lewis, Robert. *The Church of Irresistible Influence.* Grand Rapids: Zondervan, 2001.

Lings, George, and Bob Hopkins. *Mission-Shaped Church: The Inside and Outside View.* Encounters on the Edge 22. Sheffield, U.K.: Sheffield Centre, 2004.

Lipman-Blumen, Jean. *Connective Leadership.* New York: Oxford University Press, 1996.

Malphurs, Aubrey. *Being Leaders: The Nature of Authentic Christian Leadership.* Grand Rapids: Baker, 2003.

McGavran, Donald A. *The Bridges of God.* London: World Dominion, 1955.

McGrath, Alister. *The Twilight of Atheism.* New York: Doubleday, 2004.

McLaren, Brian D. *The Church on the Other Side.* Grand Rapids: Zondervan, 1998.

Meeks, Wayne A. *The First Urban Christians: The Social World of the Apostle Paul.* New Haven, Conn.: Yale University Press, 1983.

Miller, M. Rex. *The Millennium Matrix.* San Francisco: Jossey-Bass, 2004.

Mission-Shaped Church: Church Planting and Fresh Expressions of Church in a Changing Context. London: Church House, 2004.

Newbigin, Lesslie. *Foolishness to the Greeks: The Gospel in Western Cultures.* Grand Rapids: Eerdmans, 1986.

Ogden, Greg. *Transforming Discipleship.* Downers Grove, Ill.: InterVarsity Press, 2003.

Paine, Claude E., and Hamilton Beazley. *Reclaiming the Great Commission.* San Francisco: Jossey-Bass, 2000.

Peterson, Eugene. *A Long Obedience in the Same Direction: Discipleship in an Instant Society.* 2nd ed. Downers Grove, Ill.: InterVarsity Press, 1980.

Regele, Mike. *Death of the Church.* Grand Rapids: Zondervan, 1995.

Roels, Shirley. *Moving Beyond Servant Leadership.* Leadership Briefing. Pasadena, Calif.: De Pree Leadership Center, 1999.

Roof, Wade Clark. *Spiritual Marketplace.* Princeton, N.J.: Princeton University Press, 1999.

Sanders, J. Oswald. *Spiritual Leadership.* Chicago: Moody Press, 1967.

Schaller, Lyle E. *The New Reformation: Tomorrow Arrived Yesterday.* Nashville: Abingdon, 1995.

————. *Tattered Trust: Is There Hope for Your Denomination?* Nashville, Tenn.: Abingdon, 1996.

Schwartz, Peter, *The Art of the Long View: Planning for the Future in an Uncertain World.* Chichester, U.K.: John Wiley and Sons, 1998. First published in the U.S. by Doubleday, 1991, 1996.

Shenk, Wilbert R. *Exploring Church Growth.* Grand Rapids: Eerdmans, 1983.

Stackhouse, John G., Jr. *Humble Apologetics.* New York: Oxford University Press, 2002.

Stark, Rodney. *The Rise of Christianity.* San Francisco: HarperSanFrancisco, 1997.

Swindoll, Charles. *Quest for Character.* Portland, Ore.: Multnomah Press, 1987.

Theissen, Gerd, ed. Translated by Margaret Kohl. *Social Reality and the Early Christians: Theology, Ethics, and the World of the New Testament.* Minneapolis: Fortress Press, 1992.

Webber, Robert. *Ancient-Future Evangelism.* Grand Rapids: Baker, 2003.

Wenham, Gordon J. *Genesis.* Word Biblical Commentary. Dallas: Word, 1987.

Whitacre, Rodney A. *John.* IVP New Testament Commentary 4. Downers Grove, Ill.: InterVarsity Press, 1999.

White, James Emery. *Embracing the Mysterious God: Loving the God We Don't Understand.* Downers Grove, Ill.: InterVarsity Press, 2003.

Woodberry, Dudley J., et al. *Missiological Education for the Twenty-First Century.* Maryknoll, N.Y.: Orbis, 1996.

Wright, Walter. *Relational Leadership.* Carlisle, U.K.: Paternoster, 2000.

Yancey, George. *One Body, One Spirit: Principles of Successful Multiracial Churches.* Downers Grove, Ill.: InterVarsity Press, 2003.

Subject Index